BOLLINGEN SERIES XLV

The Collected Works of Paul Valéry

Edited by Jackson Mathews

VOLUME 9

PAUL VALÉRY

MASTERS AND FRIENDS

Translated by
Martin Turnell

With an Introduction by
Joseph Frank

BOLLINGEN SERIES XLV · 9

PRINCETON UNIVERSITY PRESS

Copyright © 1968 by Bollingen Foundation
Published for Bollingen Foundation, New York, N. Y.
by Princeton University Press, Princeton, New Jersey

THIS IS VOLUME NINE OF THE
COLLECTED WORKS OF PAUL VALÉRY
CONSTITUTING NUMBER XLV IN BOLLINGEN SERIES
SPONSORED BY AND PUBLISHED FOR
BOLLINGEN FOUNDATION.
IT IS THE EIGHTH VOLUME OF THE
COLLECTED WORKS TO APPEAR

Library of Congress catalogue card no. 56-9337
Printed in the United States by
Clarke & Way, New York, N.Y.
DESIGNED BY ANDOR BRAUN

CONTENTS

v

Introduction

A LARGE PART of the published work of Paul Valéry consists of occasional literary and cultural reflections on the most varied and diverse topics. Essays, prefaces, official speeches, reminiscences of old friends and literary comrades-in-arms— all poured forth from Valéry's pen in a steady stream during the latter part of his life. Collected in the five volumes of his *Variétés* (which do not, however, by any means exhaust all his published prose of this kind), these casually incisive and elegant articles did much to spread the prestige of Valéry's name among a wide circle of readers. They are much more easily accessible than his dense and hermetic poetry, his subtle and chiseled Socratic dialogues, or his several volumes of gnomic fragments and aphorisms which can only really appeal to the *cognoscenti* of his work. And if the average cultivated reader has made some firsthand contact with Valéry, it is probably in the pages of his famous *La Crise de l'esprit*, which in 1919 stated with classic brevity the theme of the decline of the West through an excess of the very rationalism whose discovery had been its greatest triumph.

Valéry's essays were called out by the most haphazard occasions, and many were speeches delivered as part of his functions as a member of the French Academy. So many and so varied were the chores imposed on Valéry by this august

body that he once, in a letter to Gide, jokingly called himself "the Bossuet of the Third Republic." It is a tribute to Valéry's independence and originality that, despite such ceremonial auspices, he always managed to produce something far surpassing the level of conventional eulogy or ritual celebration. Valéry, as a matter of fact, never approached any subject except in terms of his own peculiar intellectual concerns and philosophical preoccupations; and these were quite different from the historical and literary interests of the scholar or critic, as well as from the doctrines of the major philosophical currents in France during his lifetime. (Though personally friendly with Bergson and Alain, Valéry perhaps comes closest of all in tendency to the Neo-Kantianism of Léon Brunschvicg, who, as he notes in a letter, "quotes me in all his books.") Not until the appearance of Sartre's *Situations* can we find any French essayist who matches Valéry's literary authority and stylistic brilliance, and who combines these qualities with so strongly marked and sharply individual an intellectual personality.

Valéry's thought, however, is the product of an extremely idiosyncratic blend of heterogeneous elements, which are much more difficult to pin down than Sartre's obvious philosophical affiliations. And perhaps the most useful task one can perform, as an introduction to the essays collected in *Masters and Friends*, is to use them for the purpose of disengaging the various aspects of the *Weltanschauung* that forms their common background.

I

The first complex of ideas that may be noted in Valéry's essays derives from his early and crucial contact with the spiritual world of French Symbolism. Like all important

literary movements, French Symbolism carried with it a freight of values and attitudes that went far beyond the merely "literary"; and these values became a permanent part of Valéry's sensibility. Certainly the most important of such values was the Symbolist *mystique* of art and the artist; and in his farewell to Pierre Louÿs, Valéry recalls the fervor of their common participation in this cult of the aesthetic. "Thirty years ago, the word 'artist' meant for us someone who lived apart, a dedicated person, at once victim and priest, a person who was singled out by his gifts and whose virtues and weaknesses were not those of other men." At the age of eighteen Valéry announced to Louÿs that his bible had become Huysmans' *A Rebours*; and while he soon discarded the musky trappings of this breviary of Symbolist decadence, the influence of the climate of ideas it represented can hardly be mistaken in his outlook.

It explains, for one thing, his reverence for the rare and precious personality, the creative source and center of all culture, whose disappearance he was so often to lament later on. Valéry's idea of culture always remained an aristocratic one, centered around discreetly charismatic individuals and small spiritual elites whose features are strongly suggestive of the Symbolist *cénacles* (and particularly the *cénacle* of Mallarmé) that he had known as a young man. It also helps to explain his contemptuous disdain for politics, and his indifference (at least on a theoretical level) to the ordinary issues of morality. The Symbolists turned their back on the whole realm of the political and social as inimical to the pursuit of the highest refinements of art; and Valéry notes, with some satisfaction, that Descartes had also assumed the same indifference to the politics of religion in his day in order to pursue the highest refinements of thought. Similarly, if the virtues and weak-

nesses of the artist are not those of other men, then morality has no right to impose its prescriptions on the creative spirit. Valéry takes a slyly malicious delight in pointing out this highly amoral moral to the eminently respectable audience attending his lecture on "Villon and Verlaine."

Another example of this indelible Symbolist impress on Valéry's thought may be found in his persistent preoccupation with mysticism and with other irrational currents of speculation such as Illuminism and Theosophy. Valéry, as we shall soon see, is perhaps the most intransigent rationalist to have appeared among major European writers since the eighteenth century; but his fascination with such a figure as Swedenborg, to whom he devotes a lengthy essay, can easily be understood if we remember his Symbolist origins. For the metaphysics of Symbolism was very close to that "spectral learning" which Valéry mentions in connection with Gérard de Nerval—a learning "tinged with theurgy, gnosis, the cabala, deciphered myths, and every kind of mystery that could be absorbed by a mind longing too avidly for light."

Just how imbued Valéry himself was with such "spectral learning" may be gleaned from a letter that he wrote to Mallarmé at the age of twenty, in which he confides to his *cher Maître* that the poet "defines the mysterious echo of things and their secret harmony, as real, as certain as a mathematical relation to all artistic spirits . . ." The only novels of Balzac that Valéry mentions, and the ones he clearly knows best, are those in which the theosophic, Swedenborgian tendencies of the great realist are most prominent (*Séraphitus-Séraphita, Louis Lambert, La Peau de chagrin*); the work of Flaubert that he prefers to all others is that compendium of mystagogical heresies, *La Tentation de Saint Antoine*. Valéry also admires Huysmans' trilogy of novels

about a religious conversion, and accords special praise to the final volume, *La Cathédrale*, for consisting of an "extraordinary network of modern metaphors in which we catch, as though in its entirety, the tremor of the vast and exact alphabet of symbols willed by the Middle Ages."

The poetic impulse in these novels of Huysmans is carefully contrasted with the standard products of French turn-of-the-century Naturalism; and Valéry's attacks on the novel as a form, which gained him a great deal of notoriety, are unquestionably the echo of a taste inculcated by Symbolist aesthetics. Nothing was more opposed to the Symbolist ambition to transform the world into art, to find the poetic talisman that would liberate its secret harmonies and reveal its magic unity, than the apparent ambition of the Naturalists to reproduce the thousand and one insignificant details of everyday life. And behind Valéry's sallies at the expense of the novel looms the rivalry between Zola and Mallarmé, with the one gaining the plaudits of the vulgar and the other the adoration of a handful of the elect. Whatever their origin, however, some of Valéry's barbs are extremely shrewd criticism. He remarks aptly that the Realism of the 1850s confused scientific observation with the crude unselectiveness of the naked eye; and he notes that such writers as Flaubert and the Goncourts, who lavished the most sophisticated prose on the most ordinary and commonplace characters, only succeeded, as a result, in obtaining an effect of extreme artifice rather than of reality.

For Valéry, the art of the novel always remained identical with the Naturalism he had rejected as a young man; and in an "Homage to Marcel Proust," of all places, he still continues to define the essence of the form exclusively in terms of verisimilitude. "There must be no essential difference be-

tween the novel and the natural description of things that we have seen and heard," he writes. "Neither rhythm, forms and figures of speech, nor even any definite structure are obligatory." One is hardly surprised, after this, at Valéry's admission that he had "scarcely read a single volume of Marcel Proust's great work." But as is so often the case with Valéry, his direct literary insight and his power of generalization somehow manage to overcome the limits of his taste. Proust's genius, he also remarks brilliantly, consists in being able to convey the "infinity of possibilities" which is the very essence of human consciousness, but which is usually suppressed because the business of living requires selection and choice.

Stendhal is the only major novelist to whom Valéry devotes an important essay; but, as he intimates rather coyly, there are special reasons for his attachment to this paradoxical figure. He had read *Lucien Leuwen* at a moment in his life when the love affair in the book became entangled with a romantic infatuation of his own; and this trapped him into a betrayal of his critical principles, which required a strict avoidance of confusion between his private feelings and those stimulated by the author's craft. Moreover, Valéry sees Stendhal's novels primarily as "vaudeville" or "operetta"; the highest praise he can give is to compare them with Voltaire's wittily extravagant *contes philosophiques*. Valéry shows an acute sense of literary history in linking Stendhal with this eighteenth-century tradition, whose influence is patent in the fragments of his own *contes philosophiques* (published as *Histoires brisées*). The point is, though, that Valéry could tolerate prose fiction only when its authors disregarded the canons of Realism, like Voltaire and Montesquieu, or played fast and loose with them like Stendhal.

It was the formlessness of the novel of Realism, the fact that

it presumably modeled itself on the fluidity and aimlessness of quotidian experience, that impelled Valéry to exclude it from the realm of true art; and no concept, of course, was more important for Symbolism than that of form. For Mallarmé, the world existed solely to be transmuted into his *grand œuvre*; the function of life, with all its passions and values, could only be to dissolve its identity into the structure of this grandiose creation. Valéry too never tires of affirming the importance of form, and he assigns to it, like Mallarmé, a superiority over all other human concerns. Bossuet, he asserts, is important not as a defender of the Christian tradition but as a great stylist; and in a comparison that recalls both Gautier and Malraux, Valéry praises Bossuet's prose because its structures can be enjoyed "just as passionately as . . . the architecture of a temple when its sanctuaries are deserted and the feelings and causes which led to its construction have long lost their force." It would be difficult to find a critic who gave more weight to the purely formal properties of literature than Valéry, though for the most part his comments do not go beyond general appreciations of the type just quoted. Strangely enough, however, it was this very devotion to the concept of form that prompted Valéry to react against Mallarmé and the Symbolist worship of art, and to turn away from literature entirely for a period of about fifteen years.

II

If the experience of Symbolism accounts for one strand of the ideas that come together in Valéry's essays, then another strand may be traced to his remarkable way of reacting against this very same movement. This reaction is the most important event in Valéry's literary biography, and unquestionably has

deep personal and emotional roots. It is linked, in the first place, with the sentimental-intellectual crisis that he went through in 1892—a crisis that was resolved during a sleepless night in Genoa punctuated by the lightning flashes of a violent thunderstorm. The upshot of this crisis was Valéry's determination to master his sensibility by turning it into an object for rational scrutiny and investigation. "This crisis set me against my 'sensibility' so far as it threatened the freedom of my mind," Valéry wrote in 1944, the year before his death. "I tried, without any great success at first, to oppose the awareness of my state to that state itself, and the observer to the sufferer." This effort could not help but lead Valéry away from the purely emotive world of literary expression, and hence, too, away from the idolatry of art that was the cornerstone of Symbolist values. These latter were now all immolated "to the one that had to be created to rule over the others, the *Idol of the Intellect*."

Another factor to be considered here is Valéry's personal relation to Mallarmé. Valéry had the greatest admiration for this master of verbal music and mysteriously evocative imagery; but there could hardly fail to be, all the same, a certain rivalry between an elder poet and a gifted young disciple filled with insatiable creative ambition. Valéry was acutely conscious of this inevitable competition between the literary generations, and often uses it as a critical schema—for example, when he explains the baroque affectations of Huysmans' style by the necessity of distinguishing himself from Gautier, Flaubert, and the Goncourts. The same tension existed between Mallarmé and his most talented follower; but rather than seeking a further nuance or complication of style, Valéry broke with literature altogether as the first step in discovering his own literary path.

To understand Valéry's development at this period (the mid 1890s), when he gradually abandoned literature to study mathematics and physics, we must remember that he had always been haunted by the dream of uniting science and art. Valéry's interest in the exact sciences had been originally stimulated by a reading of Poe's *Eureka*, that extraordinary and isolated effort to imagine a poetic cosmos in scientific terms; and he had always been fascinated by Poe's suggestion of a scientific poetics, based on an infallible knowledge of the psychological responses of the reader. Even at the very height of his Mallarmé-ism, we have seen him speaking of the "mysterious echo of things" being "as real, as certain as a mathematical relation." Art and science had thus never been inseparably opposed for Valéry, though they had always been for Mallarmé; and this is the point at which Valéry asserted his originality vis-à-vis the Master. "I told him [Mallarmé] one day that he had the makings of a great scientist," Valéry writes disingenuously in his *Letter on Mallarmé*. "I do not know if the compliment was to his taste because he had no idea of science that would make it comparable to poetry. *He opposed them, on the contrary* [italics added]. But I could not help making a *rapprochement*, which seemed to me inevitable, between the construction of an exact science and the design—evident in Mallarmé—of reconstituting the entire system of poetry by means of pure and distinct notions. . . ."

Valéry was certainly aided in making this *rapprochement* by the influence of the writings of Henri Poincaré, the great mathematician and philosopher of science, whose physical silhouette is sketched in "Verlaine Passes By." Poincaré's writings, Madame Valéry has told us, remained constantly on her husband's night table; and one can imagine Valéry's excitement when he began to grasp the implications of Poin-

caré's stress on the pure formalism of mathematics, which, like Symbolist poetry, strove to "donner un sens plus pur aux mots de la tribu." "Matter has no importance for them [mathematicians]," writes Poincaré in his *La Science et l'hypothèse*, "they are only interested in form." Symbolism and science became one in this search for forms which, depending only on human creativity, were yet capable of endowing reality with a new and more profound significance.

The conception of "form" thus provided a bridge by which Valéry could move from art to science without really abandoning one for the other. Indeed, what Valéry accentuates in the *Introduction to the Method of Leonardo da Vinci* (his declaration of intellectual independence) is the unity of the two rather than their diversity. This unity derives from their common ability to create forms and structures from an agglomeration of raw materials, and to impose continuity on the seemingly haphazard and disorderly; and Valéry's intellectual aim henceforth was both to establish this unity and to clarify its operations. What Mallarmé had done for poetry, Valéry could see as only a particular solution of a much larger task; what Mallarmé had tried to do only intuitively, Valéry would try to do for the activity of the mind as a whole—the common source of both science and art—with the rigorous tools of mathematical analysis.

The recent publication of Valéry's *Cahiers*, which he always considered his most important work, has shown with what tenacity and application he pursued this ambition all his life —the ambition of working out nothing less than a "mathematics of mental structures," which would illuminate the *forms* of all types of mental activity. Using his considerable knowledge of modern science as a guide, Valéry tried to find ways of describing mental activity in its most general pattern

based on analogies with mathematical and physical models. Judith Robinson, who discusses these efforts in detail in her excellent *L'Analyse de l'esprit dans les Cahiers de Valéry*, also points out how close he came, quite independently, to many of the ideas of such thinkers as the Vienna school of logical positivists and their English disciples, the Wittgenstein of the *Tractatus*, and Norbert Wiener's theory of cybernetics. Nothing definitive came of these efforts during Valéry's lifetime; and the ultimate value of his *Cahiers* from this point of view still remains to be decided. What is important here, however, is not so much the substance of these speculations as their spirit. For they reveal the scientific cast of Valéry's mind, and his conviction that only the axiomatic clarity of mathematics furnishes a standard by which all knowledge should ultimately be judged.

III

Valéry evolved, then, from the enchanted world of late-Symbolist occultism to what might be called the aesthetic rationalism (or, more exactly, mathematicism) that constitutes the unique position of his maturity. One would have to go back to Taine and Renan to find any French essayist displaying a comparably intransigent belief in science; and it is amusing to recall that these precursors of Valéry were the progenitors of the Naturalism he abhorred. The "science" that Valéry admired, however, was not biology or historical positivism but mathematics; and this made it possible for him to reconcile his passion for lucidity with his aesthetic sensibility. For mathematics, as Valéry had learned from Poincaré, was the creation of pure "forms" which dominated and transformed the empirical rather than conforming to its exigencies. Moreover, it was not too difficult to transfer the emotional

attitudes developed in the exquisitely rarefied mandarin-world of Symbolism to the equally select world of a scientific elite. The language of higher mathematics was perhaps even more baffling than the poems of Mallarmé; and the stance of superiority and aloofness to the common herd cultivated in the *cénacle* could easily be assimilated to the objectivity and neutrality that science ideally demands of its initiates.

If Valéry did not succeed in working out his quixotic project of a "mathematics of mental structures" (or at least of putting such a "mathematics" into communicable form), the traces of his private cogitations are everywhere discernible in his essays, emerging, like the tip of an iceberg, to reveal the hidden mass beneath. Nothing is more central to Valéry than the desire to use the methods of ratiocination developed by mathematics to dissolve the mysteries of mental life—among which, of course, is the mystery of artistic creation itself. Valéry abhors such words as "genius" and "inspiration" because they imply an ultimate barrier to rational comprehension; and it is precisely this barrier that he wishes to break through. Hence his unbounded admiration for a figure like Descartes, who was determined to apply mathematical reason to *all* the problems of traditional philosophy and metaphysics.

Leonardo the artist-scientist is the hero of Valéry's youth; Descartes—the mathematician-philosopher determined to master the universe of the spirit—is the idol of his maturity. No more in the one case than in the other do Valéry's essays on his heroes jibe with all the historical facts; but as he said in a marginal note, appended, thirty-five years after publication, to his first Leonardo essay: "In reality, I named as *a man* and *Leonardo* what appeared to me then as the power of the mind." The same may be said of most of Valéry's major essays, which, whatever their nominal subject, turn out to be

one or another variation on the powers, attributes, and functions of the mind; and this point must be understood if we are to do justice to Valéry's essay on Pascal, "Variations on a *Pensée*." For if the heroes of what Valéry called his *Comédie de l'esprit* bear the names, at various times, of Leonardo, Poe, Mallarmé, and Descartes, the villain of this Comedy is never anyone other than Pascal. No one is hounded by Valéry as relentlessly as the great mathematician who was also a great *prosateur*, and who disgracefully preferred the God of Abraham, Isaac, and Jacob to Valéry's Idol of the Intellect.

Valéry's essay on Pascal is so obviously a hostile philippic that there is little point in assessing the fairness or validity of its arguments. More important is to understand that, in Valéry's eyes, Pascal had committed the great betrayal: he had renounced his superb mathematical gifts for the sake of Christian salvation. Even worse, his baneful distinction between *l'esprit de finesse* and *l'esprit de géométrie* would have outlawed as futile the whole Cartesian attempt to master the realm of the spirit by mathematics. Nor could Valéry's haughty temperament endure the lack of pride and dignity natural to the whole Christian attitude of humility and self-degradation. Pascal's intellect, he writes scornfully, "cannot bear to think that it has fallen into the nets of time, number, and dimension, that it is trapped in the terrestrial system." To this we may contrast Valéry's own attitude in *Le Cimetière marin*, where, after contemplating the full extent of man's nothingness, the poet refuses to renounce life and affirms his ecstatic submission to these very same "nets of time, number and dimension":

> Non, non! . . . Debout! Dans l'ère successive!
> Brisez, mon corps, cette forme pensive!

Buvez, mon sein, la naissance du vent!
. . .
Courons à l'onde en rejaillir vivant!

Nietzsche would certainly have sympathized with Valéry's feeling that to dwell too long on man's weakness and misery is unhealthy and vitally debilitating. And the essay on Pascal is not the only point at which we can detect a convergence between the impeccably mannered (if mordantly ironic) member of the Academy and "the nervous poet Nietzsche," who took "to the idea of energy as to a drug," and who philosophized with a hammer rather than with a stiletto. Valéry's "Four Letters on Nietzsche," which do little more than acknowledge the receipt of some volumes from Nietzsche's French translator, hardly do justice to the extent and complexity of their mutual interrelation. Along with the writings of Henri Poincaré, the works of Nietzsche were constantly at Valéry's bedside; and according to Édouard Gaède, who has thoroughly investigated the matter in his brilliant *Nietzsche et Valéry*, the poet was among the first readers of Nietzsche in France.

Both share, as we have seen, the same attitude to Christianity and indeed to any form of the supernatural or transcendent: Valéry's repugnance for what Nietzsche called the *Hinterwelten* may be less violently expressed, but it is no less deep and intractable. And there is a good deal of Nietzsche's manner as an essayist in Valéry's tendency to see his subjects not as private individuals but as "types of the creative life," as characters in his *Comédie de l'esprit*. Unlike Nietzsche, however, Valéry was not at all interested in unmasking the hidden emotive impulses stirring behind ideological disguises. He wishes, rather, only to understand the immanent psychic

mechanisms of the mind by which these structures are pro-
duced. Mysticism for Valéry is simply a kind of non-Euclidian
geometry whose axioms and postulates have not yet been
ascertained; and in the essay on Swedenborg, he struggles to
find analogies in artistic experience for the mystic's certainty
of the "truth" of his visions.

The name of Nietzsche occurs several times in Valéry's
essay on Stendhal; and both are united, to be sure, in their
admiration for this quirky and capricious figure, whose vivac-
ity and loquacity remind Valéry of Balzac's illustrious
Gaudissart—the literary prototype "of those prehistoric com-
mercial travelers who dazzled and exasperated their corner
of the inn table in the days of the last stagecoaches and the
first railways." As a sheer piece of literary and historical
criticism, Valéry's scintillating pages on Stendhal are the
finest in the book; but Valéry would not have been true to
himself if he had remained simply on this literary level.
Stendhal's *égotisme*—his continual effort, as Valéry sees it, to
dramatize and enjoy the spectacle of the multiple facets of
his own personality—inevitably leads to reflections on the
need of the personality both for absolute independence and
autonomy and, at the same time, for the approval and
admiration of others.

Valéry, however, is no La Rochefoucauld who delights in
exposing the essence of human nature to be vanity and self-
love; he distinguishes very carefully between the noble pride
which spurs to creative achievement and the ignoble vanity
that searches merely for tawdry self-advantage. One of
Valéry's profoundest and most characteristic insights is to
attribute the origin of pride, not to any base motive, but to an
instinctive negation of the common fate of death. "And so
the horror of death produces out of its darkness some insane

will to be *unlike*, to be independence itself and the absolutely singular being, that is to say, a god." It is little wonder that Valéry himself finds such remarks to be more appropriate "as a marginal comment on *Ecce Homo* than on *Henri Brulard*." The shadow of Nietzsche's Superman may indeed be discerned lurking behind these reflections on the Absolute Self, whose need for autonomy and singularity deeply appealed to Valéry; and Nietzsche's insistence that man should strive to surpass himself often echoes more restrainedly in Valéry's pages. But rather than involving the creation of a new table of values for mankind, what this means for Valéry is the attainment by the mind of the highest degree of reflexive self-consciousness.

Despite this indebtedness to Nietzsche, and the intense admiration for Wagner that he shared with all the progeny of Baudelaire, Valéry's knowledge of German literature did not go very deep. He knew English well enough to translate some of Poe's *Marginalia* as well as a poem of Thomas Hardy's; once he had even intended to translate *The Red Badge of Courage*; but though he was acquainted with Rilke personally, and much impressed by the necromantic quality that emanated from the latter's presence, he was unable to read his work. This lack of any intimate contact with German literature (despite Valéry's employment of the Faust theme) no doubt accounts for the weakness of his essay on Goethe, which is the only place where one feels that he is not quite up to a subject imposed by chance. (It might be remarked that the problem of coming to terms with Goethe has been a stumbling block for more than one non-German man of letters. T. S. Eliot does little better in the Goethe essay included in *On Poetry and Poets*; only Santayana and Ortega y Gasset come to mind as having acquitted themselves honorably of

the formidable task of tackling the German colossus.) The strength of Valéry's literary essays derives from the quality of their personal insight, the refractions of Valéry's ideas projected through the prism of other creations or personalities; and when his sensibility has not been truly engaged, as in the Goethe essay, the result is more rhetoric than substance.

Valéry does his best, to be sure, to find the points at which his own interests might give him some access to Goethe. Like Leonardo, Goethe too aspired to be a universal man and combine art and science; certainly he is the greatest incarnation in modern times of this perennial Valéryan aspiration. As a result, Valéry dwells a good deal on Goethe's scientific side, and implicitly turns him into an anti-Pascal whose love of sober, scientific knowledge saves him from a Hamlet-like despair before the terrors of death and dissolution. Goethe's attitude, however, as Valéry rightly remarks, was based on a "*mystique* of objectivity," a refusal to believe that "there was anything in the *subject* more significant or more important than was to be observed in the least *object*." Valéry could sympathize with this cult of Appearance so far as it tended towards the dispassionate study of nature and seemed to coincide with his own emphasis on "form"; but he knew very well that Goethe's idea of science was very far from being his own.

Goethe, after all, had been the great opponent of Newton and hence also of Descartes—the opponent of all the mathematical, quantifying tendencies of modern science that Valéry so much admired. If Goethe also wished to wipe out the Pascalian distinction between *finesse* and *géométrie*, he unquestionably preferred to give the hegemony over knowledge to the former, rather than to assign it, like Valéry, to the latter. This is why Goethe attempted to substitute his own

science, based on qualitative observation, for one that dissolved appearance into a network of mathematical relations. Valéry could hardly fail to pick up this challenge to his own most cherished principles; and it is no surprise to find that Goethe, though a universal genius, "was perhaps lacking in mathematical sense."

Luckily, though, there is a passage in *The Metamorphosis of Plants* in which Goethe expresses the desire to have botanical concepts so clearly defined that they could be used "in the same way as algebraic formulas." This harmless phrase is enough for Valéry to exclaim that he has caught the anti-Newtonian Goethe "en flagrant délit d'intention géométrique," i.e., reaching out despite himself for "a variety of symbolic calculus, analogous to those so frequently invented and used in modern dynamics and physics." In this manner, Valéry gracefully glides over the hiatus separating Goethe's conception of universality from his own "universal man," and sacrifices the chance to measure his position against a truly intimidating foe. The essay concludes with a dazzling display of fireworks and capital letters describing the meeting of Goethe and Napoleon, which is sufficiently characterized in Valéry's laconic comment on this article in a letter to Gide: "Napoleon: external stuffing."

IV

Valéry was fond of declaring that his favorite historical period was the late eighteenth century, and that, if given the choice, he would prefer to have lived during the years in which the resplendent civilization of *Le Roi Soleil* was beginning to set. "I imagine this period must have been one of the most brilliant and satisfying ever known to men," Valéry writes. "It was

marked by the glittering close of one world and the powerful struggles of another to come to birth, also by a highly refined art, by forms and manners that were still very temperate, by all the strength and all the graces of the mind. There were magic and the differential calculus; as many atheists as mystics; the most cynical of cynics and the oddest of dreamers. The excesses of the intellect were not unknown, yet were counter-balanced—sometimes in the same head—by an astonishing credulity."

Passages embodying the same idea turn up so frequently in Valéry that one may take them, not only as the expression of an historical predilection, but also as the fulfillment of an emotional need. Nor is it difficult to explain why the contemplation of this personally selected golden age should have given Valéry so much satisfaction. It images a world in which French neoclassical taste still reigned supreme, and in which —though precariously—it was still able to contain and master the extremest tensions of the free play of the intellect and the emotions; and this world appealed so powerfully to Valéry because its various aspects reappear in his own work. Do we not find in his own creations an adherence to neoclassical forms combined with a never-ending thematic struggle between consciousness and being—the struggle that the mind always discovers between "what it can know and what it is?" Valéry's delight in a world where both magic and differential calculus were equally powerful currents of thought reflects his own creative universe, which could produce both a volume of poetry called *Charmes* and conceive the project of a "mathematics of mental structures." The same weave of tensions and contrasts defines the spiritual horizon of the admirer of Poe, Mallarmé, and Baudelaire on the one hand, and of Descartes, Riemann, Poincaré, and Einstein on the other.

The interest and fascination of Valéry's essays derives precisely from the scope and variety of his intellectual ambitions, which aimed at nothing less than to unite what the whole history of modern culture has driven apart. But one can understand why, like his own Monsieur Teste, Valéry liked to dwell so loftily in the realm of pure abstraction and possibility, or, to use his own term, of pure "form." For the moment he looked at the reality and actuality of the world created by his mathematical predilections, the poet and man of letters could not prevent himself from uttering a cry of protest. This protest is heard very clearly in "The Return from Holland," a group of reflections devoted to the revered memory of Descartes. "Is not the Method, after all, the Charter of a realm of Number whose whole ambition is now apparent to us, even if we cannot yet grasp its full power? . . . Life itself, which is already half enslaved, circumscribed, streamlined, or reduced to a state of subjection, has great difficulty in defending itself against the tyranny of timetables, statistics, quantitative measurements, and precision instruments, a whole development that goes on reducing life's diversity, diminishing its uncertainty, improving the functioning of the whole, making its course surer, larger, and more mechanical." Valéry's paeans to the triumphs of mathematical reason are often accompanied by such a menacing bass, warning of the insidious destruction of the *quality* of life brought about by the transformation of man's environment.

Another type of warning can be found in his speech on Voltaire, delivered at a solemn séance in the Sorbonne shortly after the liberation of Paris in 1944. In what sounds as close to being a *cri du cœur* as we can find in Valéry, he declares: "It might be said that all our intellectual efforts, the whole of the incredible increase in our positive knowledge have served

only to raise to a savage and crushing power the means of bringing the human race to an end, having first destroyed the hopes it had nourished for centuries of taming its own nature." The desperation that one hears in these lines may well explain the unusual nature of this essay, which speaks a different language from the one generally audible in Valéry's pages. Whether this language is only Valéry's response and adaptation to the demands of a particular occasion, or whether it indicates a genuine modification of his point of view, is difficult to say; but the whole emphasis of the essay, in any case, runs counter to positions he had taken in the past.

For Valéry does not celebrate, as we might have expected, Voltaire the antagonist of the Church and the supernatural, and the enemy of his enemy Pascal; nor does he so much as mention those marvelously lively *contes* that he was inclined to consider the very apogee of French prose fiction. Rather, he invokes the shade of Voltaire the crusader against inhumanity and oppression, the advocate of humanity who, with the pen as his sole weapon, successfully fought against the much more formidable arsenal of the French monarchy. "The decisive event of [Voltaire's] career, the guarantee of his immortality, was his metamorphosis into the friend and defender of the human race." Such "defenders of humanity" had received short shrift from Valéry in the past, as we can see from a passage in his *Cahiers* (1907) on the same subject. Here we find him excoriating "the charlatanism discovered by Voltaire who, at a favorable moment, made of the man of letters a universal, political, prostitute-idol, a sort of Augustus Caesar elevated by popular opinion—as if the truly superior man could be recognized by the crowd." This facile and self-complacent contempt for the mob is one of Valéry's least attractive traits; and it is, regrettably, far more typical

than his panegyric on Voltaire for devoting himself to the service of mankind, or for dedicating his literary gifts to a moral-political cause. It is possible, however, that the harrowing events of the war years had shaken Valéry's faith in the Idol of the Intellect which he had hitherto revered so ardently and exclusively, and had opened his eyes to the need for other values as well.

However that may be, several other passages in the same essay reinforce the impression of novelty and possible metamorphosis. "After all," Valéry says, "the Gospels and the Rights of Man are in agreement on the one essential point: the infinite value of the human person." This "infinite value," as we see, is no longer identified solely with the geniuses who embody the Absolute Self and its ruthless will to autonomy and power. Valéry also praises Voltaire for appealing to men's hearts as well as to their reason (though he was far from having accorded the same privilege to Pascal). "He [Voltaire] invoked reason, *but he aimed at men's hearts. What could prevail against this alliance between truth and pity?"* This implicit avowal that pity could *aid* reason and truth is perhaps the most startling about-face in Valéry's last public utterance. It may be supplemented by the following extract from the *Cahiers*, written a few months before Valéry's death in July 1945. "—That is the *fact*. The most obscure of facts. Stronger than the desire to live and the power to understand is, after all, this blasted H[eart]."*

Taken along with Valéry's constant laments about the state of the modern world, such passages reveal the gnawing cleavage that he could never assuage between his humanist

*It is impossible to translate the nuance, both blasphemous and reverential at the same time, contained in the play on the words "*sacré C[œur]*."

sensibility and his conceptual commitments. This cleavage, to be sure, provides the major theme for all his work; but while he can turn it into superb poetry, and dramatize its antinomies effectively in various prose and semi-poetic genres (*Monsieur Teste, Eupalinos, L'Idée fixe,* the fragments of *Mon Faust*), he could never find any convincing way of bridging this contradiction in his essays. These latter remain, as Émile Faguet once said of Voltaire, "a chaos of clear ideas," in which every part is beautifully perspicuous and the whole a blooming, buzzing confusion. It would be unfair to come down too heavily on this lack of consistency, especially since Valéry always disclaimed any ambition to construct a philosophical "system"; but one can legitimately object, it seems to me, to his refusal ever to acknowledge this contradiction as a problem that he had an obligation to admit or to confront. Even in the Voltaire essay, it is significant that the change of position is not accompanied by any hint of *personal* retraction or reconsideration.

The Valéry who laments the degradation of the quality of life conveniently forgets that he is the same Valéry who accepted, as his sole and highest value, the intellectual method and outlook that brought this degradation about. The advocate of intellectual exactitude and Leonardo's *ostinato rigore* criticizes mercilessly on the one hand what he glorifies extravagantly on the other—and never a word betrays the suspicion that perhaps his views might require some adjustment or modification. More precisely: if we accept Valéry's own criterion of mathematical rigor, by what conceptual standard can he justify the values that lead him to speak of life as being "enslaved" because of its increasing quantification? Neither the idea of "life" nor that of "enslavement" (in this sense) can be unequivocally defined. One can imagine the

withering scorn with which Valéry would have treated a mere "philosopher" who had attempted to denigrate science by means of such concepts. Their lack of precision would have been tartly thrown in his face, and he would be disposed of in this way without a moment's hesitation.

As a thinker, then, Valéry is much too inclined to evade the implications of his own thought, much too eager to maintain an imposing posture of infallibility. He is forever having his intellectual cake and eating it too by assuming the simultaneous stance both of a high priest of science and a humanistic prophet of doom. The major criticism that can be made of him on this score is not so much conceptual or logical as it is personal: Valéry is simply too self-indulgent toward his own position, and never measures himself by the standards he applies so sternly to others. This is one respect in which the zealot of the highest intellectual self-awareness falls distressingly short of even a modest approximation to his own goal.

Rather than dwelling on Valéry's shortcomings, however, it is much more profitable to conclude by stressing his achievements. No modern writer has *lived* the adventure of the scientific mind with as much depth and intensity as Valéry; and it is never superfluous to defend the virtues inculcated by science against the distortions of passion and prejudice (though one wishes that Valéry had imbibed a little more of the personal humility that science—as well as religion—is supposed to foster among its devotees). The creations of Valéry proved that the highest abstractions of the intellect could be united with the most subtle refinements of the aesthetic sensibility, even if this was a personal feat that could not be generalized into a doctrine or "method." Moreover, in a Western world presently divided, so far as philosophy is concerned, between an irrationalism parading as ontology

and a rationalism that cannot get beyond skeptical self-destruction and methodological paralysis, the example of Valéry's aspiration towards universality is not to be ignored. Henri Bergson is once reported to have said: "What Valéry has done had to be attempted." One may add that, if Western culture is to remain faithful to its great tradition, it will have to be attempted again and again.

JOSEPH FRANK

MASTERS AND FRIENDS

Pontus de Tyard

PONTUS DE TYARD is no very great figure. His name simply makes us think of the *Pléiade*, a constellation from which he borrows a little of the light that has helped him to find his way down to our time.

But if learned attention will concentrate on and linger over this companion of Ronsard and du Bellay, it will discover in Tyard almost all the noble qualities which went to the making of the great men of his period. We know that they were equipped with all the talents, and the whole gamut of human desires was implanted in their fiery souls.

The century from Leonardo to Francis Bacon is particularly rich in universal minds. The curiosity to feel, the voluptuous pleasure of knowing, the passion for creation were carried, in those fabulous times, to an unprecedented pitch. The arts, the sciences, Hebrew, Greek, mathematics, speculative or practical politics, war, theology . . . there was nothing that did not seem desirable and, as it were, delightful and easy to those multifarious monsters, thirsting after knowledge and power, who devoured the whole of the past and gave birth to a whole future.

Our Pontus was a man of the same stamp though of smaller stature. The poet was an astronomer; the astronomer a bishop; the bishop an agent of the King, and served as his pen in the

polemics of the day. The emblems of the lyre, the miter, the astrolabe might have figured on his tomb. But the fourth corner of the tombstone could well have been decorated with another emblem which, it seems, would be as suitable for Tyard as the others. It would be one of those sublime big-bellied bottles of which he made large and joyous use provided they were filled with Burgundy, which was the wine of his country as well as his own choice.

As for love, Tyard, like everybody else, did not fail to pay the tribute due as of right to that inescapable master. He was much occupied with a certain Pasithée. But in exchange, love made him a present of quite a number of charming lines; it inspired the *Livre des erreurs amoureuses*, where we find graceful things like this:

> *O calme nuit qui doucement composes*
> *En ma faveur l'ombre mieux animée*
> *Qu'onque Morphée en sa salle enfumée*
> *Peignit du rien de ses métamorphoses . . .*

I must not forget, in speaking of Pontus de Tyard, that one tradition credits him with having been the first poet to write sonnets in our language. There is some doubt about the merits of our bishop's claim, but this very doubt is a source of fame, for the sonnet is one of the happiest of poetical inventions: the sonnet, whose brevity and strictness of form were feared by neither Michelangelo nor Shakespeare, a form which condemns the poet to perfection, so that the mere suspicion of introducing it to the French is infinitely honorable.

Tyard had a weakness for inversion, which he used a little too often and too markedly; but in poetry it is a useful and

significant liberty, for it inflicts a noble torture on the normal and humdrum course of expression.

Taking advantage of a total eclipse of the sun to disappear from this life, Tyard died in 1605, aged but not bowed by eighty-four revolutions of our planet; having loyally, and without getting them too mixed up, served Apollo, Venus, Urania, Henri III, Bacchus, and the Church.

Sketch for a Portrait of Descartes

FIFTEEN YEARS ago you could still see, in a street near the Place Royale, a police barracks where soldiers in the reserve came to have their papers checked and stamped.

A man would go in and take his bearings across a dignified but home-like courtyard. The offices he was looking for were on the left, in one of the arcades shaped like basket handles—all that remained of a fairly ancient cloister. Its ruined majesty fitted in very well with the easygoing life, half public and half private, which the First Empire had brought with it. There was an absent-minded orderly; a few canary cages fixed to the pillars; forage caps and pots of flowers in the windows; here and there white breeches were hanging on a line to dry. Year in and year out, about a hundred thousand men who were liable for the call-up had to cross this courtyard. I do not know whether it ever occurred to a single one of them that he was being made to undertake a pilgrimage. The very authorities who ordered it, high as they were, did not know its real objective. They imagined they were simply maneuvering the reserves for their own purposes; but they were compelling us, without realizing it, to pay a visit to one of the greatest monuments in the history of thought.

The barracks had taken the place of a convent, and the

police that of the Minim friars. It was there that Father
Mersenne, a very useful and quite an important man in intel-
lectual circles at the beginning of the seventeenth century,
lived and died; he was an easygoing, inquisitive religious who
propounded problems and sometimes conundrums for the
whole of intellectual Europe—a somewhat different Europe
from the one we know; he was the agent of scientific ferment
and the intermediary between scholars of differing religious
creeds; the childhood friend, the loyal and overzealous
friend of Descartes, the propagator of his theories, and one
of the most engaging of those lesser men whose role is possibly
essential to the development of great men and the unleashing
of great events. Some systematic research into the history of
such assistants, hangers-on, confidants, or intermediaries, al-
ways to be found in the proximity of genius and among the
tiny active causes which produce the great events, would be
quite a novel and, I imagine, quite a rewarding study.

When Descartes was in Paris people used to call on him in
the morning in the rooms of the invaluable Father Mersenne
at the convent of the Minims in the Place Royale. It was there
that he met M. Mélian on July 11, 1644. When he arrived
from The Hague in June 1647, he went to stay with the Abbé
Picot in the Rue Geoffroy-Lasnier, where he wrote the pref-
ace to the *Principles*. He left for Brittany, where he had some
business to transact, came back by way of Poitou and Tou-
raine, and was greeted on his return to Paris at the beginning
of September by the good news that a pension of three thous-
and livres had just been granted him by the King at the
instigation of the Cardinal Minister. News of this kind has
grown rare.

It was then that "M. Pascal the younger, who was in Paris,
felt a desire to make his acquaintance and had the satisfaction

7

of a talk with him at the Minims' convent, where he had been told that he would find him. M. Descartes had the pleasure of hearing him describe the experiments on the Vacuum which he had performed at Rouen, an account of which was being printed and a copy of which he sent to him in Holland some time after his return there. M. Descartes was delighted with M. Pascal's conversation."

I am too much concerned for the fame of the latter to transcribe the rest of the story.

One day when I was passing by, I noticed with distress that on the site of the ancient home of the Minims there was a cube-shaped building, whose whitewash was far too fresh and bright, surmounted by cannon balls with plumes of flame carved in soft stone. The police had been moved into this block. I liked them better when they were in the former convent, the police being a sort of military order, though it appears to have no objection whatever to the marriage of its members.

There are few countries in Europe where a house that was consecrated by the presence of so great a man and had heard such a conversation could have vanished as discreetly as in France. There was no tablet on the wall of the Minims to tell what it had seen. No one seems to have known what I have just related, which I found in Baillet, since not a single soul complained, or opposed the destruction of the building. Everything disappeared in the cloud of dust raised by the demolition squad.

In this respect Descartes has been unlucky. No statue of this admirable man in Paris—an omission that I am content should remain unremedied. He has been given only a rather poor street, though it is enlivened by noises from the Polytechnique and faintly haunted by the ghost of Verlaine, who

died there. Lastly, we have allowed his bones to be mislaid somewhere around Saint-Germain-des-Prés; and I have not heard that anyone is looking for them for the crypt of the Pantheon.

But, prudent man that he was and an incomparable artist when it came to working on the most intractable materials, he built a tomb for himself with his own hands—a truly enviable tomb. In it he placed the statue of his mind, a statue so clear and lifelike that you would swear it is alive and speaking to us in person, that there are not three centuries between us but rather a possibility of contact, a distance no greater than between one mind and another, or between a mind and itself. His monument is the *Discourse*, which, like everything that is precisely expressed, is virtually incorruptible. A decorous yet homely language, which is not without its pride or its modesty, transmits to us the fundamental intuitions and attitudes shared by all thoughtful men, in such sensitive and remarkable form that the result is less a masterpiece of resemblance or verisimilitude than a real presence, and one actually nourished by our own.

There are no difficulties, no images, no scholastic trappings, nothing in the text which is not said in an inward tone of the simplest and most human kind, and only just a little more precise than the natural one. The author, who might be speaking to us, seems to have confined himself to clarifying, exactly recounting, and at times very clearly articulating the immediate expression inspired by his memories and his hopes. He has assumed that tone which first teaches us our own thoughts, and rises in silence from our concentrated attention.

An inner word, striving after no effect or artifice, being our own closest and surest possession, however much our own it may be, cannot but be universal.

A part of Descartes' aim was to make us hear and under-

stand *himself*, that is, to inspire in us the kind of monologue that was his own necessity, and make us repeat his own vows. *He wanted us to discover in ourselves what he had found in himself.*

This was his prime intention. Every innovator of an intellectual order must find a way of making himself irresistible. Some captivate us by their charm; others wear us down by the rigor of their method; Descartes communicates his own life to us, so that the sequence of his impressions and actions may initiate us into the ways of his thought by the same natural path of events and meditations which he had followed since youth, and which is similar to many other paths though it leads to very different points of view.

By making us identify ourselves with his beginnings, thus easily involving us in his career, he succeeds with little difficulty in enlisting our sympathy for his rebellious adolescence, for he speaks to us of our own—our resistances and our lordly judgments. Having completed his education and dismissed it as virtually useless (for in fact, education is more or less useless to the man who is unable to use what he would never have discovered for himself), he wandered all over Europe, purging his mind by travel and by action in a war which was then in progress, in which he seems to have participated as fancy moved him. He kept away from books, which can be rather a nuisance in the army; he went in for mathematics, an art that needs nothing but a pen and can be practiced anywhere, at any time, and for as long as our heads will stand it.

What a luxurious form of freedom! What an elegant and voluptuous way of being oneself, when a man can thus lose himself in *things*, and yet grow stronger in his ideas! . . .

The accidental, the superficial with its rapid changes, stimulate and clarify what is deepest and most constant in a person who is really born for a high intellectual destiny. In full in-

dependence of mind, he enjoys the pleasure of existing simply in order to understand. The properly organized consciousness turns everything to account. Everything contributes to its detachment; everything serves to engage it; it stops at nothing. The more relationships it absorbs, or endures, the more closely integrated it is and the freer and more flexible it becomes. A mind completely *connected* would certainly be, at this extreme, a mind infinitely *free*, because in the last resort freedom is simply the use of the *possible*, and the essence of the mind is a desire to be at one with its whole potential.

Descartes shuts himself up with the *whole* of his awareness and he pushes the use of his own potentialities to the point of casting doubt on his own *existence* in the very middle of his account of his *life!* . . . The same man who traveled all over the world and indulged in amateur soldiering suddenly turns around inside the frame of himself and his body, and transforms the whole of his own system of reference, and of our common certainties, into something relative; he changes himself into *another*, just as a sleeping man who makes a sudden movement, as a result of something in his dream, alters, *transcends* the dream, changing it into a mere dream. He creates an opposition between the being and the man.

But to be aware of the being in the man and to draw such a sharp distinction between the two, to seek a higher degree of certainty by a sort of special procedure, are the first signs of a *philosophy*. . . .

Perhaps I ought to stop at that word, at the very point where I no longer know what I am talking about. There is still time to avoid involving myself in difficulties that are not the kind I would have chosen, and of which the most formidable are those which are hidden from me. I am not at ease with

philosophy. I know that it is inescapable, and that we can hardly open our mouths without paying tribute to it. But how can we help that, when philosophy itself cannot tell us precisely what it is? It is almost meaningless to say, as people often do, that every man is a philosopher without knowing it, since the very man who takes it up consciously is unable to explain exactly what he is up to.

When it comes to philosophy, I myself am rather like a barbarian in some Athens where he knows that he is surrounded by priceless things and that everything he sees deserves respect; yet in the midst of this Athens he becomes worried; he is bored and embarrassed, conscious of a vague feeling of veneration mixed with superstitious fear, and of a brutal desire to smash everything or set fire to so many wonderful and mysterious things which have no counterpart in his own mind. How can you tolerate the fact that such things exist and are so famous, if the very idea of them would never have occurred to you? I also compare myself to those unfortunate people whose hearing is good and who are capable of distinguishing every sound; but the interconnections and blendings of sounds, the forms and figures, the delicate weavings, the infinities of sounds, in short the *music*, escapes them. The music of the philosophers is almost imperceptible to me.

So if I venture to talk about Descartes, it is no doubt because I draw a distinction between him and them. . . .

Descartes

Mr. President,
Mr. Minister,
Ladies and Gentlemen:

THE FRENCH ACADEMY could not fail to accept the invitation so graciously extended by the Organizing Committee of the Ninth International Congress of Philosophy, and my first duty is to thank the Committee in its name. It was the Academy's duty to itself to be represented at a gathering in honor of Descartes on the third centenary of the publication of the *Discourse on Method*.

The great influence that Descartes seems to have had on our literature; the event for which he was responsible, the first appearance in the French language of a philosophical work; the world-wide fame that his works have brought to the nation, are three factors that touch the Academy very closely, three strong and palpable reasons why it should join all those who are today paying homage to the great man's memory.

As for the honor that our Society has done me by choosing me as its representative, I hardly need to tell you that I owe it to the unavoidable absence of the most eminent philosopher of our time. The state of his health has prevented our

colleague M. Henri Bergson from occupying the place in which everyone expected to find him and where he would have spoken to you about Descartes with the magic authority, the natural depth, and the beauty of expression which are his. But he is with us in spirit, and in a few minutes you will hear the letter that he has been kind enough to write to us.

Gentlemen of the Foreign Delegations:
The Organizing Committee has made the modest gesture of appointing me to welcome you, and to express its gratitude to you for contributing to the distinction and importance of this Congress.

The name of Descartes which has been bestowed on it gives it a very special significance. You are aware of the extent to which the clearest and most forcible characteristics of the French mind are exemplified in the great man's thought. That is why the celebration of his fame assumes for us the solemnity of a national occasion, distinguished by the presence of the head of the State.

We thank you, gentlemen, for associating yourselves with our tribute and for coming to repay the visits that Descartes himself made to more than one country. No one has been a better European than our intellectual hero who came and went with such ease. He thought wherever he could think: he meditated, he made discoveries and calculations wherever he happened to be: in a well-warmed room in Germany, on the quays in Amsterdam, and as far afield as Sweden, where death overtook the traveler whose freedom of mind was the very precious gift which he had never ceased to preserve by his freedom of movement.

I hope, gentlemen, that while you are in France you may meet everywhere with that sympathy which we like to dis-

play toward all men of thought, and that you will be as favored during your philosophical visit as Descartes was in the different places where his fancy took him.

I must now say a few words on the particular subject which has brought us together, and deal, as best I can, with Descartes and philosophy. It will be a case of touching lightly on tremendous themes. The philosophers, who are of necessity hard men, have no doubt called on me to try my hand in much the same way as experiments are performed on a living body, or perhaps they are resolved to sacrifice an innocent and propitiatory victim on the Altar of Reason.

To tell the truth, the moment I knew they had me caught and bound, and realizing to the full the difficulties and dangers of a task for which I was in no way equipped, I reflected at once on the almost insurmountable obstacle created by the prodigious amount that had been written on the subject. What could I say that was not certain to be found in one of those volumes? Could I even invent an error which would at least be a *new* error? Could I think up a misinterpretation which had not been heard before?

Descartes. . . . For three centuries men of the highest intelligence have been rethinking his philosophy; it has been "dissected" and commented on by so many painstaking exponents; condensed by so many schoolmasters for so many pupils—but where is Descartes? I dare not say that there is an infinite number of possible Descartes; but you know better than I that there are a good many, all vouched for, text in hand, and curiously different from one another. The plurality of plausible Descartes is a fact. Whether it is a question of the Method or of the metaphysical developments which followed, the diversity of judgments and the divergences of

opinion are there, and are astonishing. And yet Descartes is by definition a clear writer.

As we might expect, it is the most delicate and, in some respects, the most inward elements of his philosophy that are the most warmly contested and the most variously interpreted.

To some people, for example, the God of Descartes is only an expedient, who serves to guarantee the correctness of his speculations and to act as prime mover. Pascal, with the excessive clear-sightedness that springs from perfect antipathy, committed himself wholeheartedly to this view.

Others, on the contrary, who understand him differently, present us with a Descartes who was sincerely and even fundamentally religious. In the very foundations of the Method and beneath the structure of rational knowledge, they show us a crypt where, they say, a light gleamed which was not the light of nature.

But what greater glory can there be, for man or book, than to provoke such conflicting views? The surest sign that you are really dead is universal acceptance. Whereas the number of different and incompatible faces with which we can reasonably endow a man is a clear demonstration of the richness of his make-up. How many Napoleons have there not been? My own view is that we cannot really circumscribe a man's life, imprison him in his ideas and his actions, reduce him to what he appeared to be and, so to speak, lay siege to him in his works. We are much more (and sometimes much less) than what we have done. We know from our own experience that our identity and our unity are, as it were, external and almost alien to us, that they lie far more in what we learn indirectly about ourselves than in what we learn through our immediate awareness. A man who had never looked at himself in a mirror would at first glance find nothing to tell

him that the unknown face he saw there was connected by the most mysterious link in the world to what he felt and what he thought on his side of the glass.

Each of us, therefore, can create a Descartes of his own, since those who set out to make the closest study of him seem to diverge all the more radically from one another the more carefully they consider their subject. I repeat, for the point appears to me to be an important one, that the divergence of opinions is most marked when it comes to the real core of Descartes' thought.

I confess, gentlemen, that I like this difference of opinion among the experts and authorities on Descartes. If they cannot agree among themselves, the amateur at once begins to breathe more freely, and feels rather more disposed to listen to himself and to follow the promptings of his own thought.

The fact is that in such matters I have nothing to offer but a very lively curiosity, and I am more interested in the mind itself than in the things that are imagined, argued, and decided in the mind. What excites my most natural inclination is the vain attempt to discover the actual workings of thought. To interest myself in the subject, the problems, the reach of that thought requires an effort of the will. It is the substitutions and the transmutations that I imagine at work in it, the vicissitudes of its lucidity and its power, the interventions and interferences which take place in it that delight the true student of the life of the mind. The strange desire to observe that which observes and to image that which imagines is not without a certain naïveté: it reminds us of those quaint woodcuts such as we find in Descartes' *Dioptrique*, which explain the phenomenon of sight by the figure of a little man posted behind a huge eye, busy looking at the image that forms on the retina.

But though the temptation is irresistible, it implies no

system of philosophy, no point of view, and no conclusion, because the mind in itself has no means of setting a limit on its own fundamental activity, and there is no such thing as a thought which is its last thought. Mechanics teaches us that it is impossible to give to a solid body a form such that, when placed on a horizontal plane, that body can never reach a state of equilibrium. But the mind has solved the problem and gives some very painful and very exhausting demonstrations during times of anxiety and on sleepless nights. Yet the student of the mind simply enjoys these combinations and fluctuations of the intellect, and finds much to marvel at: he sees, for example, fundamental disorder producing a momentary order; a necessity arising or being constituted out of some arbitrary arrangement; the incidental giving birth to the rule; the part replacing the whole. He also sees personal pride creating imaginary obstacles against which it can expend and measure its powers of analysis and concentration.

And he may then go so far as to claim that no poetic material in the world is richer than this; that the life of the intelligence offers an incomparable lyrical universe, a whole theater in which neither adventure, passion, suffering of a very particular kind, nor comedy, nor anything human is lacking. He will maintain that there exists a vast area of intellectual sensibility, under appearances sometimes so denuded of the usual attractions that most people avoid them as though they were reservoirs of boredom promising nothing but painful debate. This world of thought, in which we catch a glimpse of the mind thinking about its own processes, and which extends from the central mystery of consciousness to that luminous zone where the passion for clarity comes into play, is as varied, as moving, as surprising in its dramatic revelations and the intervention of chance, and as admirable in itself, as

the world of the affective life, governed by the instincts alone. What after all can be more specifically human, more specially the prerogative of the man who is most a man, than intellectual effort divorced from any practical consideration; and what is purer or more daring than his progress along the path of abstract thought which sometimes dips so strangely toward the depths of human potentiality?

In a time like ours, when there is no lack of futility or anxiety, no lack of facility or confusion, kept alive and continually fed with fresh pretexts by the powerful media you are all aware of, at such a time it might not be altogether unprofitable to celebrate the nobler exercises of the mind.

But up to the present, literature has not, so far as I am aware, paid much attention to this immense treasure house of subjects and situations. The reasons for its neglect are obvious. I must, however, mention one which is only too well known to you. It lies in the extreme difficulty presented by language when we try to force it to describe mental phenomena. What are we to make of terms that cannot be precisely defined unless we re-create them? *Thought, mind* itself, *reason, intelligence, understanding, intuition*, or *inspiration?* . . . Each of these terms is both a means and an end in turn, a problem and a solution, a state and an idea; and each of them, in each of us, is adequate or inadequate according to the function which circumstances impose on it. You are aware that at this point the philosopher becomes a poet, and often a great poet: he borrows metaphor from us and, by means of splendid images which we might well envy, he draws on all nature for the expression of his profoundest thought.

The poet is not so fortunate when he tries the corresponding procedure. Nevertheless, gentlemen, from time to time I find myself trying to imagine, with the model of the *Human*

or even the *Divine Comedy* in mind, what some great writer might be able to produce in the sphere of the purely intellectual life that would be comparable to those great works. The urge to understand and to create; the urge to surpass what others have achieved and to become the equal of the greatest; or, on the contrary, the self-denial and the renunciation of fame which are found in some. And then the details themselves of the moments of intellectual activity: the waiting for the gift of a form or an idea; for the simple word that will transform the impossible into a thing achieved; the desires and the sacrifices, the victories and disasters; and the surprises, the infinite patience, the dawn of a "truth"; and such extraordinary moments as, for example, the sudden awareness of a sort of solitude that may come without warning even in the midst of a crowd, and descend on a man like a veil beneath which the mystery of a direct revelation occurs. ... And how much more? All this suggests a poetry whose resources are inexhaustible. The creative sensibility, in its noblest forms and its most exquisite productions, seems to me to be just as much a subject for art as all that is moving or dramatic in our everyday life.

However, I cannot conceal from you, my philosophical friends (from whom in any case it is impossible to conceal very much), that this manner of looking at the mind leads us quite naturally to regard philosophy as an application of thought to itself; and the eye that is interested in interior events is satisfied by the spectacle of the transformations of thought, and is content to treat conclusions as mere incidentals, or brief pauses, like rests in music. But this is how the universe of the mind, seen purely in itself, though provided with all the necessary illusions, must strike the eye of the poet; it is a system lacking neither in verbal *nebulae* to be resolved,

nor in the infinite perspectives of a kind of space, which may even be *curved space*.

The great advantage of this point of view is that it allows the greatest possible generality in the treatment of purely intellectual matters; and, in particular, you can see how interesting it may be for philosophy itself, though appearing at first to treat philosophy more lightly than it should.

Think of the fate of all those doctrines which to us seem to have been refuted, all the hypotheses and arguments which the advancement of knowledge, the development of the means and the habit of precise observation, the discovery of entirely new facts, have reduced to nonsense. Think of the many famous works that ask questions we can no longer ask, or which answer questions we can no longer even understand. Must they be condemned to the sort of death signified by a mention in the history books or inclusion in school syllabuses?

You can no longer argue with such mummies. Their weird names exist only for a few uncomfortable moments in the minds of schoolboys. Yet in order to restore, not their original vigor, but something of the virtue which brought them into being, it is sufficient to think of the living act of their creators and of the form taken by that act, of its once vital necessity. We then realize that refutation, exposure of errors, rejection—and even the abundance of commentaries— though all these can weaken, ruin, and exhaust a philosophy, making it unusable and even unintelligible for the next generation, they nevertheless cannot but leave intact, if it ever possessed them, its structural value and its solidity as a work of art.

In a few moments I may venture to tell you why it seems to me that this suggestion must be made, or rather whispered,

to an audience of philosophers. Philosophy—and please take my ignorance as the excuse for this remark—appears to me, like all the rest of human affairs today, to have reached a critical stage in its evolution, and from the same cause, which is the extraordinary progress in the natural sciences.

Do not imagine, gentlemen, that I have wandered a long way from our Descartes. On the contrary, I am still talking about him. He was undoubtedly one of the first and most enterprising of those who have created the present state of human affairs. In that vast Comedy of the Mind which, as I said, calls for a Balzac if not a Dante, Descartes would occupy a place in the first rank. But in a work of this nature, death by no means puts an end to the adventures of the characters. Their life is sometimes only a prologue to their never-ending careers: the exposition, as it were, of the tragedy of their thought. Descartes is among those whose posthumous fate has been of the most varied. He is the one very great man of modern times who has no tomb. His bones lie somewhere, but nothing certain is known about them. What is thought to be his skull is in the Museum of Natural History, where they were kind enough to allow me to see it and hold it in my hands for a moment or two. There is no statue of him in Paris any more than there is of Racine: I am not complaining about that, but I wonder how sculptors can tolerate such a thing.

As for his work, that is a very different story.

Everybody knows that the purely mathematical part has more than survived for its own sake: it was so richly alive, so full of the future, so luminously necessary that it seems less an invention than a discovery, and we cannot conceive how science, or rather how the human mind, failed to forge for

itself long before Descartes an instrument whose importance is almost comparable to that of the mind's most valuable conventions, such as number or language. But it was obviously necessary for algebra itself to have reached a stage where it admitted of the conception of a system of reciprocal relations between number and magnitude. Nothing is more interesting than Descartes' remarks on the subject, or the way in which he explains the psychology of its creation, which he links to the minute observations he had made concerning the limits of our powers of attention. Moreover, the intention to reduce the effort expended on each occasion, and to substitute a uniform procedure (sometimes a kind of automatism) for the necessity of discovering a particular solution to each problem, is fundamental in Descartes: it is the essence of his Method. With the help of his geometry, it won him the most brilliant success ever achieved by a man whose genius was applied to reducing the need for genius, and to securing a tremendous economy of thought. The search for a method is the search for a series of operations that can be performed externally, thus doing the work of the mind better than the mind can; and this approaches what can be achieved, or what we imagine could be achieved, by mechanical means. All the amazing machines that enable us to calculate and to integrate at high speeds are directly derived from the inventions and aims of Descartes. Descartes was greatly struck by the fact "that a child who has been taught arithmetic and has made an addition according to the rules can be sure he has discovered all that the human mind could possibly discover about the sum he is examining"; and when he showed that by working according to the rules of algebra on the projections of a point in space, you could find by a few well-designed formulas all that you wanted to know about shapes and their

properties and, in addition, a number of analogies or relations that no intuition would have uncovered, he enriched at one stroke that fortunate child, now a young man, with knowledge whose existence the greatest geometers of earlier times could not even have suspected.

It is not impossible that Pascal was infected with a bitter and tormenting jealousy when confronted with this sort of creation of the sum total of geometrical possibilities. All the profound skill that he felt he possessed for solving particular questions in geometry was, as a result, diminished in scope.

Descartes himself could not have foreseen where the development of his inexhaustible device would lead. From those illustrious co-ordinates of his have come a countless aggregate of discoveries, a transfinite number of ideas yielding to the strange power of the geometric mind, which grows endlessly by means of the increasingly subtle analysis that it performs on itself, discovering hidden treasures beneath the apparent obviousness of its first axioms or in the structure of its simplest operations, and taking everything to pieces down to the mechanism of those "groups" which constitute the most primitive and the most abstract element in our intuition of space.

But none of the prodigies wrought by his genius would astonish the magnificent pride of our Descartes. And even if, granting him the victory in geometry, we drew his attention to his errors in the field of mechanics and physics, I should not be altogether surprised if the confidence that came from his ambitious thinking provided him with a retort in the manner of Corneille.

"Someone had to make a mistake," he might reply, "but a mistake of the kind that I alone could make. No one before me had thought of a universe expressed entirely in mathe-

matical terms, a world system which was a numerical system. I wanted nothing obscure in it: no occult powers. And no *action at a distance*: I do not understand that sort of thing. But it appears that in the latest state of your science, a most exalted form of geometry, which is the great-granddaughter of mine, has at last relieved you of Newtonian physics. That is quite in the spirit of my own work. People have made fun of my vortices and my subtle matter as though, a century and a half after my death, they were not still explaining magnets and the movement of light by the action of an environment fitted up with little spinning tops."

You must forgive me for making the great Shade speak so freely. Perhaps It was going on to talk about the famous question of the quantity of movement. Or perhaps It would rather keep silent, leaving to us the task of putting up some sort of defense of It. Is not that the duty of a pious posterity?

Descartes earned the signal honor of being the first to construct an entirely metrical universe, by means of conceptions —let us call them fictions—which allowed it to be treated as an outsize mechanism. Pascal, once again, did not care for a design which his logical, rather more than intuitive, mind as well as his feelings rejected. Indeed, he wagered that the plan would end by coming to grief; and it is true that the vortices and the rest did not have a very long run. On the other hand, the idea of a universal physics has never ceased to gain in favor. If Descartes' world did not last, what a number of others have suffered the same fate! The universe of action at a distance; the different ether concepts—Fresnel, Maxwell, and Lord Kelvin; and fifty years ago, the system wholly based on energy: all have followed one another. But each of those broken vessels, though incapable of containing the world, has left impressive ruins behind. Even that indolent celebrity

Maupertuis, by a turn of fortune that Voltaire could not fore-see, has found his "least action" coming back into some use. I am not saying that he would not be taken aback by the novel meaning now given to it.

But there is one other thing that I want to say, at my own risk, in favor of our Descartes. Being a physicist of the universe, he wanted to reduce it to a mathematical representation; he was therefore bound to impose upon it conditions that can be expressed in equations. The result was that the mathematical form itself drove him to look for some magnitude which would remain constant beneath the transformations of phenomena. He thought he had found it in the product of mass multiplied by movement. Leibnitz pointed out the error. But an idea of capital importance had been introduced into science, the idea of *conservation*; an idea which in fact replaced the confused notion of causality by a simple conception that may seem clear enough. This idea was no doubt already implicit in pure geometry, where, in order to give it some basis, it must obviously be assumed that solid bodies are not changed by movement. We know the vicissitudes of the idea of constancy: it might be said that since Descartes we have done nothing but change the unchanging: conservation of the quantity of movement, conservation of kinetic energy, conservation of mass, and of potential energy; we must agree that the transformations of the idea of conservation have been decidedly rapid. But, nearly a century ago now, Carnot's famous discovery compelled science to inscribe the fatal sign of *inequality*, which for a time seemed to condemn the world to inevitable ruin, alongside the sign of *equality*, which Descartes' purely mathematical sense had an inkling of without actually formulating it. I am not altogether clear what is conserved today. . . . I think that we can add to

the defense of Descartes this observation of my own—perhaps a naïve one—that in order to state his theory of conservation, he had worked out the constituents of motion in the form of a *product*. Now this *form*, for which he provided no adequate content, was to become in a sense the natural form for all expressions of energy.

As for his physiology, gentlemen, which seems to have been the subject to which he applied himself most constantly toward the end of his life, it testifies to the same will to *construct* that dominates all his work. It is easy today to make fun of his mechanistic views, with their crude simplifications and ingenuous details. But what else could a man do at that time? It is incredible to us and almost a disgrace to the human mind, almost an argument against the intellect's capacity for observation, that a fact which appears so obvious to us and so easy to discover—the fact of the circulation of the blood—was only discovered in Descartes' own lifetime. He could not fail to be struck by this mechanical phenomenon and to use it as a powerful argument in favor of his theory of the automaton. Besides, if we know far more about it, the very growth of our knowledge has up to the present carried us further away from a satisfactory conception of the phenomena of life. Biology, like the other sciences, produces one surprise after another; because, like the others, it moves from one new method of investigation to another. We are aware that we cannot for a moment think of halting on this fatal slope of discoveries in order to work out, on a certain day, at a certain time, a solidly based conception of the living being. No one today can sit down in front of this picture of things and set to work. But in Descartes' time there was nothing absurd in imagining that one could. There was nothing against it but metaphysical reasons, that is to say, reasons *that can be wiped off the slate*. But

for us it is different: we are up against the vast unknown possibilities of experimental knowledge. We are therefore faced with the task of solving problems in which both the data and the terms vary from moment to moment, unpredictably. Let us suppose that we have decided to try giving an account of the vital functions; let us suppose also that like Descartes we have rejected occult forces and entities (which were already so extensively used in medicine), and we discover by that very fact that he was bound to borrow from the mechanics of the period its whole paraphernalia of pumps and bellows in order to represent an organism which was capable of the main, or the most obvious, functions of life.

But should not this consideration be extended to our general opinion of Descartes, as a defense of his reputation and a means of forming a worthy picture of him? We must strive to estimate the demands of his thought and the instruments at its disposal in such a way and so closely that in the last resort to think of him must inevitably make us think of ourselves. That would be the greatest tribute of all.

I ask myself, therefore, what it is that strikes me most in him, for that is precisely the part that can and must still be alive. The quality in his work which throws me back on myself and my own problems—that is what quickens his work with something of my own life. It is not, I confess, his metaphysics that I can bring to life in this way; it is not even his Method, or at any rate not in the way he formulates it in the *Discourse*.

What delights me in him and makes him so alive for me is his consciousness of himself—*his whole being* summoned to his own attention; a penetrating consciousness of the workings of his own thought; a consciousness so precise and so dominating that it transforms the Self into an instrument

whose infallibility depends only on the degree of his consciousness of it.

You will see at once that this view, which I put forward without apology, leads to judgments of a rather special kind, and to an estimate of the value of Descartes' various works which is not at all the usual one.

I would, in fact, distinguish in him those *problems which emanated from himself* and for which he felt within him the spur of personal necessity, from those *problems which he would not have thought of for himself* and which were in a sense the artificial needs of his mind. I think that it may have been the influence of his education, his circumstances, his desire to appear as complete a philosopher as was expected, one who must have an answer to everything, that made him wish to satisfy these secondary impulses, which seem quite external or alien to his true nature.

You will observe one thing: that in every question to which he could reply by an act of his Self, he triumphed. His Self was a geometer. Without insisting on the point, I shall say, with certain reservations, that the basic idea of his geometry was thoroughly characteristic of his whole personality. It would seem that, in everything, he took his Self, of which he was so powerfully aware, as the point of origin of the axes of his thought.

You will see that I have no great opinion of that substantial part of his work which deals with subjects whose existence or importance he discovered through *other people*.

I am fairly certain, gentlemen, that I am mistaken. Everything points to it, and the only thing in favor of my conviction is my inability to do anything but follow it.

I find it impossible not to accept what seems to be forced on me by the character of our hero. My feeling is that he was

not quite at ease on certain subjects. He argues about them at great length; he retraces his steps; he disposes of objections as best he can. I have the impression that he is aware at such times that he has strayed from his own will, that he is being untrue to himself, and feels obliged to think in a way contrary to the deepest inclinations of his mind.

What then do I see in the *Discourse on Method*?

We need not linger over the principles themselves. What attracts me, starting with the delightful account of his life and the circumstances which set him to work, is the presence of the man himself in this prelude to a philosophy. It is, if you like, the use of "I" and "me" in a work of this kind, the sound of the human voice; and it is that, perhaps, which is most sharply opposed to the architecture of scholasticism. The use of "I" and "me" to introduce us to ways of thinking in completely general terms: that for me is Descartes.

Borrowing a word from Stendhal, who introduced it into the language, and distorting its meaning a little for my own ends, I say that the real Method of Descartes ought to be called *egotism*: the expansion of consciousness for the purposes of knowledge.

I have thus no difficulty in concluding that the essence of the *Discourse* is simply the description of the conditions and the consequences of one event, a sort of *coup d'état*, which rids the Self of all the difficulties, obsessions, and parasitic ideas with which it is burdened, but which it never chose nor discovered in itself. Doubting one's own existence seemed to him actually a bit absurd. That particular doubt was a fashionable state of mind at the time. From Montaigne to Hamlet, it was the thing to wear. But as soon as the mind tries to express it clearly, it discovers without the least effort that the little verb "to be" possesses no special virtue at all, that its only

30

function is to join, and that to say that we are not is the same as saying that we are. No one says "I am" unless he is adopting a momentary attitude and, as a rule, one he has learned; and even then it is said with many silent hints, sometimes requiring a lengthy commentary.

The idea of doubting his own existence would never have occurred to Descartes, who had no doubt about his own value. He was profoundly aware of the value of his Self, and when he says "I think," he certainly means that it is Descartes and not just anybody who is doing the thinking.

There is no syllogism in the *Cogito*; there is not even a literal meaning. It is a piece of shock tactics, a reflex act of the intellect, a living and thinking being who shouts: "I've had enough of it! Your doubt means nothing to me. I shall invent another that is not useless. I shall call it *methodical doubt*. You'll allow me to begin by turning it on your own propositions. Your problems get me nowhere; and whether *I exist* according to one philosophy and *do not exist* according to another makes no difference either in things, or in me, or in my powers or my passions. . . ."

This is not all that could imaginably be extracted from the famous *Cogito*, which it would be wonderful to think Descartes had discovered in a dream. And that, after all, is not impossible. . . .

I have one further thought that connects with what I have said. Stendhal, to whom I return, tells us somewhere that at the critical moments of his extraordinary life Napoleon used to say—or must have said—to himself: "*Alors comme alors!*" This was his way of spurring himself onward.

The effect of the *Cogito*, to me, is like a clarion sounded by Descartes to summon up the powers of his ego. He repeats it as the watchword of the Self in a number of different places

in his work, sounding the reveille to pride and intellectual courage. That is the secret of the charm—in the magical sense of the term—of this formula which has been so much discussed, when it ought, I think, to be enough to feel it. At the sound of the words the entities vanish; the will to power invades the man, pulls the hero to his feet, reminds him of his utterly personal mission, his own destiny; even of his difference, his individual injustice. For it is possible, after all, that the man born to achieve greatness must become deaf, blind, impervious to everything, even truths and realities, which is liable to cut across his aims, his impulses, his destiny, his way of growth, his inward light, his own world-line.

And lastly, if the sense of Self achieves such consciousness and central control of our powers, if it deliberately turns itself into a system of world reference, a source of creative reforms which it sets up against the incoherence, the multiplicity, and the complexity of the world as well as against the inadequacy of conventional explanations, it feels itself nourished by an inexpressible sensation, in face of which the resources of language wither, similitudes cease to be valid, the will to know, directed toward it, is absorbed by it and no longer returns to its point of origin because there is no longer any object which can reflect it. It is no longer a case of thinking. . . .

In short, gentlemen, Descartes' real wish could only be to raise to its highest pitch what was strongest and most susceptible of generalization in himself. He wanted above all else to exploit the treasures of his intellectual vigor and desire, and *he was incapable of wanting anything else.* That is the principle against which the texts themselves cannot prevail. It is the strategic point, the key to the Cartesian position.

This great captain of the mind found two kinds of ob-

stacles in his path. The first were the natural problems that confront every man who comes into this world: phenomena, the physical universe, living beings. But there were other problems which were oddly and, as it were, arbitrarily entangled with the first, the problems that he would not have imagined and that came to him through what he had been taught, through books, inherited traditions. Lastly, there were the proprieties, requirements, obstacles, if not dangers, of a practical and social order.

Ranged against all these problems and obstructions were the Self and, in support of the Self, certain faculties. One of them had proved its worth: you could count on it, on its methods which, when properly used, were infallible, on the imperious duty it imposed to make everything clear and to reject everything that could not be sorted out into distinct operations: this was mathematics.

And now action could be joined. It was preceded and announced by an address worthy of a great leader. And the battle began to take shape.

What was it about? And what was the objective?

Its aim was to show, or to prove, what a Self is capable of achieving. What did Descartes' Self propose to do?

Since he felt no limitations in himself, he wanted to do, or to re-do, everything. But first the slate must be wiped clean. Everything that did not or might not have come from the Self was nothing but idle words. Anything that could only produce words—which themselves could only produce opinions, doubts, controversies, or mere probabilities—could not stand up to that Self and had no power comparable to it. And that Self alone would, if necessary, find its own God: would confer Him upon itself and He would be as clear and as demonstrable as a God must be to be the God of Descartes.

33

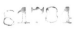

A "necessary and sufficient" God, a God who satisfied Descartes as Bourdaloue's God satisfied him: "I do not know whether Thou art satisfied with me," said that celebrated prelate, "but I myself must confess, to Thy glory, O my God, that I am satisfied with Thee, and perfectly satisfied. For to say that I am satisfied with Thee is to say that Thou art my God, since there is only one God who can satisfy me."

On the other hand, when it came to what I have called natural problems, he developed, in the course of the struggle for *his own* clarity, that heightened awareness which he called his Method and which has magnificently conquered a boundless geometrical empire.

He wanted to extend it to the most varied phenomena; he wanted to remake the whole of nature, and to the task of making it rational he deployed an astonishingly fertile imagination. It was typical of a Self whose thought would not yield to the variations of phenomena, or even to the diversity of the means and forms of life. . . .

What a man! Perhaps it would have been better not to entrust to a poet the difficult task of paying him tribute? . . .

But since that is how it is, I will push this kind of imaginative analysis to the point of wondering what sort of man a Descartes would be who was born in our own age. It is only a game.

But what slates would be left for him to wipe clean? And how would he come to terms with a science which has become impossible for any one man to comprehend, and which henceforth will be narrowly dependent on a vast and constantly developing apparatus; a science that, in some way and at every moment, is in a state of mobile equilibrium with the facilities at its disposal?

There is no answer. But it seems to me that such questions are worth asking.

34

The individual is becoming one of the problems of our time; the hierarchy of intellect is becoming a difficulty in our time, which is a kind of twilight of the demigods—I mean those men scattered in time and space to whom we owe the essentials of what we call culture, knowledge, and civilization.

That is why I have emphasized the strong, the bold, the great personality of Descartes, whose philosophy has less value for us, perhaps, than the idea that he has given us of a magnificent and memorable Self.

A View of Descartes

RENÉ DESCARTES was born at La Haye, in Touraine, on the last day of March, 1596. He came of a noble and very ancient family. They had been professional soldiers down to his father, Joachim, who secured an appointment as counselor to the Parliament of Brittany. His mother died a few days after her son was born, and was probably a victim of tuberculosis. He inherited from her "a dry cough and a pallid complexion that stayed with him until he was more than twenty." The doctors predicted an early death.*

Owing to his precarious state of health, he was kept at home for long years and was looked after by women. But his father also kept an eye on his intellectual development and very early foresaw what sort of man he might become. He called the child, who was perpetually asking questions, his "philosopher." When the philosopher was ten years old, the excellent and clear-sighted Joachim Descartes, who meant him to have the best possible education, sent him to the *collège* of La Flèche, which had just been founded by Henri IV and handed over to the Jesuits, to whom the King entrusted the task of educating France's youthful nobility. During the

*Baillet, *Vie de Descartes*, 1691. An excellent book on which I have drawn, like everyone else, for most of the biographical information given here. [P. V.]

36

whole of his course in the humanities, Descartes was a model pupil. But when he turned from the study of literature to that of logic, physics, and metaphysics, he was no less shocked by the uncertainty and obscurity of the doctrines he was taught than by the astonishing variety of opinions: he observed that nothing was too strange or too incredible to have been taught by one philosopher or another. This intellectual shock was an event of capital importance in the development of his mind. It occurred about the age of sixteen: a critical age at which the fate of the freedom and character of our thought is very often decided. His whole career can be regarded as the development of this self-realization which was to change into a powerfully creative reaction under the impetus of a second inner event, seven years later, of which I shall speak presently.

At the time that he was building up his defenses against philosophy, he embarked with extreme pleasure and zeal on the study of mathematics; but he was surprised to find that, solid and firm though its foundations were, no one had built on them anything more impressive than the practical application of mathematics to the various technical processes that used it. Thus the body of knowledge which he found in existence and which had been instilled into him by his masters presented a contradiction between the importance universally attributed to a kind of philosophy whose authority failed to compensate either for the weakness of its premises or the extravagance of its deductions, and a science which was based on observed fact and rigorous thinking but was nevertheless relegated to serving the practical needs of everyday life.

Descartes himself proceeded to draw up a balance sheet of the needs, aims, and resources of his own mind as opposed to a general estimate of the intellectual values current in his age. *This is how he must have argued:* "From childhood I have been

brought up to believe that my studies would teach me every-
thing worth knowing, and that the knowledge would be
clear and certain. I applied myself to them with enthusiasm.
I was taught by the best masters at the most famous school in
Europe. I learned everything they taught there; and in addi-
tion I read all the scientific works I could lay my hands on. I
was considered to be not inferior to any of my schoolfellows.
Now, mathematics apart, I see that all the rest is simply a
pastime, or completely worthless."

What was he to do? He left school without regrets and aban-
doned the study of literature, in which he had found nothing
but verbiage and deceit. He took up riding, and with still more
enthusiasm, fencing, in which he became so interested that he
wrote a short treatise on it. His father, who intended him for
an army career but who wished him to see the "great world"
first, sent him to Paris. He arrived in the style of a son of good
family with his valet and his lackeys, spent less time in high
society than in a society where you can have some fun, and
lost, or gained, a few months enjoying the round of amuse-
ments, outings, and above all, gambling.

But he soon ceased to find any pleasure in what passes for
pleasure. He broke away as best he could from the compan-
ions of this easygoing life in order to make new friends and
engage in very different pastimes. In particular, he became a
firm friend of M. Mydorge, at that time reputed to be the first
mathematician in France, in whom "he found some hidden
quality that appealed to him exceedingly, whether on ac-
count of his temperament or the character of his mind"; and
he renewed contact with a man whom he had known when
he was very young at school and who was to play a part of the
first importance in his life—Marin Mersenne. When he left

La Flèche, Mersenne had joined the order of the Minim friars. He was for Descartes the most loyal and useful friend, almost indeed the official representative of his thought, who filled the immensely valuable role of confidant, defender, informant, and correspondent. He was of a type often found at the elbow of great men. But Father Mersenne must undoubtedly be placed in the front rank of such acolytes of genius.

Descartes was twenty-one. The time had come for him to enter the profession of arms. He thought first of joining one of the King's regiments, but was led by circumstances to go and learn the art of war under Prince Maurice of Nassau. His campaign in Holland seems not to have been marked by much fighting or much hardship. He distinguished himself in it principally as a mathematician, and dazzled a group of scholars at Breda by solving almost instantaneously, by a method of his own, certain problems with which they had hoped to catch him out. In between times he wrote a treatise on music in Latin; then as an amateur inquisitive about human affairs and leading a military life free of active duty, he went to Germany, was present at the coronation of the Emperor Ferdinand, and afterwards volunteered for service in the Bavarian army, which was about to begin operations against the Elector Palatine.

Several months went by before the start of the campaign. It was during this period of waiting and negotiations that he went through the extraordinary phase of mental development which turned the youthful swordsman into the creator of the most daring and the most energetically conducted intellectual revolution the world has ever seen. The second half of the year 1619 and the first months of 1620 deserve to rank among the great periods in the world of ideas. Having moved into winter quarters, Descartes found himself at Ulm, and it was

probably there (or not far from there) that the decision suddenly formed in his mind to take *himself* as the source and arbiter of all value in matters of knowledge. We have become so familiar with this attitude that we can scarcely imagine the effort and the single-minded determination that were necessary to conceive it in all its clarity and to adopt it for the first time. The sudden abolition of all the privileges of authority, the declaration of the nullity of all traditional teaching, the institution of a new inner power based on self-evidence, doubt, "good sense," the observation of facts, the rigorous formulation of arguments—this ruthless cleanup of the mental laboratory amounted, in 1619, to a series of extraordinary measures adopted and decreed in his winter solitude by a young man of twenty-three, confident in his own speculations and convinced of their validity, in which he found the same strength as in the very sense of his own existence; as strong in himself and as sure of himself as a little twenty-one-year-old lieutenant was to be, in his room at Valence, a hundred and seventy years later. But Descartes created *his* Revolution and Empire at a single stroke.

All this belongs to the realm of action, since thought is of its essence powerless to withdraw from its own activity. A man dreaming is trapped in the changing phases of his dream, and can only extricate himself through some happening outside and alien to the world of dreams. Descartes was able to look back upon the whole of the doctrines and theories of ancient and scholastic philosophy and the chaos of their contradictions—which people seemed to have lost sight of and with which the teaching profession had so nicely come to terms—as a person on waking thinks over the confusion of the nightmare he has just had and reduces it to nothing by a single

40

glance at the stable, well-defined objects around him, distinct from himself and in accord with his movements. To make the whole of this dogmatic rubbish equal to zero was certainly a sort of act—almost a reflex.

But this drastic reaction, which came as the second of the events to which I referred above, would probably have remained a personal incident of no greater consequence than the first, if it had not been accompanied (unconsciously solicited, or perhaps provoked) by the formation of a plan for "an admirable Science," the idea of which came to him on November 10, 1619, with so dazzling a light that he could scarcely endure it.

The creative moment had been preceded by a state of concentration and violent agitation. "He had so wearied himself," says Baillet, "that his brain caught fire and he fell into a sort of enthusiasm, which so affected his already prostrate mind as to put it into a condition to receive the impress of dreams and visions." After he had gone to bed, he had three dreams, of which he has left an account. He even tells us that the Genius which possessed him had predicted the dreams, and that *the human mind played no part in them*. He was so struck by all this that he began to pray and made a vow to go on a pilgrimage "in order to place the affair, which he regarded as *the most important of his life, under the protection of the Blessed Virgin*."

Taken as a whole, the day of November 10 and the night that followed amount to an extraordinary intellectual drama. I assume that Descartes has not misled us and that his account of it is as accurate as the recollection of a dream can be: there is certainly no reason for doubting his sincerity. I know of several other examples of this kind of illumination following

upon prolonged interior conflict and sufferings comparable to the pains of childbirth. Someone suddenly becomes aware that his truth has taken shape as a luminous presence inside him. The comparison with light is inescapable, because nothing gives a more accurate image of this interior phenomenon than the appearance of light in surroundings so dark that one can only move gropingly. With the light comes movement in a straight line and the co-ordination of one's movement with one's desire and goal. Movement becomes a function of its object. In the cases which I mentioned, as in that of Descartes, a whole life is suddenly clarified, and every act will henceforth be subordinated to the task which is its goal. A straight line has been staked out. An intelligence has discovered or planned the work for which it was made: it has formed, once for all, the pattern which will serve for its future activities.

We must, I think, avoid confusing these intellectual *coups d'état* with religious conversions, which resemble them fairly closely in their initial ordeals and the sudden emergence of the "new man." In fact, I find one rather remarkable difference between these modes of transcendental transformation. Whereas in the mystical order the change may occur at any age, in the intellectual order it seems to take place usually between the ages of nineteen and twenty-four: such was the case, at any rate, in the few "samples" known to me personally.

But the case of Descartes is, perhaps, the strangest that can be imagined. Let us go back to the events of November 10, 1619. They are preceded by a period of concentration coupled with intense excitement during which the light and the feeling of certainty declare themselves, and the marvelous plan (*mirabilis*

42

scientiae fundamenta) dazzles its author. Drunk with fatigue and enthusiasm, he goes to bed and has three dreams. He attributes them to a Genius, a "Daimon," at work in him. Finally he has recourse to God and the Blessed Virgin, imploring their aid in order to be assured of the value of his discovery. But what is the discovery? This is the most astonishing part of the whole episode. He asks Heaven to confirm him in his conception of a method of rightly conducting his *reason*. Yet this method implied a fundamental belief and confidence in *himself*, for these were the conditions required to destroy confidence and belief in the authority of the doctrines of tradition. I do not say that there is a contradiction here, but there is clearly a glaring psychological inconsistency between states of mind following one another in such close succession. It is this very contrast that makes his account so moving, so alive, so convincing. I can conceive nothing more truly poetic than the extraordinary modulation which, in the space of a few hours, made him run the whole gamut of his untapped nervous and spiritual resources, from the tension of his analytical, critical, and constructive faculties to the elation of victory, the surge of pride at having made the find; then to *doubt* (for what he had won was so wonderful that it seemed impossible that he could really have it in his hands: he must be under some illusion about its reality); finally, after so much faith in himself, an appeal to the faith that he had received from the Church and through grace.

I am not a philosopher, and in the case of Descartes, on whom so much work has been done, I can only venture to offer a few elementary observations. It is this, however, that enables me, when I think them over, to discover in those very precious and dramatic moments a more real interest and a greater

present importance, or rather *eternal presence*, than anything I can find in the examination and discussion of the Cartesian metaphysics. His metaphysics, like many another, has not and can no longer have anything but an historical importance; that is to say, we ourselves are compelled to provide what it no longer possesses, to pretend that we do not know things we do know, things discovered since his time, to make a temporary loan of a little of our own warmth to arguments that have definitely lost their heat; in short, we have to make an effort of imagination, without the slightest hope of final proof, in order to reconstruct artificially the conditions in which a certain system of formulas and arguments was drawn up three hundred years ago, in a world vastly different from our own, which the very consequences of this same system have largely helped to make more and more alien to us.

But every system is an operation undertaken by the mind against itself. A work expresses not what the author *is* but what he *wishes to appear*, by selecting, co-ordinating, harmonizing, concealing, and exaggerating. This means that a particular purpose works on and shapes the whole range of accidents, mental games of chance, results of concentration and conscious attention which constitute the real activity of thought; but thought does not want to appear what it is: it wants that confusion of incidents and potential acts not to count, it wants its contradictions, errors, fluctuating degrees of lucidity and feeling to be resolved. The result is that the reconstitution of a thinking man, based exclusively on an examination of the text of his work, leads to the invention of monsters all the more incapable of coming to life the more the examination has been rigorous and thorough, and the more it has been necessary to reconcile opinions that were not

reconciled in the mind of the author, to clear up obscurities that did not bother him, to interpret terms whose very sounds were among the distinctive characteristics of his mind, and inexplicable to the man himself. In short, the system of a Descartes is only Descartes himself in so far as it reflects his main ambition and his manner of satisfying it. But in itself it is a representation of the world and of knowledge, and it was absolutely bound to go out of date, in the same way as a map. On the other hand, neither the passion to understand and dominate the mysteries of nature by an entirely new approach, nor the strange combination of the most ruthless intellectual pride—a pride completely convinced of its own autonomy—with sentiments of the most genuine religious devotion, nor the seeming coexistence of, or perhaps the immediate alternation between, a state of mind that would only recognize reason and another that attributed the greatest importance to dreams, can ever wholly lose the interest we take in the life of the mind—by which I mean that fluctuation whose one aim is to keep up the flow of possibility, striving to do so at every moment and by every means at its disposal.

What is more fascinating than to watch the inner Proteus passing from rigidity to intoxication, asking of prayer the strength to persevere in the way of rational thinking, begging divine persons to support him in the proudest of enterprises, and finally producing some exceedingly obscure dreams as evidence in favor of his system of clear thought? This is the most striking characteristic of Descartes' powerful and complete personality, and the one that distinguishes him from most of the other philosophers: there is no other whose character, meaning the reaction of the whole man, participates more actively in the production of abstract thought. His en-

tire philosophy—I would almost go so far as to say his science, his geometry, his physics—clearly proclaims, takes for granted, and makes use of his Self. I shall come back to this point. But how can we fail to observe, even at this stage, that the essential work, the *Discourse on Method*, is a monologue in which the passions, the ideas, the experience of life, the ambitions, the practical considerations of the hero are all, indistinguishably, expressed in the same voice? When we see this memorable work in relation to the spiritual climate of the age, we cannot avoid noticing that the age of Descartes followed the age of Montaigne, that Prince Hamlet was not unaware of Montaigne's monologues, that doubt was present in the very air of the time, stirred with the agitations of controversy, and that this doubt, reflected in a certain head with mathematical tendencies and habits, had every chance of developing into a system, and of finally attaining its limit by registering the very act that expresses it. I doubt, therefore I am certain of at least one thing—that I doubt.

For the rest of Descartes' biography, I recommend the reader to consult the works specially devoted to it, from which I could only borrow. What I am attempting in my own way is to give a sketch of his intellectual character. If I have dwelt on his early years, it is because the formative period of the man of intellect, the age when the adolescent is turning into a man, is the time when ambitions take shape and perspectives unfold. It is the age when we are most vividly aware of what is to be our outstanding quality, to be developed and used to the utmost. Now, *in everything to which he turned his hand*, Descartes felt that at heart he was a geometer. He took geometry as his model. It was also the thing that most deeply stimulated his thought—and not merely his thought but his will to power. There is, in all born geometers—and it is noticeable

46

even in their early years—an astonishingly simple, sincere, and totally unconcealed pride, the natural outcome of the superiority they have shown themselves to possess by their ability to understand and answer a host of questions to which the majority of people apply their minds in vain. A consciousness of this kind of superiority was the origin of the youthful Descartes' decision to outdistance every thinker of his age, and to see further than any of them into the future of knowledge. He himself said: "What I have to offer . . . concerning the nature and properties of curved lines . . . is, so it seems to me, as far above ordinary geometry as Cicero's rhetoric is above a child's A B C." At a very early age he conceived the possibility of inventing a means of dealing systematically with *all* the problems of geometry by reducing them to problems of algebra, and this could be done if he could find a way of making the operations of geometry correspond to those of arithmetic. He found it. By the reciprocal correspondences that he established between numbers and forms, he freed speculation from the necessity of holding and referring to the image while the mind proceeded by way of logical deduction. He taught us to formulate geometrical relations in a homogeneous language entirely composed of relations between magnitudes, providing the mathematician not only with the most precise picture of the problem under discussion, but in addition with a view of the different ways in which it could be developed. He introduced the admirable idea of deducing solutions from the supposition that the problem was already solved. "We must," he said, "survey the difficulty without considering the difference between known and unknown lines," and he invented the very simple device which brought the idea to fruition and made possible, by the use of a combination of known and unknown quantities alike, the construction of a machine whose functioning would extract from

its own structure all that could be known about a given set of data.

To a reader of today, no doubt, Descartes' *Geometry* looks very different from the treatises on analytical geometry of our own time. But the way was open, the principle established, which for the past three centuries has never ceased "to permit the solution of an unlimited number of problems" and to suggest a vast number of others of which no one had ever dreamed. What is more, the Cartesian discovery proved so powerful as a stimulus and an instrument of speculation that its use could not be restricted to the domain of pure mathematics. It soon invaded the field of mechanics, then physics; and, in close association with the infinitesimal calculus, it became as indispensable to our interpretation of the world as, for example, the decimal system. This extraordinary development presents the mind with a somewhat fantastic intellectual spectacle. We see those "few straight lines" "moved by one another," which Descartes used as the universal instrument of metrical relations, become the system of axes of co-ordinates, representing sometimes the phenomenon itself as the trajectory of a moving body, sometimes the law governing the phenomenon; then we see the system enriched by the addition of another variable, time; finally we see it undergoing the prodigious modification required by the theory of relativity, which substituted for Descartes' straight lines the n-tuple flexibility of Gauss's curvilinear co-ordinates, and the non-Euclidean continuum for his three-dimensional space.

Nor is that all. The Cartesian method of representing all sorts of measurable variations has acquired a continually increasing practical importance. Whether it is a question of prices on the stock exchange, the temperature of a feverish patient, the distribution of statistical information, meteoro-

logical fluctuations, etc., the translation of observed numbers
into graphs that enable us to measure at a glance the rate of
any change that is occurring has become familiar and almost
indispensable in the present state of human society, where
rapid forecasts are required by the extreme complexity of
social organization. Descartes is certainly one of those who
have been mainly responsible for the pace and the physi-
ognomy of the modern era, which is specially characterized
by what I shall call the "quantification of life." The replace-
ment of diagrams by numbers, the practice of submitting all
knowledge to quantitative tests, and the inevitable *depreciation
of all those forms of knowledge that cannot be translated into arith-
metical terms* has been of the utmost consequence in every field.
On the one hand, the measurable; on the other, everything
that evades measurement. We need only observe a single day
of our existence to see how it is divided, valued, ordered, and
preordained by the dials and charts of various kinds of measur-
ing apparatus.

Thus, at twenty-three, our Descartes was already marvelously
sure of his powers as a mathematician; and being convinced
of the effectiveness of his method by its great successes in
geometry, he "promised himself that he would apply it to the
difficulties of the other sciences as usefully as he had done to
those of algebra." It seemed to him there was nothing in ex-
perience that could not be clarified, acquired, transformed
into solid and usable knowledge by the "admirable science"
of this method that so enchanted him. A method is not a doc-
trine: it is a system of operations which performs the work of
the mind better than the mind itself, left to its own devices.
Such operations are necessarily of a quasi-material nature,
that is to say, they can be conceived, if not carried out, by

mechanical means. A doctrine can claim to teach us something of which we knew absolutely nothing; while a method can hope only to bring about changes in something of which we already have a partial knowledge, in order to extract or deduce from it everything that can be known about it. That is what Descartes means when he writes "that a child who has been taught arithmetic and has made an addition according to the rules can be sure he has discovered all that the human mind could possibly discover about the sum he is examining." The child has therefore made himself into a machine for changing several numbers into a single number, and the greatest mind in the world could do no more than that, because a given machine, in principle and by definition, is equivalent to any other machine of the same construction. But the facts of arithmetic and geometry are simple, compared with all the other facts we might take it into our heads to examine, and are actually the simplest possible because they can be reduced to the simplest of acts: a number to the act of counting, a line to the act of drawing.

At this point we come to Descartes' metaphysical moment and his decision to embark on his great intellectual adventure, since he would not submit to being nothing more than the foremost geometer of his time.

His aim was nothing less than to arrive at a *view of all things* which would enable him to apply his method to them, and in such a way that he could reason about them with the same boldness and confidence as a geometer could, once he had settled his definitions, drawn up and stated his axioms and postulates, and so found the paths to a particular truth, as it were, predetermined and unfolding in front of him. In order to flourish and develop "to infinity" in the mind, mathe-

matical entities and acts need only a few conventions that can always be held to be as arbitrary and therefore as invulnerable as the rules of a game. Here method creates its own object and becomes part of it.

But what about the whole range of given existences and things? What about the world of sense perceptions, the living world, the physical world, man, the moral world? Here is something whose diversity and complexity confront the intellect, in its will to represent and to dominate by means of symbols, with the invincible obstacle of the real—the indivisible and the indefinable. Science draws on reality for the means of action which it turns against it; but the mind cannot withdraw from the reciprocal relationship it always ends by discovering between what it can know and what it is.

Yet the whole of Descartes' intellectual life was inspired by the idea of creating and imposing on everything belonging to the realm of knowledge a uniform method of treatment that would turn every question into a particular form of geometric space. He was not the only man who had dreamed of fitting everything into a system of rules drawn up once for all, "thanks to which all those who observe them exactly will never think that what is false is true, and will, without wearying themselves by useless exertion, arrive . . . at a true knowledge of what is within their reach" (*Regulae*).* This may remind us, for example, of Lully and Leibnitz. Scholasticism itself claimed to offer something no less comprehensive and certain; and besides, is not all philosophy an enterprise whose aim is the completion of knowledge in so far as knowledge can be reduced to the functions and combinations of language?

*Valéry's reference.

We see him, therefore, at the age of thirty-two, faced with the enormous problem of devising a universal method. But in spite of all his self-confidence and self-assurance, which were certainly justified by his brilliant successes as a mathematician, a task of this magnitude was an adventure on which a man reckons to pledge his whole future. A mind prepared to commit all its powers to this vital undertaking must be freed from worldly cares, protected from the trials and worries that authorities of various kinds can create even for the most retiring and meditative of beings. Descartes therefore devised a policy of caution, reserve, and withdrawal, even of mistrust toward his fellow men. To himself he preached renunciation; he forbade himself to desire things; he wanted to be certain that nothing was within his power except his own thoughts; and he ended by making up his mind to go and live in Holland, where he did not understand the language and where, in the midst of a people who were engrossed in commerce and "more attentive to their own business than inquisitive about other people's," his relations would be confined to those he desired and deliberately cultivated. Once and for all he took up a firm stand against anything that could distract him from his great design; he would keep on the right side of the law, would respect custom, religion, public opinion and the opinions of individuals, *reserving the right to change his own according to mood and circumstance*. This was *probabilism*, or in modern jargon, *conformism* and *opportunism*. Accordingly, he worked out for himself a kind of prudence that woud allow free play to his boldness in the realm of abstract thought. Not everybody is agreed on the way a man of intellect should behave toward his social environment, with its temptations, persecutions, and solicitations. Vanity attacks his pride. Pleasure corrupts his inner joys. Material needs cut across this thought with their worries and use up his strength

and his time. Public authorities and political parties can only regard him as dangerous, or useless, or serviceable, because they cannot see people in any other way.

In short, the urge to embark on a long and exacting intellectual task is necessarily obstructed by the fact that a man is not simply a disembodied mind and cannot live by his mind only. It sometimes happens, however, that these obstructions give birth in this same mind to unexpected powers and insights. The external accident sometimes provokes the internal accident that will turn out to be what is called a "stroke of genius," so that in the end one has to agree with Leibnitz and Pangloss that everything is for the best even in the worst of worlds.

Descartes had settled his accounts with philosophy—the philosophy of other people. He had planned or worked out his own personal way of life. He had complete confidence in his own armory of mathematical models and ideals, and he was now free, without any return to the past, without regard to any tradition, to engage in the struggle: the struggle of his own will to clarify and organize knowledge against the uncertain, the haphazard, the muddled, the inconsequential, which are the likeliest attributes of most of our thinking.

He worked out one basic certainty: he told himself "that he must reject as completely false everything in which he could imagine the slightest element of doubt, in order to see whether after that there did not remain something in his beliefs which was absolutely beyond doubt." And basing himself on the common experience of dreams, he suggested that everything might perhaps be only a dream. The one thing that seemed to him unshakable in its truth was the famous proposition "I think, therefore I am," which was to be taken as a first principle and which in addition revealed to him that

he was a substance whose whole essence was to think, a substance entirely independent of body, place, and every material thing.

The position is a remarkable one from every point of view. I mean it is remarkable also in various ways that have not perhaps been noticed. It has given rise to innumerable commentaries and to a certain number of quite different interpretations. Each of them consists of treating the formula "I think, therefore I am" as a proposition whose meaning is beyond discussion and whose logical function is all that remains to be established: some people see in it a sort of postulate; others, the final term of a syllogism.

At this point I am going to take a considerable risk. I say that we can consider it from a very different point of view—we can assert that this brief and pregnant expression of its author's personality *has no meaning whatever*. But I must add that it has *a very great value*, entirely characteristic of the man himself.

I maintain that *Cogito ergo sum* has no meaning because that little word *sum* has no meaning. No one dreams of saying or needs to say "I am" unless he is taken for dead and wants to protest that he is not. In any case he would say "I'm alive." But a cry or the slightest movement would be quite sufficient. No, "I am" cannot tell anyone anything and is no answer to any intelligible question. But the remark does correspond here to something else, which I shall explain presently. Furthermore, what meaning can be attributed to a proposition whose negative form would express its content just as well as the positive? If "I am" means anything, "I am not" tells us neither more nor less.

When he came back to these words ten years after he had first thought them up and put them into the *Discourse on Method*, Descartes repeated them with a certain embarrassment, denied that they proceeded from a syllogism, but asserted that they were a statement of something self-evident, "*simplici mentis intuitu*" (*Entretien avec Burman*).* In saying this, however, he touched on the very point at which language is linked to what no doubt happens at an earlier stage, what provokes and gives content to a particular expression. It may be a mental representation; but it may equally well be a sensation, or some sensory event akin to it. In the latter case, the spoken word, emerging as an immediate consequence, has both the meaninglessness and the value of a reflex action, as we can see from an exclamation, an interjection, an oath, a war cry, a prayer, or a curse. For when the mind reflects on them in retrospect, it realizes that in themselves they mean nothing, but that they play a *momentary* part in registering a sudden alteration in the expectations or the inner orientation of a living system. It is precisely this that I think I see in the *Cogito*. Neither syllogism nor even meaning in the literal sense; but a reflex action of the man, or more accurately, the explosion of an act, a shattering blow. There is, in any thinker of such intellectual power, what might be described as a home policy and a foreign policy of thought; he sets up certain "reasons of state" against which nothing can prevail and which always end by delivering the Self, by force, from all the difficulties and parasitic ideas with which it is encumbered *without having found them in itself*. Descartes would never have thought of doubting his existence, having no doubt at all about his value. If the *Cogito* turns up so often in his work, if

*Valéry's reference.

it is found again and again in the *Discourse*, the *Meditations*, the *Principles*, it is because it is an appeal to his essential *egotism*. He takes it up as the theme of the lucid Self; it is the clarion call to his pride and the resources of his being. Never, until he came, had a philosopher so deliberately exhibited himself on the stage of his own thought, risking his own neck, daring to write "I" for whole pages on end; he does it above all, and in an admirable style, when writing the *Meditations*, applying himself to the task of describing in detail his interior debates and maneuvers, making us participate in them, and become like himself: uncertain at first, then growing confident like him, having followed and, so to speak, embraced doubt after doubt with him until we reach the purest, least personal Self, which must be the same in all, and universal in each.

I have called his style admirable. We have only to read this passage:

Let us take, for example, this piece of wax which has just been re-moved from the hive; it has not yet lost the sweetness of the honey it contained; it still keeps something of the scent of the flowers from which it was gathered; its color, its shape, its size are apparent; it is hard, it is cold; we touch it, and if it is tapped, it gives off a sound. In short, all the things by which we can distinctly recognize a body are to be found in it.

But while I am still speaking, someone takes it over to the fire . . .

These few lines are perfect. They are untroubled by any appeal extraneous to what they have to say; no desire to create an effect mars their purity of tone or the sober simplicity of their restrained movement. There is not a word which is not inevitable and which does not appear at the same time to have been chosen with exquisite taste. I see in them a model of the way in which language is adapted to thought, blending the smooth and detached manner that belongs to the geometer

who is propounding a problem, with a certain discreetly poetic grace, heightened by the rhythm, the harmony, and the careful construction of this tiny fragment.

If we were to judge philosophers by their language, we might perhaps gain some special insight into the processes of their thought: its way of bringing itself to their attention, declaring itself, getting itself accepted and cherished to the point of becoming a permanent mode. But I do not want to insist unduly on this somewhat heretical and paradoxical notion, though it may help in understanding a little better the ideas I have suggested about the *Cogito* and even my reasons for suggesting them. The theme of the *Cogito* seems to me to recur all through Descartes' work, which, to tell the truth, is a monologue in which his person and almost the sound of his voice never cease to make themselves felt and heard—like a theme of *certainty* that teaches him nothing, can teach him nothing, but which each time it appears recalls and gives fresh life to the initial impetus that produced the great design.

Once assured of his own existence, Descartes decided that he ought to imagine he was certain of nothing else. Yet as soon as he stopped meditating, he was certain of a great many other things. But he considered, great innovator though he was, that he must adopt the traditional attitude in metaphysics: that of universal doubt, which you could take with you into your study and leave behind you when you came out. It was a professional act. So we see him at grips with a hoary problem. The experience of dreams, the errors of perception, the illusions of touch and sight, hallucinations of various kinds have raised from time immemorial this theoretical question—a question so completely *theoretical* that we may wonder in our hearts whether it is not purely *verbal*. We go to a great deal

of trouble to convince ourselves that we are dreaming when in fact we are doing nothing of the sort; but this amounts to extending to the sum total of our knowledge the suspicion that it is all as vain and deceptive as the phantasmagoria of sleep and the other aberrations of our minds. We do not scruple to conclude that we are living in a world of appearances, and this leads to many other inferences which, in any case, are of no practical consequence in our lives. Whether or not we are deceived, or dreaming, does not affect our sensations or even our actions. It appears, however, that such a position is essential to philosophy: it allows the philosopher to declare that anything he pleases, or anything that his fancy suggests, is *reality*. But this unfortunate word has no meaning except as one of the terms of a comparison. To reduce all things to dreams is to abolish the comparison; from that point *there is no more dream*, and the reaction against the dream, which consists of opposing it to "reality," vanishes at the same time.

We must, however, dispose of this artificial doubt, which is a residue of tradition, and which I describe as artificial because it demands an act of the will, as it requires the intermediary of language, to make its appearance at all. It supposes in short that we have an idea of some operation or transformation which, when applied to our knowledge of things, would replace it by some reality of a second kind, and change into the memory of a dream what we regard naturally, ordinarily, and for practical purposes as reality. Statistical evidence in favor of the reality known to common sense is overwhelming. It is no doubt permissible to think that some sort of awakening could sweep away, as a dream is swept away, all that our senses, our understanding, and our experience pro-

vide us in the way of data about our environment, the sources, modes, and determinants of our actions, and the probability of our expectations being fulfilled; but this hyperphenomenon has never been observed, and I am very much afraid that all the efforts that might be made to imagine it with any accuracy are doomed to failure.

Descartes was therefore obliged to pretend. He indulged in some rather strange suppositions. He pretended that there was "not a true God, but a certain evil genius, no less cunning and deceitful than powerful, who used all his wiles to deceive him." And to prevent himself from being taken in, Descartes decided to suspend judgment and "to prepare his mind so well against all the tricks of the great deceiver that, however powerful and cunning he was, he could never impose on him."

Socrates had his Daimon. For the purposes of his argument, Descartes provided himself with a Devil. If, for example, we invented every conceivable hypothesis for explaining why a world of appearances produces on us the impression of reality, the existence of a Devil might well be included among them, and in any case costs very little. I observe here, without drawing any conclusion whatever from it, that in the account he left us of his dreams during the famous night of November 10, 1619, we find a Genius "who foretold the dreams before he went to bed," and an evil Genius to whom he attributed a pain that woke him and the intention to lead him astray.

How could he rid himself of a doubt so absolute and so resourceful? So far as his own existence was concerned, he had already outwitted and defied the Deceiver by his magic formula of incantation: *I am, I exist*. But the question now

was to find a way of proving that everything else, his body itself and the world, either was or could be just as existent as himself. It was even a matter of safeguarding the findings of mathematics, since God may have wished to lead us astray even by our geometrical arguments.

He proceeded toward "truth" by means of an astonishingly ingenious detour. He found no certainty except in his own thought. It could be employed, without appealing to anything outside itself, in self-analysis: this would provide the pure elements for a synthesis that would be *certainty*.

He began by putting forward the view that "nothing was easier for him to know than his own mind." He examined its ideas, which he divided into two classes: those which came to him through his senses and which he could always regard as illusory, though "so long as we do not think there is anything outside us which resembles these ideas," we are "in no danger of making mistakes about them"; the others, which are in the soul, represent "substances," a term borrowed from scholasticism which he used to designate things which were self-existent: they contained an "objective reality." He meant by this that these substantial ideas could not fail to represent something real outside him. But what was this *real* par excellence, this only complete and absolute reality?

At this point we come to the famous argument which led to the appearance of God in Descartes' philosophy. He had learned through doubt that his own being was not absolutely perfect, and "that it was a greater form of perfection to know than to doubt." But where could the idea of a greater perfection have come from? Since he could not have acquired it either from things or from himself, for the more perfect could

not have come from the less perfect, he deduced the existence of God from the presence in his mind of the idea of perfection. I have abridged and shockingly mutilated the argument which he refashioned, corrected, and developed in a succession of great works, sometimes revising it under the stimulus of the criticisms and objections which were inevitably directed against this cornerstone of his system. It would be interesting to ask ourselves what would become of his argument in a modern mind, and in particular, whether the fundamental idea of perfection would subsist in it with the same force and necessity.

In one of the treatises relating to the existence of God, we find a remarkable piece of quantitative reasoning. He classifies substances according to their degree of objective reality, that is to say, according to the degrees of being or perfection which the ideas that represent them imply, a scale which ascends from nothingness to the idea of a "sovereign, eternal, infinite, all-powerful, all-knowing God, the universal Creator of all things that are outside Him." There you have a progression from zero to a positive infinity. Each of the terms in this ordered series receives whatever objective reality it contains from the term just above, which surrenders to it some portion of its own perfection, just as a warm body surrenders some of its warmth to one less warm that comes into contact with it.

From this point onward, certainty is based on the theory of the existence of a Perfection that cannot deceive. What is more, the theory of an objective reality opposed to an actual reality demonstrates that we cannot attribute to our body the power of thought, because everything belonging to the body and the things that surround it can be resolved into extension,

shape, position, and local movement, and because "in the clear and distinct idea of them there is certainly contained some sort of extension, but no intelligence at all."

The argument can be summed up in this way: My thought is made up of ideas not all of which are derived from experience. There are some which come from a different source. They are classified according to their richness. "Our natural insight shows us that we know a thing or a substance all the better the more properties we observe in it." The idea of perfection, an infinity of perfection, and the necessity of the existence of a being who fulfills it, follow, since existence is a condition imposed by an idea.

This argument can give rise to many difficulties. Like every metaphysics, it slides over the problem of the value of any results produced by language when it is used to express things of the mind itself, that is to say, those things on which different minds cannot reach agreement by referring to the common sensory objects on which agreement is based. Metaphysicians are therefore led into drawing up "definitions" of terms already in existence and endowed with meaning by current usage, which itself only needs a medium of exchange immediately convertible into acts, which in turn require nothing more than instantaneous signals; and these attempts to transform words, which are only the vague and unstable products of age-old gropings after exact expression, into precision instruments and resources of knowledge to be exploited to the very limit of their supposed content, are never satisfying to anyone but their own authors. Descartes, for example, defines clear and distinct ideas: *clear*, what is present and evident to an attentive mind. "*Distinct*, what is so precise and different from anything else that it only includes within itself what appears plainly to anyone who reflects on it as he ought."

When he uses the word *Doubt*, which is of such importance in his work, he himself does not distinguish between natural, spontaneous doubt, which comes from not knowing what name or what attribute to ascribe to a thing insufficiently known, and artificial or philosophical doubt, which we place like an algebraic sign in front of anything we choose and especially in front of what we know best. . . .

Nevertheless, the development of his metaphysics produced results very different from those of the abstract constructions of his predecessors.

The notion of Method fully developed and displayed; the capital distinction between the world of the mind and the world of extension; as a result, the abandonment of the fruitless attempt to discover by way of logical analysis what experience alone can teach; next, an entirely mechanical view of the universe and of living beings, and an outline of a completely mathematical conception of the world; furthermore, the Self as the point of reference for All Things, each individual mind with its "evident truth" being taken as the origin of the axes of its knowledge; in a word, a highly productive dividing up of the chaos of observations and deductions which represented the state of knowledge and the means of knowing which he had found when he embarked on a life of thought—such were the almost immediate results of a deliberate act of the intellect.

He developed this philosophy in a whole series of virtually parallel applications carried out in the fields of mind and extension: dioptrics, mechanics, the passions of the soul.

But when he reached a certain age, it was the study of living beings that seemed to take precedence in the use of his time and his researches. The mechanics of life interested him

above all else. He appeared to have fallen rather out of love with geometry and physics, and liked to imagine (for this apostle of reason was singularly prone to imagining) the workings of the living organism. Indeed, in spite of his efforts to separate Psyche from the body and from extension, he went to great lengths to find her a cerebral habitation and to demonstrate that this location was indispensable for the purpose of feeling. He observed that there was in the brain a little gland that appeared to him to be the seat of the soul, and the reason he gave was that the other parts of the brain, like our eyes and ears, were all double, that it was necessary "that there should be some place where the two images which entered by the two eyes could merge into one before they reached the soul"; and he did not see any other part of the body in which they could be united except in this gland. This was highly ingenious. We have very different ideas about the functions of the pituitary gland, which seems to be an organ of control of the first importance; but when it comes to the co-ordination of images, I fear we are not much wiser. It is the same with the workings of the nervous system: according to Descartes we are inhabited by "a very subtle wind" which he calls "animal spirits," and which in his view accounts for all our vital energy, going from the pineal gland to the brain and from the brain to every corner of the body, whose changes, actions and reactions, he wanted to explain. Our movements, our mental images, our memories, our passions are the result of the power of the soul over the distribution and flow of that subtle matter which is carried by the blood to whatever point it should go but which also runs through our nervous system. We are still in the position of wondering what it is that circulates in our nervous system—an electric current or some diffusion of a chemical nature? The problem

remains; it has been stated with much greater accuracy, but it nevertheless remains. As for the relations between the physical organism and the "facts of consciousness," or subjective sensibility, there has been nothing new since 1650.

What most strikes and excites the public when it happens to learn of the existence of a new thinker and his work is always and inevitably some formula or pronouncement out of context, coming with the powerful effect of paradox or the comic effect of a simplification pushed to the point of absurdity. To the crowds of people who knew his name in the last third of the last century, Darwin's work meant nothing but the words: "Man is descended from the monkey." In the seventeenth century, Descartes' name made a good many people think of the "animal-machine." Some protested, some laughed, some argued with the idea, some found it delightful, while others did not forbear, nor were slow, to pass from animal to man. The next century did not hesitate to put into circulation and to popularize the concept of the man-machine.

What is the value today of Descartes' analysis and conclusion? I find it very difficult to say, and shall confine myself to a few comments.

In the first place, I must point out that the meaning of the word "machine" has changed considerably, while the idea of an "animal" has become peculiarly complicated. We have introduced into our machines a great many devices comparable to those suggested by the reflex actions of living beings; and the number of different forms of energy used simultaneously in the same machine, whereas in the time of Descartes there were only one or two, has grown so much as to be comparable to the number necessarily involved in the processes of transformation that constitute the physical aspect of life.

In short, Descartes could still come down on the side of vital mechanism. Moreover, we can only theorize about the animal in so far as we reduce it to a system that repeats itself and that draws from its environment something whose transformation is essential to the process of repetition. This strongly resembles a machine. What is more, we can only study the facts of animal life by the same methods, the same physical and intellectual means, as those which enable us to understand or invent machines. Even if our study is the behavior of animals, we subject them to tests and reagents, we are trying to disturb instincts or to create habits, that is to say, to disrupt a certain process of repetition which was due to take place, or to introduce one which did not previously exist. But all this is only an experiment based on the idea of the machine (which itself, in turn—we should not forget—derives from a sort of imitation of the actions of living beings and the organs that produce these actions). For in the last resort, we can only conceive ourselves to the extent that we imagine that we repeat ourselves. Our own identity lies in the probability of recurrence. We cannot form a plan, for example, unless it is based on the assumption that we shall perform many series of actions which we think we can perform because we have done so before. But a plan cannot be reduced to its mere execution. At this point insurmountable difficulties appear. Up till now there has never been a machine that formed a plan. And in the end, I am convinced that a hurt animal suffers and does not merely mimic all the actions necessary to convince us that it is suffering. A kick no doubt operates on two levels: on the one, it *hurts*; on the other, it makes the animal cry out or flee. But in fact I know nothing about it. Nor does anybody else.

I must now go on to say a few words about the Cartesian con-
ception of physics, in order to indicate briefly the importance
of two very new and very fertile ideas which he introduced
along with a quantity of notions now, and long since, dis-
carded and forgotten. These ideas and errors arose from the
same speculation and the same determination to provide a
model explanation of the world by means of mathematics
alone. If everything belonging to bodies is reduced to shape
and movement, shape and movement are translatable into
magnitudes and measurable relations. But the magnitudes of
shapes may, in turn, be translated by his method of geometry
into equations. Algebra holds the world as one of its possi-
bilities. This was an immense step forward in the way of
representing the measurable universe. Nobody had previ-
ously been able to conceive that a system of reference might
make possible the expression of all material phenomena in a
homogeneous language, or rather in a language restricted to
the fundamental variables: Extent, Time, Mass. It was a
radical rejection of the profusion of qualities which made up
scholastic physics. For nearly three centuries, science has
never ceased to pursue the work dreamed of and broadly
sketched out by Descartes. The progress of analysis has en-
abled a succession of scientists to chart the development of the
Cartesian conception of mechanics and physics, up to and in-
cluding the theory of relativity, which in itself is an almost
monstrous development in subjecting phenomena to the
geometry of the continuum. It appears, however, that the
method may have reached its limit, quite recently, when cer-
tain entirely unknown and unexpected facts, revealed by new
methods of investigation, have tended to make us think, if not
conceive, that the continuum vanishes on the verge of the
excessively small. Atomic physics tries to see, as through the

eye of a needle, what is happening in a world that no longer resembles our world of immemorial experience. I am mistaken: it is not a matter of seeing; *seeing* no longer has any meaning; space and time, and the idea of a body located in one place at a given moment, all vanish when it becomes impossible to separate the thing observed from the influence exerted by the means of observation.

The fate of the Cartesian universe has been that of all representations of the world or of its inner structure. They are provisional conceptions, more or less in keeping with the methods of observation and verification available at a certain period or a particular moment in the history of science. Ether has gone to join the vortices, and contemporary theories of the atom scarcely last more than ten years on an average. But Descartes' imaginings remain nevertheless the first attempt at a physicomechanical synthesis reduced to mathematical terms and applying to a whole system. To say that they are mathematical terms is to say that they are expressed in equations, and that they force the mind to search for "what remains the same" during the evolution of the system it has set out to study. Descartes thought that in "quantity of movement" he had discovered the universal constant which remains unaltered beneath the transformations of phenomena. Leibnitz pointed out the error. But an idea of capital importance had been introduced into science, the idea of conservation. . . .*

*Except for minor variations, the essay from this point on is the same as "Descartes" above, pp. 26–35.

A Second View of Descartes

Descartes and his greatness can be summed up for me in two points.

He made a personal matter of what had before his time been treated in dogmatic form, dominated by tradition. He decided that there was no authority which could prevail against the impression it might give of the vanity of its teaching: he had no use for anything except evidence or observation scrupulously verified. What this amounted to was a refusal to attach to language any value derived merely from people or books. He therefore threw the whole weight of his being into one side of the scales; the other was loaded with all the philosophical work that had gone before. He discovered that his Self tipped the balance. He felt strong in his own solitude; but was able to answer for everything that he thought, observed, deduced, or defined *himself*, as opposed to the quantity of doctrines, formulas, and purely verbal constructions kept alive only by the arguments of the schools and handed down from century to century like a fiduciary issue that could never be converted into gold.

Descartes was first and foremost a will. This man wanted above everything to exploit the resources of desire and intellectual vigor that he felt in himself, and *he could not want anything else*. That is the central point, the key to the Cartesian

position. It is useless to seek any other principle in his philosophy.

Whence comes that superb confidence in his own mental powers which is apparent in his style and in his disdain, and which he was too lucid as well as too prudent to base merely on his hopes, on a chimerical faith in his own value?

Descartes believed in the power of his own thought from the time he became aware of his gift for geometry. It gave him an intoxicating sense of his superiority. He knew that, in this field of study, he was the inventor of a method which seemed to him "as far above ordinary geometry as Cicero's rhetoric is above a child's A B C." This youthful discovery dominated the whole of his intellectual life. He had no doubt about the nature of his conquest, and felt sure that the same man and the same intellectual application which had won such a brilliant and outstanding success in the abstract analysis of space must attack the physical world, and then the problems of life, and that they could not fail to obtain results of equal importance.

He proceeded to invent a *Universe* and an *Animal* by imagining that he was explaining them. Whatever illusions he may have harbored in this field, his efforts have been of the greatest importance. That is my second point. If the Cartesian universe has suffered the fate of all the universes conceived and conceivable, the world in which our "civilization" exists still bears the marks of his will and his characteristic way of thinking.

Our world is permeated by the various uses of measurement. Our life is becoming increasingly governed by numerical determinants, and everything that cannot be represented by numbers, any knowledge that is not measurable, is dismissed as being of little value. The name "science" is increas-

ingly denied to all knowledge that cannot be translated into figures.

And here is the curious observation with which I shall end this note: the outstanding characteristic of this change in our life, which consists of organizing it in accordance with number and magnitude, is *objectivity*, as purely impersonal as possible, so much so that what is *true* for modern man, which is directly related to his ability to control nature, seems to become more and more opposed to what our imagination and our feeling *would like to be true*. But, as has been said, at the source of this prodigious transformation of the human world we find a Self, we find the daring and powerful personality of Descartes, whose philosophy has, perhaps, less value in our eyes than the image he has left us of a magnificent and memorable *Him*.

The Return from Holland

A JOURNEY is a process that links towns to certain times. For me, however, the most exciting, the most philosophical thing about a journey is the interval between stops.

I do not know whether there are genuine lovers of railways, enthusiasts who love *trains for trains' sake*, and I hardly know of anyone except children capable of enjoying as one should the noise, the rush, the endlessness, and the surprises of a train journey. Children are the great masters of absolute enjoyment. As soon as the row of carriages begins to move, I myself am always lulled into a state of naïve metaphysical speculation mixed with fantasy.

I am leaving Holland. . . . I suddenly have the feeling that Time is beginning; that Time has started to move; that the moving train has become a symbol of Time with all its relentlessness and its powers. It devours all visible things, shakes up all mental things, flings its massive body into a savage attack on the very face of the earth, sends bushes, houses, provinces scurrying to the devil; mows down trees, shoots through arches, dispatches telegraph poles, rudely flattening in its wake all the lines it crosses, canals, furrows, roads. It turns bridges into thunder, cows into projectiles, the pebbly surface of the roadbed into a curtain of machine-gun fire.

Even one's ideas, continually overtaken, and dragged along as though stretched thin by the rush of images, undergo a change like a sound whose source flies past and away.

I easily surrender to the feeling that I am no longer any-where—reduced, so to speak, to the sort of abstract being who, wherever he happens to be, can tell himself that he is thinking, reasoning, making decisions, functioning, ordering his life in the usual way; that he is alive and that nothing essential has altered; that he is therefore not changing places. Would it not take the most extraordinary changes, upheavals so inconceivable as to be incompatible with life or reason, to convince the pure logician who dwells in all of us that he is on the move?

It is a marvelous thing that there are so many delicate mechanisms inside us practically impervious to transport.

On the other hand, the whole man, the real soul of the traveler whose journey is coming to an end, as every turn of the wheels brings him nearer home and a link in his life is about to close, falls prey to the strange effects of this transition. What he leaves behind, what he feels at the moment, what he foresees and looks forward to—these things fight for possession of him, push, jostle, change places inside him. His mind oscillates between the different stages of the journey, clearly marked by the mechanical precision of his departure and the probable punctuality of his arrival; he is beset hap-hazardly by hopes, regrets, and fears; forgets them, and finds them again working on his emotions. His past, his present, his immediate future *sound* in his mind like three distinct bells whose possible combinations are all rung, then re-echo, become confused, and mingle in a curious harmony. Playing over and endlessly taking up again all the *themes* of existence,

a chime of events—past, expected, or at hand—accompanies the traveling body, fills the drooping head, beguiles it, disturbs it, taking on the rhythms of the roadbed, orchestrating dreams, distracting, lulling, awakening its traveler. . . .

Night falls. Terrestrial fires flare and die—sudden signal boxes, shrill warnings, rapid flickers of unknown lives we brush against in passing. . . . Between two lights, my eyes, dimmed by the haze obscuring the windows, gradually cease to see a countryside already deadened and simplified by the evening light, streaming away unendingly toward the places and days of the past.

In the end I have the impression of seeing nothing but water in all its different states: water as snow; water as ice; running water; water as puddles reflecting water as cloud; water as steam whose loosened rolls unfurl, come apart, hang back, and melt away behind us. The many forms of water make up almost alone the substance of the misty, changing landscape where the last gleams of dusk still play upon the racing mass of whites and pallid grays.

When the lights go on, the fragment of a face is suddenly reflected in the windowpane. A sort of mask is interposed, the portrait of a man, luminous and unmoving against the background flight of somber, snow-clad shores.

I see myself motionless and warmly colored behind the glass; and if I lean forward a little toward this *me*, a fragmentary shadow looking at me, I blot it out, annihilate myself, become one with the nocturnal chaos.

Philosophers have always had a taste for tiny experiments of this nature. A chance illusion, some simple and striking effect

of dioptrics or acoustics, some queer accident of perception sends them into a daydream which at their leisure they turn into a theoretical meditation. From the lighting of a cave and the shadows it produced, Plato found no great difficulty in deducing some admirable if perhaps sinister conclusions. His natural darkroom provides one of the most celebrated examples of the *transmutation of values.*

But being no philosopher, I have never been able to push to excessive lengths—for there must be excess—all those thoughts which the sight of my motionless face, standing out luminously against a background of rushing night broken by sudden apparitions, might have put into my mind.

But I have just been in Amsterdam, where Descartes and Rembrandt had been contemporaries. We can still see the houses where they lived.* One cannot help trying to imagine their thoughts. We put ourselves naïvely in their place, on the banks of canals, on the footbridges over the Amstel, or at some crowded spot in the middle of that labyrinth of waters swarming with boats, pontoons, heavily laden barges, old varnished tubs with swollen bellies and bulging poops, something between a junk, a piece of furniture, and a barrel. . . . The passing hours chime a little sadly in the air of the pale sky. Men cross from one bank to another by the narrow bridges. The onlooker watches life, and lives.

Descartes was particularly fond of this town "where, since there was not a single man except himself who was not engaged in commerce, he could remain all his life without ever

*Descartes' house has been identified thanks to the work of M. Gustave Cohen, whose researches have singularly enriched and clarified our knowledge of French literary history. [P. V.]

being noticed by anyone and could walk round every day lost in the throng of a great people."

I do not know if he understood their language. I certainly hope not. What could be more conducive to a thoughtful withdrawal into oneself, to the clear delimitation of an external world, exactly defined and separated from this other world—what could more isolate a man than ignorance of the reigning conventions that co-ordinate the spectacle of the life around him? It is an essential part of the philosopher's profession not to understand. They have to be as though fallen from a star, eternal aliens. They must practice gasping in amazement at the most commonplace of things. Go into the temple of an unknown god, gaze at an Etruscan manuscript, sit down beside the players of a game you have never learned, and enjoy your hypotheses. The philosopher is much the same nearly everywhere.

But not to possess the key, not to have learned the rules, the signs, the connections, to be unable to guess the meaning of what he sees—is not this to reduce what is seen to what it merely is, to *shape and movement*? Nothing could be more Cartesian, I imagine. Still more, does not this incomprehension offer a golden opportunity for not overlooking anything, for *omitting nothing*, since we do not even know what to overlook, what to retain, and everything we observe is of the same value; so that we must take notice of everything or reject everything?

Thus, in the midst of their commerce and of the Dutch at work, Descartes, isolated and not unaware, gazed at their business and their mode of life as he would have gazed at some completely unknown machine. Descartes absent and present, ab-

stracted from their language, their interests, their tastes, their passions, their manners, strong in the fact that nothing of himself mingled with them, found himself plunged into the living mass of a foreign people like a measuring rod which is thrust into some medium and withdrawn from time to time to take readings. Descartes' was a well-ordered mind, was indeed the very genius of order and definition. His thought could pursue itself untouched by the feverish activity of the people around him. He would say that their noise was no more to him than the babble of a stream. He was not the man of crowds. . . .

The man of crowds is a poet, a storyteller, or a spiritual drunkard.

He sinks into the mass of wandering souls; he becomes intoxicated from absorbing an inexhaustible number of faces and expressions, and in the flow of the streets he feels giddy with the passing of an infinite number of *individuals*. . . . He senses and confuses the sound of thousands of feet and as many rhythms of walking; his eyes catch and lose thousands of eyes, as he looks upstream into their visions, aims, and separate wills.

At certain times of the day, the bustle of great towns creates a marvelously disturbing sense of the *multiplication* of lonely *ones*. We observe naïvely, with a sort of horror and a touch of panic, that *individuals* cannot be added up. So many private persons, each of them of capital importance to himself and of little or no importance in the eyes of most of the others, and all of them together vaguely giving one another the impression of a walking cemetery, or a procession of ghosts, because the stream of faces, the general sense of the sound of conversation and feet, the steady flow of dissimilar beings, force on us the idea of an indistinguishable total of quite dis-

tinct destinies, give us the same feeling of detachment—
sometimes depressing, sometimes cheering—that grips us
among a group of tombs.

Nothing takes away from life the impression of life, but
nothing removes from death the solemnity of death, so much
as the overwhelming consciousness of the number of the liv-
ing or the dead. The effect of number and repetition is to
make us feel the force of law and the machine, and in a way
their absurdity. There are times when they numb the mind,
and times when they drive it to invent, in self-defense, what-
ever allows it to believe itself unique and its own master.

We might end by saying that, in a man of the crowd,
thought becomes a part of the movement, that the swarm of
images *carries away*, so to speak, the very faculty that perceives
them.

A Descartes is a very different matter.

While turning over in my mind a thousand and one ideas
about him, it would amuse me to look out of my window, in
Amsterdam, at the pedestrians tripping along in the newly
fallen snow, or at the heavily muffled seamen maneuvering
on the black and white water, half frozen over and half
thawed. They would shuttle their long, heavy barges with
extraordinary adroitness, the barges sometimes so huddled
and clogged together that the men had to go at it as though
they were playing a game of draughts, operating in carefully
thought-out moves, creating ahead of them the space they
intended to occupy, finding another for the vessel they were
dislodging, then waiting, edging in, steering until they finally
reached the entry of a dark narrow tunnel where they disap-
peared to the dull throb of the engine, the man at the helm

ducking just when his head was about to strike the top of the arch. The innumerable sea gulls distracted my attention, delighted and refreshed my mind by wafting it into space. Their pure smooth bodies, held exactly against the wind, glided down invisible slopes, brushed against the balcony, turned, stopped in their flight, and landed on the larger floes, where the white creatures who had taken up their position there fought among themselves over the scraps of refuse trembling in their beaks and the revolting remains of fish thrown back into the water.

The flash of two sudden birds brought me back to my first thought. Absent-mindedly resuming a semi-Cartesian meditation, I imagined as best I could the great man's feelings. I brought together and in my own fashion linked what I saw around me to a vague idea of his philosophy. . . . Let not the illustrious Shade be annoyed! I cannot grow fond of anyone without making him so vividly present to my mind that he becomes very different from himself.

I count also on the fact that the thoughts of the living man were not quite the same as the one he put into his books. Books always deceive us to some degree, more or less. What they fail to tell us about the writer and what they add leaves plenty of room for anyone who wishes to imagine the author as he may have been.

Let us imagine my Descartes in Amsterdam looking at all the things at which I like to think he looked. Among the many objects on which his eyes may well have rested, I can think of none more likely to have brought him back with the shortest possible delay to his usual methods of thought than the whole

paraphernalia of commerce which covers the banks and quays with barrels, packing cases, piles of merchandise, and machinery.

Winches, pulleys, all the simple contrivances, and all the maneuvering needed to transfer merchandise from the quay to the hold and from the hold to the quay; they are delightful objects for such a lover of *mechanics* and measurable things to contemplate. When he stood on those busy banks he was surrounded by opportunities for the mathematician, his attention continually attracted by a multitude of tiny problems which, in that well-ordered mind, were very likely to develop into large problems. Very little is needed—a barrel starting to roll, a heap of grain piling up, a cable breaking and lashing against its mooring, or even a falling apple—to plunge a man of intellect into the problems of universal dynamics. The man comes to a stop; but the mind pursues its strange course toward I know not what point, whence it will work its passage back by syllogisms. . . .

No place is more favorable, no environment more stimulating to meditation on the grand design of our intellectual Richelieu than this center of trade, where *measure* reigns supreme. Everything in a port is manifestly, openly, brutally metrical. The whole of its visible activity is concentrated on counting, weighing, classifying, and stowing away; number and order plainly dictate every action, and nothing passes through it which cannot be gauged in terms of tons, pounds. bushels, and sundry other measures. . . .

Is not the Method, after all, the Charter of a realm of Number whose whole ambition is now apparent to us, even if we cannot yet grasp its full power? The measurable has conquered almost the entire field of the sciences and has dis-

credited every branch in which it is not valid. The applied sciences are almost completely dominated by measurement. Life itself, which is already half enslaved, circumscribed, streamlined, or reduced to a state of subjection, has great difficulty in defending itself against the tyranny of timetables, statistics, quantitative measurements, and precision instruments, a whole development that goes on reducing life's diversity, diminishing its uncertainty, improving the functioning of the whole, making its course surer, longer, and more mechanical.

When I was in Holland, I asked whether anyone knew the circumstances in which Hals and Descartes first met. But it seems that there are no documents relating to this fascinating encounter. We should love to know who introduced the painter to the philosopher, or the philosopher to the painter; how many sittings there were and how long they lasted; whether Descartes was a good sitter, what they said to one another, and even whether the model thought that painting was vanity? . . . I do not know, even, whether the two men could understand one another without the help of an interpreter.

At that time a painter was living in Amsterdam who specialized in portraits of minor philosophers. There are two or three admirable examples of his work in the Louvre. His philosophers remind us more of Spinoza than of Descartes. They are not spending their time musing or strolling along the banks of the Amstel or on the Dam, their minds sometimes *intus* and sometimes *extra*, passing from one world to another and from a theory of the universe to an incident in the street or on the canal.

Rembrandt's little philosophers are shut-ins. They are still

maturing in the *stove*. A ray of sunlight shut in with them illuminates their stone-built rooms or, more accurately, creates a cone of light in the room's huge obscurity. The spiral of a winding stair leading down from the darkness, the perspective of a deserted gallery creates or heightens imperceptibly the impression that we are looking into the interior of a strange sea shell inhabited by the tiny intellectual animal who has secreted its luminous substance. The idea of withdrawing into the self, the idea of *depth*, of the creature himself creating his own sphere of knowledge, are suggested by the arrangement of the picture, which points, vaguely but irresistibly, to spiritual analogies. The unequal distribution of the light, the shape of the illuminated zone, the cramped habitation of a sun imprisoned in a cell, where it picks out and places certain objects while leaving others vaguely mysterious, gives us the feeling that *attention* and the *waiting upon an idea* are the real subject of the picture. The very face of the tiny thinking creature is remarkably placed in relation to the beam of light.

Many years ago, I meditated at some length on this subtle art of placing some quite arbitrary element in such a way that it works surreptitiously on the spectator while his eye is attracted and held by objects sharply defined and easily recognizable. While consciousness is rediscovering and giving names to the things which are clearly defined, to the significant data of the picture, we are subjected at the same time to the subterranean and, as it were, contingent action of the darker patches and the areas of chiaroscuro. This geography of light and shade is meaningless for the intellect; it appears shapeless to it, in the same way that the diagrams of continents and seas on maps appear shapeless to it; but the eye perceives

what the mind cannot define; and the artist, who is in the secret of this incomplete perception, can speculate on it, give to the ensemble of light and shadow a countenance that serves some purpose, some hidden function in the effect produced by the work. Thus the same picture might consist of two simultaneous compositions, one of the bodies and the objects represented, the other of the placing of the light. When I used to admire certain of Rembrandt's paintings as models of this indirect effect (which I believe his researches as an etcher had brought him to observe and analyze), I could not help thinking about the *contingent* effects that can be produced by the divided harmonies of an orchestra. . . . Wagner, like Rembrandt, had found a way of linking the mind of his victim to one of the principal and most brilliant parts of the music; and while the mind was riveted to and carried away by this powerful sequence, he would bring into play, in what might be called the *shadow of one's hearing*, in the dreamy defenseless corners of the sensitive soul, a hint of far-off preparatory events, presentiments, a sense of expectancy, questions, riddles, ineffable beginnings. . . .

This amounts to creating an art of several dimensions or, in a sense, elaborating the *surroundings* and the *depths* of things explicitly stated.

I remember that a very long time ago I tried to discover whether similar effects might reasonably be achieved in literature. I was not a *practicing* writer. . . . So I could venture on all sorts of hypotheses. Now is not the moment to explain in what way and by what methods I thought the experiment should be attempted. I will simply state the essential condition: the device must be imperceptible to the unforewarned reader, and the effect must not reveal its origin.

I was perhaps inclined to assume too easily (but when all is said, I still assume) that the art of writing contains great potential resources, a wealth of combinations and forms of composition which are barely suspected if not unknown. . . . They are hidden from us by the idea we still entertain of the mechanics of literary composition, a strangely vague and crude idea in the midst of general precision. There has been no Descartes in this field. The ancients were subtler and more "scientific" in these matters than we. We are still at the mythological stage.

Moreover, it is quite easy to see that an art whose medium —the spoken word—is always on our lips and enables us to communicate at any time with ourself as with other people, becomes so easily and so intimately identified with life itself that it is difficult, if not impossible, for it to arrive at any formal development of its powers. I must add that when I was at the delightful age at which these imaginary problems occupied my mind, it appeared to me that attempts to solve them called for an enormous amount of preliminary analysis and a painful effort of co-ordination in putting them into practice. In the days when time did not count, a simple sonnet has been known to exact of its author years of solicitude and slow growth, with all the fervor, the despair, the new starts, and what may almost be called the reconciliations required to turn the poet's relationship to his fourteen lines into a long and dramatic love story. I think that these times have passed and we are now in the golden age. Never has there been so much fruit, and heaven knows how many harvests every year.

In short, I doubt whether literature will ever find its Nicolas Rameau or its Sebastian Bach. . . . If they ever do appear, let us not be envious of their fate. They will have a hard life.

The train slows down and comes to a stop on the outskirts of Paris. It picks up again slowly for the *finale*. . . . A journey is rather like a symphony. The analogy extends even to the impatience of the people who stand up, put on their hats, get ready, and make for the corridors.

Variations on a *Pensée*

Notes

[1930]

"*The eternal Silence of these infinite spaces TERRIFIES ME.*"
*This eloquent phrase, which the powerful impression it seeks to
produce on our minds and the magnificence of its form have made
one of the most famous sayings ever uttered, is a* Poem *and not a*
Thought *at all.*

*For "eternal" and "infinite" are symbols of nonthinking. Their
impact is entirely emotional. They have an effect only on a certain
kind of sensibility. They arouse* the particular feeling of being
unable to imagine.

*Pascal introduces into literature the use or abuse of those words
which are excellent for poetry, and only for that.*

He makes of them a balanced arrangement, a sort of formidable
figure of equilibrium, *and quite apart from it, he sets off in opposi-
tion (like man, isolated, lost in the skies, insignificant and thinking)
his: "TERRIFIES ME." Notice how, in the heavens, the whole
realm of the inhuman is* solidly based, *represented by the form of a
great line of verse, in which those words that have the same function
add up and reinforce one another in their effect: noun with noun
("silence" and "spaces"); adjective with adjective ("infinite" pro-
longs "eternal").*

*This tremendous line creates the rhetorical image of a system
complete in itself, a UNIVERSE. . . .*

Variations on a *Pensée*

Text

[1923]

THE ETERNAL SILENCE...

"What soft and powerful sounds," said Eustathius to Pythagoras, "what strangely pure harmonies do I seem to hear in the very substance of the night that envelops us? My soul, at the limit of its sense of hearing, is surprised to catch the far-off sounds of music. It strains, like hope, to the furthest verge of my senses to pick up these crystalline vibrations and that sublimely slow murmuring which fill me with wonder. What is the mysterious instrument of my delight?"

"Heaven itself," replied Pythagoras. "You are listening to the sounds that charm the gods. There is no silence in the universe. A concert of eternal voices is inseparable from the movement of the heavenly bodies. Each of the moving stars, making the ether vibrate according to its speed, transmits to space the sound which is proper to its number. The most distant stars, which are necessarily those that move fastest, provide the firmament with its highest notes. The deeper notes come from the slowest, which are nearest to us; and the motionless earth is dumb. Just as the spheres are obedient to a law, so the sounds which they engender form the soft and gently varying harmony which is that of the heavens with the heavens. The world of pure order delights your ears. Intelli-

As for the human element, life, consciousness, terror, it is all contained in a sort of run-on line: "TERRIFIES ME."

The poem is perfect.

I shall go on to say about this poem:

True poetry always tends, to some extent, to imitate the thing it signifies by means of the substance *of language or by the way in which this substance is arranged.*

But since the physical properties of words and the tactics of arranging them in grammatical form are independent of the conventional values which correspond to them and constitute their meaning, there is very little chance that the direct expression of an idea will come into the mind in poetic form.

There would be no poetry, it would never have been invented, if this peculiar accident never occurred.

There would be no poetry, were it not that industry and artifice enable the poet, by the practice of numerous substitutions, to multiply the number of lucky finds and to put together as many as necessary to compose a wholly pleasing continuity.

But although the occasional lucky finds of which I am speaking— the sort that poets wait for, watch for, accumulate, growing cultures of them, trying to increase their virulence—may occur by accident or as a mere conjunction in anyone's head, the person in whom the link occurs will not necessarily observe and appreciate them. The majority of people are unaware of these products of their life.

So it is with children's sayings, sometimes so remarkable, whose grace and import are unperceived by their authors.

Nothing of the kind in the case of Pascal.

88

gence, justice, love, and the other forms of perfection, which reign in the sublime regions of the universe, become perceptible to the senses; and the ecstasy that you feel is only the effect of a divine and rigorous analogy. . . ."

That is what the deep desire of the ancient Greeks attributed to the abysses of the night.

As for the Jews, they never speak of the heavens but to pay tribute to its eloquence. The Biblical nights resound with the praises of the Lord. The stars sometimes appear to be confused with the sons of God who are the angels, and the countless tribes of spirits and stars resound over the whole earth in an immense acclamation.

"The heavens declare the glory of God, and the work of His hands is proclaimed by the firmament."

The author of the Psalms cannot find terms strong enough to express the full power of this extraordinary voice:

"Day vomits unto day the divine word, and the night instructs the night. This is no mere idle babbling nor idle talk that can escape the ear, but echoes that resound to the ends of the earth. . . . *Non sunt loquelae neque sermones quorum non audiantur voces eorum. In omnem terram exivit sonus eorum et in fines orbis terrae verba eorum.*"

And Jehovah himself says to Job: "The stars of the morning shouted for joy."

Whether as poem or thought, the "ETERNAL SILENCE" provides the theme of the present "Variations," which are in no way intended to suggest to the reader anything that could not be deduced almost inevitably from the brief and beautiful text itself.

By the light of those few words, the present writer thought he could make out in Pascal's depths certain rather remarkable intentions and contradictions. He thought he could define or describe them.

In the first place, he found it amusing to point out that in general the response of religious men in the presence of the night sky, clear and swarming with stars, is wonderfully unlike what Pascal tells us he felt.

They see God in that void strewn with fires.

They hear Him. In their ears the eternal silence resounds—a concert ringing with universal praise.

But whereas contemplation of the night excites and exalts pagans, Jews, and Christians to such a pitch, it crushes and oppresses the man who had already found what he wanted.

The fact is beyond dispute. The contrast is obvious. A difference so manifest must have some meaning.

I quite realize that Pascal's heaven is not the heaven of the ancient ecstatics.

Copernicus and Kepler had arrived on the scene; and Galileo. The Earth had become a very small thing in the firmament. Man was no longer the center of All. He was beginning to find it difficult to convince himself that All was created for him, that he was the object of special attention on the part of Omnipotence. In a heaven swept by telescopes and modified by the new astronomy, Pascal found, for his own part, new reasons for fear.

He saw nothing in the world from which he couldn't extract his poison. He drew some even from the heavens. He was appallingly avid of everything that depressed him, and incapable of detaching

For Pascal, the infinite spaces have nothing to offer but silence. He describes himself as "terrified." He complains bitterly of being left alone in the world. He cannot discover in it Him who declared through Jeremiah: *Coelum et terram ego impleo*. Neither does this strange Christian find his Father in the heavens. . . . On the contrary, "as he looks on the whole dumb universe, he is filled with dread," he tells us, "like a man who has been transported asleep to a terrifying desert island. . . ."

"Terror"; "terrified"; "frightful"; "eternal silence"; "dumb universe"—such are the terms in which one of the greatest intellects that ever existed speaks of what surrounds him.

That intellect suffers, describes itself, and bewails its lot like a hunted animal; and moreover, one that hunts itself and incites the great resources within it—the power of its logic, the admirable virtues of its language—to corrupt everything in sight that is not distressing. It wants to be fragile and desperately threatened, surrounded on all sides by danger and loneliness, by everything that causes terror and despair. It cannot bear to think that it has fallen into the nets of time, number, and dimension, that it is trapped in the terrestrial system. There is no created thing that does not remind it of its appalling state; some of them wound, others deceive it; all terrify it, so much so that contemplation never fails to make it howl for death. It reminds me inevitably of the intolerable baying of dogs at the moon; but this desperate man, capable of formulating the theory of the moon, would quite as readily wail against his own calculations.

Not merely what happens in the sky, but everything; and not merely everything in itself, but even the most innocent representation of things, irritates him and makes him hate it. "What vanity painting is. . . ." For the images created by the arts, he invents a sort of contempt of the second degree.

*himself from his own self-interest. He could not accept being simply
what he was. It was not enough to be Pascal. . . . Who knows
whether he did not resent too deeply and bitterly the fame of* Des
Cartes, *whose merits he constantly tried to belittle and whose great
hopes he attempted to deride; who knows if some stab of excruciating
jealousy, some secret thorn in his heart. . . .*

*The origin of his undertaking to destroy human values in general
is perhaps to be traced to some particular wound to his self-esteem.
There are rivals so formidable that they can only be brought down by
bringing down the whole of the human race with them.*

*The course of our "Variations" has brought us naturally to the op-
position between the* idea *of himself which we get from Pascal (or
from tradition), and the* idea *we may have formed of him* by our-
selves.

(*We must not flatter ourselves that one may be* truer *than the
other. Neither claim would have any meaning.*)

*Without overstraining it at all, I found in our celebrated versicle
a show of power and will very difficult to reconcile with the simplicity
of heart and the integrity of despair befitting the purest and most
somber character in the Legend of the Intellect.*

That was to run the risk of making Pascal more human, *and
perhaps more* profound.

*All the same, this fresh aspect of a famous person has not been
to everybody's taste.*

*What seemed to me obvious seemed to others to be of my own
making. Some were disturbed; a few declared it a scandal. Indeed
several of the most eminent men of our time took as a personal affront
to themselves what was merely the result of observation such as any-
one can make. Must I therefore return to the point? What had I
done? To what Pascal said that he experienced, which is all that
the legend allows him, I simply added that he said it* with art. *I was*

92

I cannot help suspecting that there is something systematic and labored about this attitude of perfect misery, this absolute disgust. A well-turned sentence is incompatible with total renunciation.

A distress that writes so well is not so complete that it hasn't salvaged some freedom of mind from the shipwreck, some sense of harmony, some show of logic or imagination, in contradiction to what the words themselves say. There is also something rather dubious, something rather facile, in making a specialty of tragic themes and imposing subjects. What do we teach other people by continually telling them that they are nothing, that life is vain, nature hostile, knowledge an illusion? What is the point of belaboring their nothingness, or telling them over and over what they already know?

I do not feel comfortable with this mixture of art and nature. When I find a writer working on man's true feelings in order to worsen them, bringing studied effort to bear in doing so, and asking us at the same time to take his industry for his emotions, I regard his methods as impure and ambiguous. This confusion of true and false in a work becomes shocking when we suspect that it is intended to convince us or to induce

distinctly aware of the writer, *even of the* poet *and almost of the rhetorician, in his few words on the* Eternal Silence.

Who cannot see this? And seeing it, who can fail to imagine a very different Pascal from the headstrong, rude, totally and hopelessly appalling *Pascal of the Romantics?*

This almost venerable tradition exhibits him as a sort of Hero of total and bitter disparagement. He must therefore exemplify the very perfection of contempt for what is, *and the ideal terror of* what may be; *and the formula for this famous character may be written more or less as follows:*

The operations of the most precocious, the most precise, and the most profound intelligence ever known can produce only one net result: an almost animal anguish.

This is the equivalent of saying that the horror of life is at least proportional to the knowledge that we may have of it.

(From which we should at once infer that God must feel an infinite disgust for His handiwork.)

But I wondered naïvely whether a man who no longer looks anywhere but in himself and toward God, who no longer thinks of himself except as suspended between salvation and damnation, who is no longer concerned about his future in the minds of others—as befits a desperate man wretchedly naked and alone, with his nothingness close beside him—still has the heart to think of the game of writing?

It seemed to me that no one ever writes except for someone, and that no one writes with art except for more than one. As long as somebody still matters to us, our distress remains manageable; *it may still be of use to us. And our faith, if we have any, is therefore not so completely fixed on God that there is not some left over, some small faith in the judgment of people of taste, and some hope in the connoisseurs of fine literature.*

a particular point of view in us. If you want to attract or impress me, take care that I do not see your hand more distinctly than what it writes.

I see Pascal's hand all too clearly.

Moreover, even if the intention were honest, the mere ambition to write and the care devoted to it naturally produce the effect of an ulterior motive. We inevitably make what was moderate extreme, what was rarefied dense, what was partial whole, and what was merely animated pathetic. . . . Sham windows appear of their own accord. The artist can scarcely prevent himself from heightening the intensity of his observed impression, and he develops his original idea in parallels, very much as the nervous system does when it generalizes some local change, extending it to the whole man. That is not an objection against the artist, but a warning never to confuse the real man who produced the work with the man whom the work leads us to imagine.

This confusion is the rule with Pascal. People have written so much about him, have spent so much time imagining what sort of man he was, have considered him with such passion, that he has become a character from tragedy, an extraordinary actor and almost a "stock figure" in the comedy of knowledge. Some people play at being Pascals. This practice has turned him into a sort of French Jansenist Hamlet who weighs his own skull—the skull of a great geometer; who stands shivering and dreaming on a terrace overlooking the universe. He is chilled to the marrow by the bitter wind of the infinite; he talks to himself on the verge of the abyss exactly as though he were standing before the footlights, and he argues publicly with his own ghost.

If I feel that all is vanity, the very thought prevents me from writing it down.

But at bottom we want to have it both ways; we want heaven and fame; and it is in this respect that Pascal becomes more real, and therefore a great deal less Pascalian than some would like him to be.

Did I invent the idea that when he looked at nature, Pascal said that he had a feeling which is the exact opposite of the one which most believers claim to experience?

Can it or can it not be proved that he deliberately set out to experience this peculiar reaction—Pascal, who only felt the joy of renunciation after first sufficiently corrupting, vilifying, and poisoning the thing that he renounced? He would not vomit up the world if he had not already tainted it.

His panic-stricken horror, which is the opposite of the religious trust inspired by heaven, is no less contrary to scientific observation. (By placing a little emphasis on etymology, it could be said, with some degree of accuracy, that the believer contemplates *the heaven which the scientist* observes.)

The man of science looks at the starry firmament without attaching any significance to it. He switches off *the whole emotive system of his personality. He tries to turn himself into a kind of machine which, after recording observations, sets about formulating definitions and laws, finally replacing phenomena by their expression in terms of conscious, deliberate, and definite potentials.*

And so our poet of silence and terror stands quite apart from nearly all the mystics and the general run of scientists.

Having added to this twofold distinction the remark we made about the immense pains that he took to write well; having convicted him of very fine and very skillful workmanship in his style and therefore of mixing his terror and disgust with a secret ambition to dazzle and to

Yet it is a rather remarkable fact that the majority of religions have placed the seat of Omnipotence at the highest possible altitude, in the same way that they have discovered its sign and the proof of its existence in the astral order which, on the other hand, has given men the idea, the earliest model, and the first demonstrations of the laws of nature.

It is toward the heavens that men lift their hands, in the heavens that their eyes seek refuge or lose themselves; it is to the heavens that a prophet's or a comforter's finger points; it is from those heights that certain words have fallen, and that certain trumpet blasts will be heard.

And doubtless neither the First Cause nor the Pure Act nor the Spirit has any physical location any more than it has shape or parts; but an instinct, which is perhaps the result of our vertical structure, perhaps the sense that our destiny is attached to very distant phenomena and that all earthly life depends on them, inevitably leads men who are overburdened, afflicted, or troubled in their minds by excessive questioning, to turn toward the zenith, *toward the heights*.

Exhausser (to raise) and *exaucer* (to grant) are the same word.

Kant himself, yielding secretly to a naïve mystical impulse, associated the kind of intuition that he had of a universal moral law with the sensation that he felt at the sight of a starry sky.

I have sometimes tried to observe in myself, and to trace in my mind, that mysterious effect generally produced in men by a clear night and the presence of the stars.

On such occasions we perceive only objects that have no

win admiration, we are in a position, now that we have tamed the anchorite and turned him into a man of letters, to examine the use to which he put his horrifying sensations and his outstanding gifts as a writer.

It is here that either I find him displeasing, or I become my own accuser.

I am quite willing that as a worshiper of the Creator he should only discover His absence in Creation, quite willing that as an artist, the great artist that he is, he should depreciate art. I can understand that as a geometer, and a profound geometer, he should reduce science to a form of curiosity and to certain applied uses not interesting enough to distract a soul from its essential suffering. I like the notion that we should not attach an absolute value to something which constitutes our relative value. I approve of having a clear enough idea of what we are to treat the gifts we happen to possess as fortuitous. No doubt it is not always the strongest minds that have been the most moved, as they should have been, by the fragility, inconstancy, and inadequacy of thought. But there is something lacking (a certain nobility) in all greatness which is not aware that it is accidental, and in every mind which fails to discern its own weakness and mediocrity as clearly and curiously as it recognizes in itself occasional beauties and insights which at times may be extraordinary.

In all this Pascal is worthy of Pascal.

But it is the use that he intended to make of the bitter fruits of his meditations which worries me and which I find repellent.

I cannot endure apologias. If there is one thing that a mind of great breadth ought to forbid itself, should not even conceive, it is the intention of convincing others, and the use of every means in its power to do so.

Commerce, politics, and unhappily religion, are not deterred by the impurity of their devices when it is a matter of building up a clientele and captivating people's wills.

connection with our own bodies. We are strangely simplified. Everything that is close at hand is invisible; everything that is perceptible is intangible. We float far away from ourselves. Our eye abandons itself to vision, in a field of luminous events which it cannot help joining together by its own spontaneous impulse, as though they existed in the same dimension of time; it traces lines, forms patterns that are its own creation, it imposes them on our mind and introduces them into the spectacle of reality.

The way in which all these points are distributed, however, escapes us. We are overwhelmed, pelted, engulfed, ignored by all this glittering host.

We can count the stars, though we cannot believe that we exist in their eyes. There is no form of reciprocity between them and us.

We feel something that demands a word from us, and something else that rejects it.

Since what we see in the sky and what we find in the depths of ourselves are equally beyond the scope of any action on our part, and since the one sparkles beyond our enterprises and the other lives at a level below our powers of expression, a sort of relationship is established between our attention to what is furthest from us and to what is deepest in us. They are, as it were, the poles of our expectation, responding to each other, and alike in the hope of discovering something new and decisive, in the heavens or in the heart.

When our eyes take in the prodigious number of the stars, what is deepest in us is stirred to an extreme sense of being itself, of being unique—and yet alone. I am a whole yet incomplete. I am a whole and yet a part.

The darkness that envelops us makes of us a naked soul.

Every work of propaganda implies a great contempt for human beings, and a great outrage against charity; for the man who tries to convince me is necessarily doing something to me which he would not like done to himself. He treats me as a person who must be taken in. He employs a horrible mixture of method and artifice, combines sentiment and syllogisms, conjures up ghosts, is prodigal with promises and threats, appeals in turn to the bestial and the ideal.

That is how orators go about their work; and likewise all those who want to get people onto their side. What is Eloquence? It borrows heat, images, metaphors, rhythms, to give vitality to statements which in themselves are nothing.

What is Apologetics? It is making good Christians with bad arguments, with the help of logic and death, etc. Could the Serpent do worse?

That is what I describe as impure, *what I cannot tolerate, and what seems to me an outrage. If there exists an Ethics of the Mind, nothing could be more of an offense against it.*

Let us look for a moment at the plan and the arguments in the Pensées *as though they were being examined and judged by the author of the Provincial Letters. Let him apply his ruthless scrutiny to the argument based on the Wager.*

That darkness is studded with inaccessible points of light. It is difficult to prevent ourselves from thinking of homes where people are awake. We vaguely fill the darkness with luminous and unknowable beings.

The same darkness which obliterates our physical surroundings makes us also lower our voice, reducing it to an inner voice, since we have an inclination to speak truth only to those who are close to us.

We experience a strange feeling of calm, and uneasiness. Between the "self" and the "non-self" there is no longer any communication. In full daylight our actions created a link between our thoughts and things. We exchanged sensations for thoughts; thoughts for sensations; and our actions served as intermediaries, our time as currency. But now there is no further exchange between the two; there is no longer a man in action who is the measure of things. There are now simply two distinct presences, two incommensurable natures. Nothing but two adversaries watching each other but understanding one another not at all. The immense enlargement of our perspectives is confronted by the reduction in our powers of action. For a time we lose the familiar illusion that things communicate with us. A fly trying to pass through a window-pane is the image of what we are.

We cannot remain at this neutral point. Sensibility knows no equilibrium. We might even define sensibility as a function whose role is to interrupt any equilibrium of forces occurring in living beings. Our mind must therefore rouse itself from its own torpor and recover from the solemn and fixed astonishment caused by the *feeling* that it is everything and the *evidence* that it is nothing.

We then see that essentially solitary being, the mind, trying to defend itself with its own thoughts. Our body defends itself

against the world by its reflex actions and its different secretions, and sometimes it produces them as though by chance and as though to do something quickly; and at other times it uses adapted movements and effective moods as weapons against anything that oppresses or irritates it. The soul behaves no differently toward the inhumanity of the night. It defends itself by its own creations, some of which are naïve and irresistible, like reflex actions; while others, the outcome of reflection, are delayed, combined, geared, and adapted to whatever knowledge the soul may have of our situation.

We find in ourselves therefore two kinds of response to the sensations I have described as aroused in us when we look at the sky and imagine the universe. Some are *spontaneous*, others carefully *prepared*. They are very different from one another, though they may mix and combine in the same head; but we must separate them if they are to be defined. We often try to distinguish between them by attributing some to the *heart* and others to the *head*. These are quite convenient terms.

In its battle against the terrifying image of the world, the heart almost always ends by creating, out of the very strength of its desire, the notion of some Being sufficiently powerful to control and to have constructed or put forth this monster of space and radiation which engenders, nourishes, imprisons, threatens, fascinates, intrigues, and devours us. And this Being may even be a Person, that is to say, there may be some reresemblance and some half-formed hope of an indefinable *entente* between Him and us. That is what the heart *discovers*. It tends to find its answer in a god.

Moreover, we know very well from our experience of love that the unique calls to the unique, and that the living desires the living.

Let us see now what other kind of thoughts may come to us

The Pascal reaction (*terror at the idea of the physicomechanical universe*) *and its opposite* (*exaltation*) *are no longer current nowadays.*

The progress of knowledge in this domain, the great discoveries which have emerged, the prodigious number of facts, the strangeness and instability of theories, and most particularly the more and more

if we put aside our feelings and try to resist the enormous pressure of things by using infinite patience and immense curiosity. The mind seeks.

The mind is in no hurry to imagine what it needs for a sustained consideration of the universe. It simply investigates; and without regard to time or the duration of a particular life. There is a remarkable contrast between the promptness, impatience, and restiveness of the *heart* and the slow pace that comes with the hopeful and critical approach. The effect of this delay, which may be endless, is to transform the problem. When the problem is transformed, it may in turn transform the investigator.

We shall come to see that we cannot think about our universe except by conceiving it as an *object* clearly separable from ourselves and distinctly different from our consciousness. We shall then be able to compare it to the small systems that we can describe, define, measure, test. We shall treat the whole as a part. We shall be led to apply logic to it, whose operations will enable us to predict its changes, or to limit their scope.

(We shall, for example, compare the whole assembly of the stars to a gaseous cloud; we shall apply to the astral swarm the definitions and laws discovered in the study of gases in the laboratory; we shall form a *statistical* conception of the universe, and think in terms of its *internal energy*, its *temperature*, etc.)

Our work will consist, in short, in making a sort of *rapprochement* between what appeared so astounding and so moving and what is familiar to our senses, accessible to our action, and conforms fairly closely to our modes of reasoning.

What is emerging, what must necessarily emerge in the long run from this endless work, is a certain change (already perceptible) in our notions of the *familiar*, the *possible*, the *reasonable*, which at every moment constitute the conditions necessary to our peace of mind. Just as men have accepted the

remarkable dependence of phenomena on the methods of observation, force modern men to suspend all judgment about the nature of things. We know that the "eternal silence" is no more than a figment of the imagination, and that there is not a single corner of "space" in which some resonator would not reveal the eternal presence of rays and energy.

The celebrated retort which occurs in The Mystery of Jesus: *"You would not seek me," etc., is perhaps derived from the recollection of something read.*

St. Bernard (whom Bourdaloue quotes in the Sermon on Grace*) said this:* Nisi enim prius quaesita, non quaereres; sicut nec eligeres nisi electa.

Pascal's formula is not quite the same as St. Bernard's. In Pascal the search itself is given as proof of the existence of what is sought. The search is the result of a secret discovery which preceded it.

In St. Bernard the soul seeks only in order to be sought. The soul's search for God depends on God's search for the soul. Thou wouldst not seek Me if thou wert not sought by Me. Thou wouldst not seek Me if thou wert reduced to thyself alone.

There was also Father Noël, whose definition of light moved Pascal to mockery.

It should perhaps be observed that this definition, utterly absurd though it appeared in the seventeenth century, could almost be interpreted today as a crude expression of the most recent theories of the composition of light (the granular structure of radiation).

Moreover, Pascal's ideas in physics are those of a singularly timorous mind. What he thought led nowhere. He lacked power to imagine the mechanical nature of phenomena with which Des Cartes was richly endowed, and which, however naïve and illusory it may be in itself, is the prerequisite for a vast amount of very fruitful research and real discoveries.

antipodes, so they will come to terms with the *curvature of space* and all sorts of other strange ideas. It is not impossible—it is even quite probable—that this adaptation will gradually transform not only our ideas but certain of our immediate reactions.

What might be called *the Pascal reaction* may become a rarity, and of peculiar interest to the psychologists.

Pascal had "found what he wanted," but doubtless because he was no longer seeking. Giving up the search, and the manner of giving it up, may bring a sense of discovery.

But he had never believed in the kind of search whose object is unforeseen.

He discovered in himself that *eternal silence* which neither genuinely religious nor genuinely profound men have ever observed in the universe.

He exaggerated, frightfully and crudely, the opposition between knowledge and salvation, though in his own century there were learned men who, it seems to me, were no less successful in achieving their salvation than he was, but without making the sciences suffer for it. There was Cavalieri, who tackled indivisibles; there was Saccheri who suspected, without admitting it to himself, how much had to be taken for granted in Euclid, and half opened the door to many of the future audacities of geometry. They were, to be sure, mere Jesuits.

Bossuet

IN THE HIERARCHY of writers I can think of no one who stands higher than Bossuet; none who is surer of his words, stronger in his verbs, more forcible and more subtle in all the procedures of discourse, bolder and more felicitous in his syntax, or, in a word, more a master of language—that is to say, of himself. His complete and unusual command of his instrument, extending from the vernacular to supreme magnificence, from perfect clarity of expression to the most powerful and resounding effects of art, implies an extraordinary *awareness* and *control* of all the resources and functions of language.

Bossuet says what he wants to say. Like all the writers we describe as *classics*, he is essentially a man of will. He proceeds by design where we proceed by chance; he relies on the sense of expectation he arouses while the modern writer relies on surprise. He starts off powerfully from silence, warms up by degrees, expands, lifts, organizes his sentence, which at times builds up like an arch, supported by lateral propositions marvelously distributed round the central moment, rises, casting off its incidentals, surmounting them to come at last to its keystone and move downward again, performing prodigies of subordination and balance, until it arrives at its appointed term and the complete resolution of its forces.

When we turn to Bossuet's thought, we must admit that it appears unlikely today to offer much intellectual stimulus. On the contrary, it is we who, at the expense of considerable effort and some erudition, must give it a certain life. Three centuries of deep and revolutionary changes in every field, the intervention of an enormous number of events and ideas have inevitably made the substance of works belonging to a time so different from our own look naïve, strange, and sometimes almost inconceivable to the posterity that we are. Yet something else remains. The majority of readers attribute great importance to what they call the *content* of a work, and even regard it as infinitely superior to what they call the *form*. A few, however, take the opposite view and regard the other as pure superstition. They take the bold stand that the structure of an expression has a sort of reality, while the sense or meaning is no more than a shadow. The value of the idea expressed is indeterminate; it varies according to people and period. What is profound for one person seems to another boringly obvious or unbearably absurd. Finally, we have only to look about us to see that what is still of interest to us in earlier literature does not belong to the order of knowledge but to the order of examples and models.

For these admirers of form, though a form is always created or determined by the author's thought, it has more value and even more meaning than any thought. What they value in form is the vigor and elegance of *action*: when they turn to the thought they find only the flow of *events*.

For these readers Bossuet is a treasure house of forms, combinations, and co-ordinated operations. They can admire the great style of his structures just as passionately as they admire the architecture of a temple when its sanctuaries are deserted and the feelings and causes which led to its construction have long lost their force. The arch still stands.

Swedenborg

THE FINE NAME of Swedenborg sounds strange to French ears. It awakens in me whole depths of confused notions surrounding the fantastic image of a singular personality who seems to be more a literary creation that an historical character. I confess that, until a few days ago, all I knew about him came from books read long ago.

In the far-off past, Balzac's *Séraphitus-Séraphita* and a chapter of Gérard de Nerval had been my only sources, and it is thirty years since I drew on them. . . .

There was, however, a charm about this fading memory. The mere sound of the syllables of the magic name, whenever I happened to hear it, suggested incredible intimations, the attractions of a weird science, the mystery of a great influence emanating from dreams. Above all, it pleased me to visualize the shadowy figure of the Illuminatus in that century in which I myself would have chosen to live.

I imagine this period must have been one of the most brilliant and satisfying ever known to men. It was marked by the glittering close of one world and the powerful struggles of another to come to birth, also by a highly refined art, by forms and manners that were still very temperate, by all the strength and all the graces of the mind. There were magic and

the differential calculus; as many atheists as mystics; the most cynical of cynics and the oddest of dreamers. The excesses of the intellect were not unknown, yet were counter-balanced —sometimes in the same head—by an astonishing credulity. All the subjects of that boundless intellectual curiosity which the Renaissance had inherited from antiquity, or derived from its own fine frenzy, reappeared in the eighteenth century, but more vividly, more acutely, more precisely. The folios gave place to volumes of smaller format.

The Europe of the day recognized the coexistence of completely opposing doctrines, ideals, systems. That is characteristic of what is called "modern" civilization. Rome and Alexandria had already known this accumulation of contradictory tendencies and theories, publicly paraded and debated. They seethed with different religions and philosophies; no one could fail to be aware, in an environment of such a high intellectual temperature, that there is more than one solution to every speculative problem. The result was contacts and exchanges, surprising combinations and contrasts of ideas which, often occurring in the same individual, made him the incarnation of the richness and confusion of the period.

In the eighteenth century, while the d'Alemberts, the Clairauts, the Eulers were busy constructing a relentlessly pure mechanical universe by the completely novel methods of mathematical analysis; while others were trying their hands at biology, catching glimpses of different philosophies of living nature, and attempting to deduce from them the origins of what they thought they knew about matter; while the great Linnaeus was embarking on the vast labor of classifying all the organic forms of life, there were some who were constructing a variety of metaphysical systems, still following the ancients, or else continuing the work of Gassendi, Descartes,

Spinoza, Leibnitz, or Malebranche. In the realm of theology Jansenists, Quietists, Pietists, and a good many other sects were quarreling over the possession of truth and the dominion of souls. There were also a great many freethinkers.

But if free inquiry, which had become more or less permissible in most countries, if the progress of the exact sciences and their astonishing success, and the discovery of the whole face of the earth—if these created a sort of encyclopedic appetite, a thirst for knowledge, a spirit that stopped at nothing, this same thirst for knowledge and power was not above exploring the penumbra of the mind as well, and even that suspect darkness where, since the earliest antiquity, men had imagined treasures of power and knowledge, and even secrets of supernatural importance.

At that time there existed in many minds certain interests and expectations which we are astonished to find together. The rational and the irrational were strangely blended. Men like Leibnitz or Bayle may appear to us endowed with too many different preoccupations; and we are disconcerted to find in one and the same man, Newton, an interpretation of the Apocalypse (based on hypotheses about the astronomy of the Argonauts) and the discovery of fluxional calculus and universal gravitation. But the century was bursting with research in every field, and its passion for accuracy, the cult of observation and experiment did not preserve it from the temptations and seductions of doctrines and practices which had been mysteriously handed down from the past.

(I observe, in passing, that the most prudent and positive of sciences demands of those who take it up with the passion that leads to discoveries, a certain taste for the marvelous; the prodigious and unexpected result obtained by a rigorous process of deduction or by a flawless method of experiment

provides the mind with one of the greatest joys it can know.)

In short, during the eighteenth century we witness the spread, we might almost call it the popularization, of all those normal or degenerate varieties of knowledge which are engendered by the desire to know more than we can. Adepts multiplied; initiates swarmed; charlatans abounded. The social and political role of the occult became immense.

Never have credulity and skepticism been more closely associated or, so to speak, more indiscriminately dealt out to the human race than at that time. *Symbology*, which deciphered the universe as though it were a hieroglyphic; *hermeneutics*, which gave Scripture a deeper interpretation than its literal meaning; *theosophy*, which looked for and found immediate illumination; and still more daring and disturbing in their ambitions and their modes of operation, *magic, alchemy, divination* by the stars, by dreams, by conjuring up spirits, existed in many a mind together with the most limpid classical culture and the discipline of the exact sciences.

Such was the mental climate, the intellectual drama, suggested to me by the name of Swedenborg. Its three syllables were simply a sort of musical chime, an incantatory formula that evoked a fantastic picture of the secret spiritual life of the age of Louis XV. I never dreamed that I should one day have to probe a little deeper and consider with a wholly new, with an almost personal interest, a character who for so long had appeared to me only as one of the shades of a society that was voluptuously inquisitive about arcane things.

But the book I have just been reading presents us with a very different picture of Swedenborg.* The vague and somewhat Hoffmannesque idea I had formed of him in my igno-

*This study was written as an introduction to the French translation of Mr. Martin Lamm's *Swedenborg*. [P. V.]

rance has changed into that of a figure no less enigmatic, but clear, intensely interesting, whose intellectual history raises a considerable number of problems of the first importance in the field of the psychology of cognition.

I read Mr. Martin Lamm's book with increasing pleasure; I saw emerging, chapter by chapter, the extraordinary Romance of a "Second" Life: I say "romance" because while I was reading I was naïvely aware of the intense desire to know *what happens next*, which usually grips us only in works written to make us feel the delights of *adventure*. . . .

No doubt the adventure it relates is not one of those which excite and hold the attention of the great reading public; the whole action takes place in the most secret places of the inner life, on those indeterminate frontiers where the powers, the ambitions, the light and darkness within us are revealed in opposition to one another, as they are, on the other hand, to the ordinary phenomena of the "external world." But so far as my personal taste is concerned, there are no journeys to the edge of the real, no magic tales, no epic or dramatic stories which can rival the study of that inexhaustible creator and universal transformer we call the *Mind*.

The Swedenborg who emerges from Mr. Lamm's book is a being who has known, suffered, and passed through every state or phase of the most intense and complete psychic life, since he seems to have had personal experience of the whole range of intellectual activity from the most normal to those extreme forms which might be described as abnormal if the use of this (to my mind) purely negative term did not involve too shallow and too simplified a judgment. The analysis of Swedenborg's successive works, which the author has carried out in masterly fashion, shows us the evolution of a remarkable case which every reader, according to his cast of mind,

can usefully think over and interpret; and, whether as historian or philosopher, psychiatrist or mystic—or even as a poet—can study, discuss, admire, or judge in his own way.

But whatever use the thoughtful reader of this book may make of it, he will undoubtedly be astonished at its abundance and clarity. He will observe with respect the wealth of learning, the amount of work, and the intellectual vigor which were required for an examination and exposition of the whole of Swedenborg's enormous output. This output, I imagine, is not always pleasant or easy to deal with, though here and there we come across passages of great poetic beauty, delightful visions from some transcendental childhood. But it provides an incomparable document whose interest I should not even have suspected without the trouble taken by Mr. Lamm to reduce to its essentials an immense amount of material and to act as our guide through the Swedenborgian Heavens and Hells. In his foreword he modestly describes his work as a contribution to the study of the origins of Swedenborg's theosophy—a study on which he embarked as a result of his researches into the "tradition of emotional mysticism which foreshadowed romanticism and later became a part of it." But in my opinion he has drawn the portrait of one of the strangest characters in the great drama of the human mind.

That is not all. What gives a book its value in my eyes is the number and novelty of the problems it creates, poses, or revives in my own mind. Books that presuppose or produce a passive attitude in the reader are not to my taste. I expect the books I read to rouse me to comment and reflection, to bring on the sort of arrested attention that makes us stare into space, opening up fresh perspectives and all at once engaging our deepest curiosity, our own particular preoccupations, and the immediate sense of our own living presence.

I shall therefore try, in a few words, to given an idea of some of the dormant questions that Mr. Lamm's book awakened in my mind.

Swedenborg appears to me *now* as the exemplar and subject of a most remarkable and complete inner transformation, accomplished in several stages over a period of some sixty years. This transformation of a psychic life, observed and traced through the chronological sequence of his writings, was that of a man of very wide culture who could be described at the outset as a scholar and philosopher of the type familiar to the scholars and philosophers of his time, one who gradually changed into a mystic toward his fortieth year. This was Swedenborg's first change, and it was prepared for by his early education, the mystical outlook of his father, and the environment in which he spent his childhood. All the same, how was he able to shift from a mechanistic view of the world, and from habits of mind formed by the practice of precise observation in the field of natural science, to a kind of meditation that was theological in origin, to a preoccupation with questions deriving from Scripture and tradition? How did this transfer of values come about? Yet, so far, this had amounted to no more than a switching of ordinary attention from one object to another; one form of theoretical thinking was replaced by another. Now a little later on, a deeper and much more unusual change occurred: from the theoretical and speculative phase, concerned with arguments about the dogma of the Fall or the nature of angels, Swedenborg moved forward to another state in which *not only ideas* were in question, but *knowledge itself*. The theoretical phase was followed by a phase in which interior events occurred that no longer had the purely transitory and potential char-

acter of ordinary thought, but introduced into consciousness an *awareness of powers and presences* different from those of the Self, and set off from it, not as responses or arguments or ordinary intuitions, but as phenomena. We therefore find that exposition and dialectic are replaced by *narrative* and description; which means that the conditions and methods of intellectual research—doubt, the recognition of a number of possibilities, choice, demonstration, etc.—are supplanted by an insight that carries immediate and absolute conviction. This kind of certainty has nothing in common with that expressed by the word "evidence": evidence is, briefly, a reaction of our mind in which *we are aware of participating*, whereas the certainty of the mystics takes the form of the awareness of an existence independent of us, the kind of awareness we commonly receive from physical objects and bodies which give us the impression of *being separate from us*. That is why the introduction of the powers and presences of which I have just spoken may well be regarded as the formation of a second "reality," or reality of the second order; and the possession of this kind of dual vision of things is the definition of the mystic state.

But with Swedenborg the theoretical activity of the mind does not entirely disappear with the advent of direct perception. It resumes its role of formulating and defending intellectual arguments. It was "natural" that a mind so highly endowed and cultivated should apply itself to the task of establishing, between its two realities, relations as systematic as possible, and should lay down a sort of method invested with a quasi-scientific form or procedure. That is what Swedenborg did in his famous *Theory of Correspondences*, in which he brought together, on the one hand, a number of different

metaphysical, cabalistic, or magical traditions with his earlier rationalism, and on the other, the discoveries that came with the awakening of his new faculty of cognition.

This *Theory* enabled him to draw up a table or dictionary in which, for everything in the world of ordinary experience, or for every word of the common language, there was a corresponding being or thing belonging to the "spiritual" world. Even the laws of physics were to be translated into "spiritual" terms.

This brings me to another question suggested by Mr. Lamm's book. What are we to understand by the word "spiritual"? I might easily have gone on with my reading in the belief that I understood it. I have heard the word thousands of times. I have used it myself on countless occasions. But I found that, in this book, it assumed a force and importance that made me pause.

This is what I said to myself: It is the vice of the ordinary philosophical vocabulary that though it must necessarily put on the appearances of technical language, it is nonetheless necessarily lacking in really precise definitions: for the only precise definitions are *instrumental* (that is to say, reducible to acts, such as pointing at an object or carrying out an operation). It is impossible to convince ourselves that words like *reason, universe, cause, matter,* or *idea* possess single, uniform, unchanging meanings. What usually happens is that every attempt to make the meaning of such terms clearer leads to introducing under the same name a fresh object of thought *which differs from the original object in so far as it is new.*

But the vocabulary of mysticism is far more evasive still. For here the value attributed to the parts of speech is not merely personal, but is the product of exceptional states or

moments on the part of the person concerned. Not only is it not independent of the person who thinks and speaks, but it also depends on his state of mind. Moreover, with the mystics, sense perceptions themselves are invested with values no less peculiar than those attributed to words. A chance sound or (as happened with Jakob Böhme) a reflection on a pewter plate are not taken for what they are or confined to the associations of ideas suggested by them: they have the impact of an event, and as though by an *actio praesentiae* become "catalytic," provoking a change of state.

The subject then enters without difficulty into his "second" life, as though the initial phenomenon were a pivotal element, a point of contact or junction of two separate "universes."

That is what happens with the principal terms used by the mystics: they possess an ordinary, or "dictionary" meaning, and another meaning whose reverberations are only perceived in the "interior" regions of a given individual. The ambiguity of this twofold function facilitates passage from the normal to the privileged state, providing *an effortless coming and going between two worlds*. This last observation seems to me of some importance: it makes it possible for us to avoid mistaking mysticism for delirium; delirium confuses the two worlds and their values; the Swedenborgian mystic distinguishes them to the point of regarding the Table of Correspondences between them as his particular problem and task; and moreover his everyday activities, his relations with people and things, are either perfectly normal or irreproachably adapted.

In the case with which we are concerned, "spiritual" is a *key word*, a word whose meaning lies in its echoes. It does not

guide the mind toward an object of thought, but agitates a whole hidden area of the affective and imaginative life. It answers the need to assert that the aim and value of what we say does not lie in what we see; and still more, that the aim and value of what we think does not lie in what can be thought. It is a sign which, in the form of an epithet, prompts us to reduce the objects and events of everyday life and material reality to the role of mere symbols; and besides, brings home to us the symbolic nature of thought itself. The "spiritual" world gives the visible world its true meaning, but is itself only the symbolical expression of an inaccessible world of essences, in which the distinction between *being* and *knowing* ceases.

The one fact of capital importance (for the psychologist) which is contained in all this and appears to be worth study is the following. Someone has the feeling, even the conviction, that something may be present in his thought other than his thought itself. The mystical or spiritual event par excellence is the introduction, or supposed intervention, in the group of attributes belonging to a Self, of quasi phenomena, impulsive powers, judgments, etc., which the Self does not recognize as its own and which it can only attribute to Another . . . in a realm where normally there is no Other— the indivisible realm of Oneself.

No doubt what takes place "in us" is quite often a surprise "for us"; sometimes owing to its superior quality, and sometimes, on the contrary, owing to a weakness or deficiency that becomes apparent and astonishes us. We find that we are sometimes more and sometimes less than "ourselves." But we nevertheless attribute these deviations to some subjective or functional cause, more or less as we do when we are surprised by some unexpected physical sensation. A sudden pain

transforms our idea of our Self; it is the same with a flash of acute pleasure; but we never for a moment imagine that these incidents or events do not belong to our substance itself, that they are not simply one of its properties seldom called into play. The mystic, on the contrary, has a sense of the exteriority, or rather extraneousness, of the *source* of the images, emotions, words, and impulses which reach him through some inner channel. He feels compelled to give them the force of reality; but as he cannot confuse this reality with *everyday* reality, his life is a journey between two worlds equally real, but of very unequal importance.

At this point there inevitably arises a question I cannot undertake to answer, and I am not even sure that I can formulate it clearly.

How can we conceive that a man like Swedenborg, a highly cultivated man—accustomed by serious work of a scientific nature, and by reflection in which logical thought and internal concentration are sustained over prolonged periods, to observe the formation of his own thought and to look more deeply into himself while at the same time remaining conscious of the workings of his mind—could have failed to perceive the part played by his own mind in producing the images, admonitions, "truths" which came to him as though from some secret source? These productions were no doubt strange, but not so strange that one could not recognize, on reflection, those elements borrowed from the ordinary experience of life.

How can we fail to see that whatever takes shape in our minds belongs to that group of combinations which can take shape within us out of our sensory data and our own psychic and emotional freedoms and potentialities? While Swedenborg the *scientist* had certainly regarded the world of sense

perception as the superficial aspect of the physicomechanical world of Descartes or Newton, Swedenborg the *mystic* regarded this superficial sensory world, known by naïve intuition, as the expression of a "spiritual" world. *If therefore this spiritual world is revealed by some supernatural power, that power chooses to express itself through Swedenborg by means of appearances that would have been suitable for the instruction of an ignoramus. . . .*

I have italicized these words, but I can bring home the idea they express even more forcibly by the following observation. The oddest vision of a visionary can always be related or traced back to some simple distortion of observable reality which yet conforms to the conditions of knowledge, and more than that, such a vision can be expressed in the terms of ordinary language. But think of the structure of things and the nature of the universe as they are presented by contemporary developments in the mathematical and instrumental resources of Science. On the one hand, these results are positive since they refer to powers of action; on the other hand, they form part of the unintelligible, they explode the venerable "categories of the understanding" and undermine the very concepts of law and cause—so much so that what used to be "reality" has become simply a matter of statistics, while the *imagination* itself, which is the source of all possible "visions," and the *common language*, which is their vehicle of expression, are condemned to impotence, incapable of expressing what our instruments and our calculations force us to try to conceive. . . .

The Swedenborgian Universe, the Spiritual World, the Place of Conjugal Love in the Realm of Angels and Spirits is therefore "human, all too human," too like our own world, while the universes constructed by science (even those conceivable in Swedenborg's time) are, on the contrary, more

and more "inhuman"; we find in them neither weddings, nor fine speeches, nor shining virgins; and they cannot serve as symbols for anything at all, being themselves mere symbols, tensors, operators, matrices, and symbols whose concrete meaning escapes us.

I have spoken of all this only to emphasize the question that seems to me to be paramount in the case with which we are concerned: *How is a Swedenborg possible?* From what premises must we start when we come to study the coexistence in the same person of a scientist and engineer, a high official, a man at once wise in practical affairs and learned in everything, who yet had the characteristics of an Illuminatus, who did not hesitate to write and publish an account of his visions, and who claimed to have been visited by the inhabitants of another world, to be in touch with them, and to have spent part of his life in their mysterious company?

I will go further still: it is not sufficient to speak of coexistence; we must also note a certain degree of collaboration, the most remarkable and most astonishing example of which is provided by the treatise on representations and correspondences which is to be found in the *Arcana Coelestia*.

I find it difficult to believe that this work was not conceived and written by an author who was much more systematic and more master of himself than inspired or lost in contemplation. The concern for orderly arrangement, the will to careful definition, the well-prepared introduction of new ideas, all these are much in evidence and must have called for a considerable outlay of logic, which is in strange contrast with the content of the reveries. But what is still more extraordinary is that part of the treatise in which Swedenborg develops the correspondences of organs and limbs; he displays, in this section, a remarkably exact and detailed knowledge of

anatomy, and he expresses himself like a man who has thought deeply about the problems of physiology; a knowledge and a power of thought which he uses to make every part of the human organism correspond to the strangest "spiritual" meanings, evaluations, or creations. This mixture of knowledge, method, and dream, of perfect and constant lucidity of mind with imaginary relationships, is so difficult to accept that we should sometimes feel tempted to suspect the good faith of our visionary if, on the one hand, the considerable expenditure of labor, the duration and continuity of his effort, and on the other hand, the disinterestedness, the nobility of character we recognize in him, did not make the hypothesis of trickery, of a vast lie in the grand manner, highly improbable.

Swedenborg himself replied to the anxious questionings of his own faith in his personal illumination: *Haec vera sunt quia signum habeo.*

This *sign* was sufficient to dispel all inner resistance and to maintain the close union between Swedenborg the rationalist, the physicist, the practical and sociable man, and Swedenborg the familiar companion of spirits and confidant of angels. These sublime and marvelous relationships did not prevent him from enjoying an active social life; he maintained them as he did the ordinary intercourse of a cultivated man with his own contemporaries, just as easily and as continuously as a person who frequents several "worlds" (such as that of his pleasures and that of his business) maintains and interlinks their different observances.

The nature of the *sign* is not explained. On the assumption that Swedenborg's reply was not a mere admission of defeat, we may attribute his silence to the fear of seeing the foundation of his inner life challenged, or else to the fear that

the sign might lose its virtue if the secret were revealed. But the difficulty of describing it may also have forced him to remain silent. It is well known that what makes our mind fix on a certainty is indefinable. I do not propose therefore to try to discover this one, but I shall nevertheless put forward a certain analogy as a mere suggestion.

I am thinking of the kind of power and consistency which affirms or confirms in us an opinion or a resolution that completely answers the needs of our sensibility. If we receive from an external source something we have intensely desired, it seems to us that the thing which satisfies us so completely is in a sense the product of our desire. We feel that a certain idea, put to us by someone else, delights us as though the desire to be delighted had formed the idea for itself; we find that a work has been so ideally made for us that it is as though we had done it ourselves; and we even say the same thing of a person; and this immediate and invincible feeling is for us an indubitable *sign*, because we cannot doubt that what pleases us does please us, or believe that what satisfies us so completely leaves room for the slightest hesitation.

By what "sign" does an artist know that, at a given moment, he has hit on his "truth"—by what "sign" does he sense at once the necessity and the pleasure (both of them increasing) of his creative act?

Swedenborg's *sign* was perhaps no more than the sense of energy, of blessed fulfillment and well-being that he always experienced when he let himself conjure up and organize his spiritual world, and the certainty of his creative joy could no doubt suffice to put off his doubts indefinitely and to lull his critical sense.

Nevertheless, in the Swedenborg case we are faced, it seems, with a number of supposed facts that cannot be reduced either

to mystic vision or to the admitted existence of a certain *sign*.

The fundamental metamorphosis of his thought, which had been entirely scientific and metaphysico-theological, into an intuitive "second reality" and a transcendental doctrine, came about by degrees, and the degrees were marked by "subjective" events which were, strictly speaking, hallucinatory, and of which the scene at the London inn was completely characteristic.

Must we accept the account of them which the theosophist himself gives, and which of necessity only he could give, as "accurate"? The importance of the question I am asking will soon be apparent. The accuracy I mean is not something that can depend on Swedenborg's good faith. We can take it for granted that this was absolute. But the most transparently honest of men, when it comes to telling us what he has seen and, above all, what he has seen in a realm to which he alone has access, inevitably alters the nature of his own sincerity *simply by using the common language*, which compounds the first and no less inevitable alteration due to the act of direct memory by adding a second which results from dividing that memory into *words* and combining them according to the forms and laws of syntax. In the sphere of ordinary intercourse such alterations are usually negligible and in any case are rectified by common experience: the world of common experience serves to verify our means of communication. But every *description* of our individual perceptions radically destroys that very element in those perceptions which it would be most valuable to know and to analyze.

That is why I am very far from putting confidence in the pretended analysis of dreams which is so fashionable at the present time and in which we seem to have forged a new Key to Dreams.

The dream is a hypothesis, since we never know it except as a memory, and that memory is of necessity a fabrication. We construct and refashion our dreams; we describe a dream to ourselves; we give it a meaning; it becomes *tellable*: a story, with scenes and a cast of characters, and in the scenario of memory the part played by awakening and recognition is for us indistinguishable from the part that restores, perhaps, something of the forever lost original. But in addition to this, we may take it into our heads to relate our dreams; the listener in turn translates the story into his own system of images: if he prides himself on the study of dreams he will argue in terms of what he himself imagines, which is the transmutation of a transmutation.

The translation of a translation may well preserve something, but not *that something which is nameless*. What cannot be named is precisely the thing which it would be important to grasp and which would give us some idea of what *consciousness in sleep* may be, the production and substitution of quasi phenomena, the perpetual coming to birth of a mental life which is essentially instantaneous, unrepeatable. But to base speculation on the *account* of a dream is to use the product of a waking *action* which deprives the hypothetical original of its real substance, turning it into an abstract simulacrum—just as a statue no longer represents the intimate creative relationship that existed between the form and the living substance of the model. In brief: we are basing our arguments on the *schema* of an event that has totally disappeared, and interpreting it; but a schema is the result of a number of different acts, and these acts are acts performed in the waking state: we have to be "awake" in order to *express* ourselves.

But suppose, on the contrary, that we deliberately attempt to modify the perceptions and representations we produce in

the waking state in such a way as to diminish their meaning, to exhaust their transitory and conventional value (as happens when we repeat a word *until it loses its meaning*): we shall see a few characteristic signs of a state of which the dream state *would be* the final phase. We observe it quite well, for example, when we feel our mind being overtaken by sleep: that we are stumbling, so to speak, between two worlds, the stronger of which gradually dissolves into the weaker. ... At such moments, we glimpse the mode of transformation of consciousness which will dominate the world of dreams, and admitting (on a purely hypothetical basis) that this world is distinguishable from the waking world by the way in which every impression that affects us develops, we shall have some idea of what may transpire under the sway of sleep when our remaining powers of feeling are disturbed by organic incidents or by external events that are insufficient to produce a total change in our state—an awakening.

Similar conditions must, in my opinion, be present in "visions." The ways in which appearances are transformed in them must closely resemble those in dreams. That is what I believe I have established by a detailed study of a few accounts of visionaries, chosen from among the most naïve cases. It is, indeed, of some importance that the evidence should be taken from someone as uneducated and as *unimaginative* as possible, in order that the creation of images should be as free as possible from secondary intentions and corrections.

In the case of Swedenborg, the conditions are quite the opposite and very unfavorable to any examination of the degree of accuracy of the account he gives in his writings. All the same, certain details of the celebrated London vision seem to me to be of the kind that "are not invented," that is to say,

that do not seem able to be desired, to be preceded by an intention, or to respond to some conscious need. . . .

I have indulged in reflections of which only this should be retained: that I should never finish if I pursued all the questions which Mr. Martin Lamm's book has suggested to me.

I began reading it without suspecting that I was penetrating into an enchanted forest where every step roused sudden flights of thought, and everywhere were crossroads of radiant hypotheses, psychological ambushes, and echoes; where every glance opened up perspectives bristling with enigmas, where the hunting intellect is alerted, loses the trail, wanders, then picks it up again. . . . But this does not mean that one is in any sense wasting one's time. I like the hunt for its own sake, and there are few hunts more gripping and more varied than the quest for the Swedenborg Mystery.

Voltaire

I OFTEN DREAM of an unusual work, difficult though not impossible to write, which someone will write one of these days, and which would take its place in the treasure house of our literature close beside *The Human Comedy*, providing us with a welcome development from that work, but devoted to the passions and adventures of the intelligence. It would be a Comedy of the Intellect, the drama of lives dedicated to the task of understanding and creating. We should see from it how everything that is distinctive of humanity, everything that raises it a little above the dreary animal level, is the work of a handful of individuals to whom we owe the means of thought as we owe the plowman the means of life.

Moreover, we are well aware that *every civilized country, that is, every country that attaches more importance to thought than thought actually has in practical life*, is represented, as it were, for all other countries by the names of a few writers who have lifted its language to the dignity of a medium of expression of universal value. We speak of Shakespeare, of Cervantes, of Tolstoi, and we mean England, Spain, and Russia.

But some among these great names evoke not merely a country and not merely admirable works: they also suggest types of the creative life—the characters, as it were, necessary to the Intellectual Comedy of which I have spoken.

France is rich in such persons of the first magnitude, whose celebrity is combined with a sort of presence, immortal no doubt, yet almost familiar. The world over, Montaigne, Pascal, and Rousseau are something more than authors: they are highly diverse models of significant attitudes toward life, so much so that we cannot think of their work without thinking of the men themselves. Even for those who have scarcely read them, Montaigne is someone; Pascal is someone; Voltaire too. They are significant individuals.

Montaigne, Pascal, Voltaire—the list is not by any means complete. Such as it is, however, it is sufficient to illustrate the diversity of features of a people who cannot be reduced to a single race, but who resolve into a far more subtle composite.

Our versatility is at its liveliest in Voltaire. He had, I fear, nearly all the faults that people are pleased to attribute to us: and if he did not have all our virtues, he possessed some of them at their highest intensity. We must confess or proclaim, according to our taste, that he is specifically French and unimaginable under any other skies—I would even say, under any other sky than Paris. The result is that in France, after two hundred and fifty years, his name still provokes strong and sharply conflicting reactions. Some people still fear and detest the man who delighted in ridiculing the objects of their beliefs, in heaping up mockery designed to destroy their faith, in pitting the letter of the Scriptures against their deeper meaning and their spirit. Other people see in him the apostle of freedom of thought and the defender of the sacred rights that every man owes it to himself to grant to every other man. After all, the Gospels and the Rights of Man are in agreement on the one essential point: the infinite value of the human person. It seems that France cannot do without some division of ideals and some opposition of feeling such as this; and that

is why, whether we execrate him or laud him to the skies, Voltaire, the very sound of whose name unleashes the eternal and antagonistic elements of our political life, Voltaire is alive, Voltaire remains: he is endlessly present.

Voltaire was twenty-one when Louis XIV died. He was eighty-four when he died himself, the monarch of the European mind. He led the funeral procession of a period whose own strangeness and extreme originality we overlook, being from childhood so accustomed to its language and its imposing display of order. It is a blend of stateliness and simplification; it reconciles the logical and the arbitrary; the full rigor of thought; the splendor of appearances; the power of will leaving its impress on every form of art, seeking natural effects through artifice, and sometimes achieving them through abstraction. It combines the austere and the theatrical. In the life of the monarch himself a genuine piety and an exact observance of his religious duties went together with a succession of love affairs known to all, whose illicit fruits were publicly recognized and occupied the highest places in the State.

Voltaire buried his century. Yet with what respect! What a perfect tomb he fashioned as the receptacle of its magnificence! He called it after its King. He was the first to point out that, during that reign, Europe came to recognize that in the realm of fundamental ideas and in the general style of its literature and manners, our country possessed a supremacy which neither her abuses, her military reverses, nor the final exhaustion of her resources could wrest from her. He had the highly original and very happy idea of introducing into an historical work a review of the state of literature and the arts during the period with which it deals. It was he who drew up,

without error or omission, so that posterity has neither re-
moved nor added a single name, the list of the great writers
whom we call our classics.

The undisputed inventor of the famous, imperious, and
essentially French conception of the Classic was the man who,
on the threshold of maturity, was able to take in at a single
and very lucid glance a whole literary output of the highest
order, now complete and in the process of becoming an
authoritative example of perfection. It was directly inspired
by the purest models of antiquity, so far as form and the
economy of effects were concerned; but on the other hand,
it was nourished on the sacred simplicity of the Vulgate, yet
pervaded by a sense of rigor which, since Descartes, a certain
taste for geometry had transmitted to more than one among
the respectable classes.

Nevertheless, Voltaire was destined throughout his life
to expend his energies on ruining, on consuming with all the
fire that was in him, what remained of the *grand siècle*, its
traditions, its beliefs, its pomps, but not its works. The con-
trast between the time when he was young and the moment
of his death is very striking. If he had lived another ten years,
the man who may have seen Louis XIV might have seen the
Terror ended—provided he had not perished in it—before
Thermidor.

That is why he may remind us of the god Janus, to whom
the Romans gave two faces looking in opposite directions,
and who was the god of beginnings and endings. But the face
of the young Voltaire contemplates a sumptuously melan-
choly twilight, in the deep purple of which the Sun King takes
to his bed, weighed down with his own magnificence, and
gives himself up to the night, a solemn sun that will not rise
again. But the other face of this Janus, the face of the old Vol-

taire, observes in the east an unknown dawn lighting up tremendous clouds. On the horizon's verge, there is many a flash of lightning. . . .

The interval between the two poles of his long life was filled with prodigious activity.

He was the man of wit par excellence; the freest, the quickest, the alertest of human beings. Compared with him, all others appeared to be asleep or daydreaming. He moved through his errors like a man capable of wiping them out as readily as he embraced them. He asked questions in every domain, and everywhere he gave answers. He expressed an opinion on everything, at times recklessly, but always with a vivacity that, in him, seemed to increase with age. The man was a physiological marvel. He was vitality itself, using and abusing a fragile body, which was always sickly, always suffering from giddiness, the vapors, or debility, but which, from one illness to another, from one recovery to another, bore him into extreme old age, looking incredibly desiccated but possessing until the last day of his life a power of attack that seemed inexhaustible.

With the possible exception of Napoleon Bonaparte, there is no face of a famous man better known than that of the aged Voltaire, with his withered cheeks, his extraordinarily prominent cheekbones, his eyes so deeply sunk that the fixity of the anatomical smile looked like a death's-head. But in the hollows of the skeletal sockets shone two eyes brighter than the eyes of the common run of men, and nothing in the world that was ridiculous or unjust or odious ever managed to escape them. The fact is that until the end he possessed an exquisite irritability. Escorted as he was, supported, stimulated, elated by the number, the swarm of enemies of every kind,

created by him as though for the fun of it (though it was no doubt from some organic necessity), he literally lived on his adversaries, whether they were alive or mere abstractions, and there has never been a man who owed more to everything which, in the field of conduct, writing, and people, was vulnerable and presented a target for his attacks. If he began by displaying a remarkable talent for historical narrative, he soon emerged as a caricaturist of genius. In a few words he could turn out the most marvelous cartoons; his sages, his magi, his judges, his great ladies, and his astonishing Germans are so lifelike beneath the fantasy that we cannot help thinking of our great Daumier and regretting that no one ever thought of inviting that powerful artist to illustrate *Candide* or *Zadig*. It is a misfortune for art, one of those lost opportunities, those passed-up profits which the mind dwells on and deplores.

But Voltaire's very life sounds like one of the best of his own tales. There are touches of musical comedy, of the fairy play, flashes of drama, and grand climaxes in his own story. He made himself admired, adored, abhorred, hated, and venerated, got himself cudgeled and crowned with laurel, with a sort of encyclopedic mastery of the art of arousing the most conflicting reactions, of creating mortal enemies, bands of devoted or fanatical admirers, of being regarded with indifference by no one, while nothing human was ever alien to him and an insatiable curiosity never ceased to drive him on. Everything stimulated his urge to know, to probe, to do battle; everything was fuel for him, and served to feed that bright, clear fire where a perpetual transmutation took place, in which enthusiasms succeeded one another, and the genius of dissociation dissolved those mere appearances of truth that lingered in his time and still imposed on the lazy-minded.

The philosophers who came after him would not allow

that he was a philosopher. They refused him the title that his period bestowed on him with one accord. They considered, no doubt, that a philosopher is a man who pores over technical terms, as though words had more substance and depth than the mental space and moment in which they come to life in each of us. But Voltaire soared above such things. Perhaps he felt too keenly, with the whole of that nervous temperament of his, that intellectual value lasts only for a flash, that the mind is life, and that life is essentially transitory.

No, he was not a philosopher. He was a man who tried his hand at all the forms: tragedy, epigrams, history, epic, tales, essays, and that vast correspondence; a man who made Shakespeare fashionable, who saw to it that the fame of Racine was secure; who to the best of his ability studied, acclaimed, and even sang the praises of Newton in verse; who jeered at Leibnitz, kept up a perpetual running warfare against religions; but built and dedicated to God Himself a little church at the entrance to his estate at Ferney: DEO EREXIT VOLTAIRE.

A man who has written so much and on whom so much has been written, of whom so much that is good and bad can be said—and few have failed to say it—a man on whom Joseph de Maistre, who admired and detested him, pronounced this antithetical verdict in which he combined his doctrine and his taste: "I should like," he said, "to have a statue raised to him . . . by the public executioner." No, he was no philosopher, this devil of a man, whose variety, whose resources and contradictions make up a character that music alone, the liveliest music, could keep up with, right to the end, to the moment when, unable to keep his eighty-four-year-old body still, he had himself taken to Paris, to the theater where a triumph awaited him. He was crowned with

laurel. When he died, the wrecker of idols had become an idol himself.

But just as the philosophers exiled him from their philosophy, so the poets, too, those soon to arrive on the scene, products of the new age, refused him the divine gift of poetry. They discovered in him a dryness, a lack of warmth and color, a dreary skepticism. It is true that to us he seems not very lyrical, his verse conforms too much to the detestable notion of d'Alembert, who had the audacity to say that the best verse is that which is closest to good prose. But who knows how posterity will judge the romantics in their turn? In Voltaire's time Ronsard's reputation was in a desperate state; and about 1840 Racine's was at a very low ebb. In the eternity of literature those who are most dead often have some chance of survival; the best-loved in their time are also those most likely to fade out soonest in the oblivion of libraries.

In short, almost all the arguments against Voltaire are directed at the fact that he had too much wit. Since he had so much, he must have been superficial. With too much wit he couldn't have had much heart. Such are the judgments of the world. But contrary to what the proverb says, it is not everybody who has more wit than Voltaire, and in fact everybody can be very foolish. This is, alas, too often proved by events which in the last resort are the effects of the action of everybody on everybody.

But our man of wit par excellence suddenly, when he was entering on the last third of his life, and as though all this wit had been given him and he had used, polished, sharpened, and poisoned it for forty years to turn it into a weapon destined for the noblest encounters, discovered in himself a new vocation and a new ardor. Dry and superficial, you say. Very well!

But how many profound minds, how many men of sensibility have failed to do for men in general what was done at that time by our skeptical, versatile Voltaire? We have to admit that his "hideous smile" illuminated and prepared the ruin of many a hideous thing.

The decisive event of his career, the guarantee of his immortality, was his metamorphosis into the friend and defender of the human race. At an age when most careers are coming to an end, when he already enjoyed all the renown that literature can bestow, when he was admired everywhere, rich, and having now only to bask in the light air of universality that played about in the encyclopedic atmosphere of his time, a time so stimulating to the intelligence—its golden age —we suddenly find him turning himself into the man we are honoring today. If he had died at the age of sixty he would by now be almost forgotten, and we should not have come solemnly together here to pay tribute to the author of *Mérope*, *Zaïre*, and the *Henriade*. We know perfectly well that the true aim of this gathering is less to commemorate the birth of a famous man and to pay tribute to the man and his work, however brilliant and extensive it may be, than to join as Frenchmen to do honor to the most generous and constant of his passions—the freedom of the mind. We know the value of that freedom. We know its cost. But we ought perhaps to be more aware that its worthiest use, the proof and guarantee of its durability, lie in the limits which the free mind itself must set to its own precious and formidable power of calling everything into question. For this freedom becomes imperiled and is lost as soon as it goes beyond those frontiers, sometimes difficult to discern.

It was when he was approaching sixty that Voltaire embarked on a veritable political campaign, based on judicial

procedures. We know the important part that such contests in the courts of justice have played in the public life of the country at every period of history. Starting from some judicial error or abuse, he provoked, he literally created a series of cases to which his prestige and talents gave reverberations that have not in any way been damped by the passage of time. He made immortal a number of cases whose names are still invoked in the courts today. He revealed in his later years an active generosity, an unexpected sensitiveness to the legal extortions and iniquities which until then had appeared to be the inevitable effect (if not the necessary condition) of the existence of a highly organized society. There was at that time a criminal code which intellectual progress was finding more and more questionable, but which was still enforced with appalling penalties; there was an abominable system of torture and a frightening absence of guarantees for the defense of the accused. Voltaire went to the root of these cases, reviewed the allegations, weighed them up, criticized the evidence, and compared the emptiness of the charges with the frightful excesses of the methods of repression. He invoked reason, but *he aimed at men's hearts*. What could prevail against this alliance between truth and pity? Both appeal to what is most human in man, what lives in him when he is free to be himself, when he is without hate or fear, as the Code puts it. But this was to intervene in the regular functioning of society, as a personal power not recognized yet daring to set itself up against public power, justifying itself by the nobility of its aims and the higher need of its intervention—an intervention based on talent, on talent alone. No—talent combined with courage and faith! He removed the cases that engaged him from the narrow and almost mechanical appraisal, the indifference or professional callousness of the magistrate, and brought them

before a judge who was as yet scarcely aware that he was the final arbiter, still ignorant of his competence as of his powers —*Man*. He put the law on trial before Man. That, to be sure, was to create confusion.

But there simply has to exist, here and there in the average conscience of the masses, some irritant, some agent of destruction to dissolve or corrode the dead elements, the things that were once true and are no longer true; to throw out those that won't die, and encourage the growth of those that could and should live. Anything that takes its ease and sleeps in a too unruffled state of well-being, in the possession of means or power too solidly based, must sometimes have its peace disturbed, must be awakened to its profoundly vicious state; for there are pernicious ills that for a long time cause no pain, and there are pains which even the person who feels them can neither define nor articulate, so as to complain of them and protect himself against them. Voltaire was the first and the most active of those who aroused the public conscience against detestable practices that were not yet detested and seemed inseparable from the administration of justice. He roused scruples that did not yet exist, a horror not yet aware of itself, with regard to certain procedures whose uselessness, injustice, and frightful harshness were accepted by an ingrained habit of submission, and he thus became a sort of legislator of a new kind, for he formulated and instituted an entirely new crime. Up till then the criminal law punished only offenses and injuries committed against the social order, the State, and the religion of the State. But Voltaire proclaimed that there were crimes against humanity and against thought, and he drew up the indictment against them. He also made people understand that there are times when the punishment itself becomes a crime, because the sight of ap-

palling torture reawakens and nourishes the savagery latent in some, while in the eyes of others it transforms someone who is only a wretched criminal into an innocent victim. If public authority becomes enraged and harasses the body of a guilty man, if it gives way to anger and seeks a kind of revenge, the pure and abstract idea of the State dispensing justice is thereby tarnished and degraded. We realize that the State itself is moved by impulses that should be foreign to it, and that it can suffer them only at the expense of its very *raison d'être*.

In the criminal cases he took over, Voltaire took over mankind. By the power of his pen alone, with nothing but intelligence and wit, he roused, he rocked the whole of his age. (This, if we think about it, is almost frightening.) He renewed the frontal assault, following the formidable example already set by the sixteenth century: an isolated intellectual operation which, though initiated and executed under their noses, was a threat to the very existence of the ruling powers, whose system of force was more of a fiction than a reality, and only managed to survive by the more or less conscious adherence of men's minds, but above all by their abstention. A social structure is all the more solid the less it requires force to maintain it.

It had long been known that literature can be used for other purposes besides the pure pleasure of reading. In principle, literature is no more than the freedom which language enjoys of abusing its function by providing people's leisure with entertaining stories or the beauties of form. But under cover of these pretexts, these seductive appearances, and by the roundabout way of pleasure and amusement, the criticism of manners, of the law, of the great, of the powers that be, creeps in and insinuates its poisons—all the more deadly for

being so delectable. At the beginning of the eighteenth century, men's minds were everywhere in ferment; but it was still necessary to use cunning. Montesquieu disguised himself as a Persian. In an absolute secrecy that was to last for a long time, Saint-Simon forged for his *Memoirs* that extraordinary style whose incisiveness and long sentences, constructed out of astonishing *raccourcis*, were to delight the connoisseurs of the future.

But Voltaire, who had learned from his innumerable personal controversies how to use a rapier that was quicker, less accurate, but just as dangerous as that of the redoubtable author of *The Provincial Letters* a hundred years earlier, invented for himself a prose that was lucid, aggressive, and swift, sacrificing the grand manner of the solid, high-sounding writers on whom as a young man he had been brought up. In the eyes of many, those imposing writers were difficult to read. Their learned constructions, too loftily organized, were confusing to those who were impatient or whose education was inadequate, and who were soon lost in the evolutions of their carefully ordered abstract periods.

Voltaire replaced massive argument by the tactics of speed, short thrusts, feints, and a harassing irony. He moved from the logical to the comical, from good sense to pure fantasy, exploited all the weaknesses of his opponent and then tossed him to one side looking ridiculous, if he did not end by making him completely odious.

It was in this way that he achieved one very considerable result which has not attracted sufficient attention. What is known as "opinion" had been created up to that time by the Court of Versailles; it spread from there to the City, and thence, after a certain time, might reach a comparatively small number of aristocrats and people of breeding living in the

provinces. Voltaire broke this circle and extended the sphere of action of the written word. His style, the immense interest aroused by his appeals for justice, and the sort of scandal they created, attracted throughout the kingdom and beyond its frontiers a large number of readers. What had been the attitude of the Court and the City became the opinion of the *public*. Here we can see the full import and significance of a mere change in style: *the public was created by an easy style*. Simply increase the numbers still more; relax all the rules and restraints of language, making it immediately accessible to the masses; borrow from the masses their familiar and picturesque expressions, and the word "public" can no longer be applied to that collective body at which the written word is aimed — to rouse, convince, and goad it into action. We must speak of the *people*, and *the whole of the Revolution is contained in that one word*.

Voltaire was, to my mind, the first of those men of letters who later were to use or abuse the authority conferred on them by literature when, on reaching the summit of literary fame, they could not help wishing for a different kind of celebrity, in their opinion more exciting and more enviable. They thirsted to embark on an entirely fresh career in the world of politics; they dreamed of making people act in accordance with their own ideas, whereas until then they had been content to instruct them, touch their hearts, or provide them with pictures or songs. Chateaubriand, Lamartine, Victor Hugo, and Zola, each in his own way bitten by the demon of politics, were all to work on their contemporaries with the idea of influencing events through men's minds, just as before they had influenced minds by the purely literary productions of their genius.

As for Voltaire, he never had the slightest hope of a seat in

the Legislative Assembly, or a ministerial portfolio. And so, willy-nilly, whether we like him or not, everything turned out in the last third of his life as though he had been guided and motivated solely by a concern for the common good. If he returned to this world . . . what would he see? What would he have to say?

I was speaking a few minutes ago about a Comedy of the Intellect which someone should write and which would stand beside Balzac's vast *Human Comedy*. But our age may well produce an appalling Comedy of Bestiality. No! A Mythology would be what we deserve. We are, we live and move, in the midst of heroes and monsters. At times they are fearful individuals to whom all human feelings appear alien; at other times incredible nations in whom credulity, brutality, and stupidity, this time organized, equipped, disciplined, and—an unheard-of thing—dangerously allied with the virtues of bravery and conscientiousness in doing as well as possible all the evil that imagination and science together have been able to devise; at still other times there are problems to be solved, on pain of death, which exceed in complexity everything that the best brains of man can grasp and follow in their calculations—all these are our hydras, our sphinxes, our Minotaurs, our Medusas. True, we also have our Theseus and our Perseus. . . . It is to them, to our heroes, that we owe our presence here today and our liberty to speak freely.

Voltaire, however, was also in his own way a sort of hero. But what could he do today? *What can a man of intellect do?* What voice at present could make itself heard above all the others, dominate the crash of explosions, the din of machinery, the blithering babel of propaganda broadcast everywhere, at every moment of the day and in every home? Where is the Voltaire who will denounce the modern world?

It might be said that all our intellectual efforts, the whole of the incredible increase in our positive knowledge have served only to raise to a savage and crushing power the means of bringing the human race to an end, having first destroyed the hopes it had nourished for centuries of taming its own nature. Are we obliged to accept the fact that nothing that is horrible and barbarous, nothing that has been coldly or wickedly planned, can ever be regarded as finally abolished and obliterated from the face of the earth? What has become of the royal decree that abolished torture? What has become of the treaties and agreements, the timid efforts of The Hague, the organizations and the clauses of arbitration which the unanimous vote of men—I mean *men of human countenance*—had obtained from their representatives? Where is the Voltaire, the voice that will make itself heard today? A gigantic Voltaire—able to cope with a world in flames—would be needed to denounce, confound, and reduce the enormous and worldwide scandal to the proportions of a squalid crime! The fact is that nowadays it is no longer a matter of a handful of innocent people being tortured, or victims who may be counted. ... Today the victims number millions; it is, indeed, impossible to count the Calases and the Chevaliers de la Barre. It is no longer a matter of having a few sentences reduced or a few laws reformed. It is a question of the whole structure of the political and economic world, which already in time of peace had grown unstable and disturbed by the unexpected appearance of entirely fresh demands, fluctuating between over- and underproduction, between the inertia of habit and acquired position and the disorderly spontaneity of inventions and rising ambitions, and which now is caught in the universal conflagration of war. ... And all that is present to the eye of the mind (when our mind recovers for a moment

some small degree of control over its eye), all that is present is a chaos of contradictions, a succession of reversals and recoveries of fortune. Within a few months, it sees hope change into despair, and then the opposite; it sees the closest relations turn into antagonism; and victory collapse into defeat; and defeat turn into victory.

In face of such a state of human affairs, in which man understands himself less and less, just as he seems less capable of understanding nature the more power he gains over her —in face of this fantastic spectacle, would Voltaire recover the famous smile we all know? Perhaps—if I may end on this note an address dealing with an infidel—perhaps he would be reminded of that supreme and august remark, the most profound, the simplest, the truest of sayings, once pronounced on the human race and thereby on its politics, its scientific progress, its doctrines, and its conflicts—perhaps he would murmur to himself this all-too-evident verdict: THEY KNOW NOT WHAT THEY DO.

Address in Honor of Goethe

Mr. President,
Ladies and Gentlemen:

THERE ARE men who give us an idea—or perhaps an illusion—
of the way in which the world, and especially Europe, might
have developed if political and intellectual power had been
able to join forces, or at least if the relations between them
had been less precarious. Reality might have had a sobering
effect on ideas; the spiritual order might, perhaps, have had
an elevating effect on action; and we should not feel the
strange and repellent contradiction between men's culture
and the management of their affairs, which is a matter of
astonishment to all who observe it. But the two forms of
power may well be incommensurable quantities; and it is no
doubt necessary that they should be so.

Of the handful of men of whom I am speaking, some be-
long to the twelfth and thirteenth centuries. Others were
responsible for the splendor and vitality of the Renaissance.
The last of them were born in the eighteenth century and
died at the same time as the last hopes of a civilization founded
primarily on the Myth of Beauty and the Myth of Knowledge,
both of them the creatures or inventions of the ancient Greeks.

Goethe was one of these. I must say at once that I can think
of no others after him. After him we find only conditions that
became progressively less favorable to the production of
individuals of outstanding and universal greatness.

That is why his centenary has, perhaps, a special significance and might mark an epoch in the history of the world. For among the many things disrupted and the many values called into question, the actual transformation of the world and our own consequent anxiety test and threaten in all sorts of ways the very life of the mind itself and those values which are essentially personal.

We cannot praise the University of Paris too highly for taking the view that the great writers and great scientists of all nations have their place within her walls, for deciding to pay a solemn tribute to the first poet of Germany, and here at the Sorbonne, which has counted among her students a Dante, a Villon, and many another with a glorious future. At the same time, gentlemen, honesty compels me to be less complimentary on your choice of the man to address you on the present occasion. The honor is very great, but I have every reason in the world to be fearful of what I have to say. One of the vastest and most complete geniuses who ever lived; a gigantic work, written in a language which I have the misfortune not to understand; a poetic power whose movement and harmony I can only divine through the veil of translation; an address to be delivered on such a hero and such a work, before an audience where everyone I see is better equipped than I am for the task entrusted to me, and where many have a profound knowledge of what is almost unknown to me—that, first of all, is what strikes me and challenges my undertaking.

But again, the circumstance most disturbing to my mind, and the one I find perhaps the most painful handicap, is the inexhaustible amount of writing produced by the occasion, the dazzling array of documents and opinions, the number of

ideas and theories appearing everywhere, constantly adding luster to the image of Goethe, already a century old, and disturbing the calm waters of the mirror of Time.

Even before this, he appeared the most complex figure in the world. Yet there seems to be no end to the fresh research which is afoot. All the labor has been repaid. Each new approach adds to the interest of the subject. How marvelous it is that someone who has been dead for a hundred years should still be able to give something to mankind, occupy so much thought, revive so many neglected problems in men's minds, and become the source of so much reflection and so much subtle speculation!

But for me it is a strange occasion to find myself suddenly faced with the ambiguous duty of giving a notion, sufficiently clear to be understood and sufficiently vague not to be completely false, of a personality transfigured by fame and, so to speak, become one with his own glory. We should always be wary of trying to define someone. His works, even the sayings that have been recorded, are by no means the least misleading of the data available to us, nor are they the things that can most surely lead us to the tantalizing heart of the mystery. I know with complete certainty what errors can beguile us when we try to discover the genesis of works of literature, and how easily we are led astray by the naïve ambition to re-create the person of the writer himself. Shall we really find out what we most want to know about him, what makes him completely different from other men—that is to say, the actual operations of his mind—from his works, his personal papers, the relics of his love affairs, and the outstanding events of his life? Shall we, in short, discover how he appeared to himself when he was most deeply and profitably alone? I go so far as to imagine that what is most remarkable and most apparent

in a man's life contributes very little to what gives his work its value. The taste of a tree's fruit depends not on the appearance of the surrounding country, but on the unseen richness of the soil.

How can we discern from his books what belongs to the very essence of the man, what is purely transitory, what is the result of deliberate intention, and what is due to chance? Substance and accident are combined in them. The spontaneous and the deliberate, the necessary and the arbitrary are all fused in the external form, like copper and tin in bronze; and the man whom we imagine as the creator of the work, as if he were the cause which could produce only this effect, is, in reality, a creature of it, in the same way that a life as a whole is an illusion produced only by a law of chronological perspective. What we must understand is that any writer's work could be other than it is, just as the memory of each one of us might consist of quite different recollections. An attempt to re-create a writer is an attempt to re-create a capacity for works entirely different from his own, but nevertheless of such a kind that *he alone* could have written them.

We must give up in despair—and I do give up in despair—that is to say, I shall simply follow my own feeling. I feel that we can regard the great men who dominate us as beings who are *merely* far more familiar than we ourselves with what is most profound in us. There is perhaps no better way of giving ourselves the impression that we know them than to look into our own deepest minds and observe what most attracts us among the most exalted of our desires. It amounts to the assumption that the greatest man does no more than fill certain gaps that exist in the same form in us all. There is in each of us (this is my theory) room for a genius.

So let Goethe be: *our own thirst for complete intelligence, for*

the universal outlook, and for great luck in creation. He represents for us, *My Fellow Human Beings*, one of our most effective attempts to make ourselves like gods. He took the ancient promise as his guide and paid a signal tribute to Him who had made it by bringing Him onto the stage.

The idea he gives us of himself is, in fact, that of the ability to adopt an astonishing number of different guises. Inexhaustibility was part of his nature; and that is why on the morrow of his death he at once took his place among the deities and heroes in the Mythology of the Mind; among those whose names have become symbols. We say GOETHE as we say ORPHEUS—and his name immediately, irresistibly, conjures up in our minds a prodigious Figure, a monster of comprehension and creative power, a monster of vitality, a monster of varying moods, a monster of serenity, who, after seizing, devouring, and transforming into immortal works everything that the experience of one human being could in the course of his existence grasp, assimilate, and transmute, is himself in the end transmuted into a *myth*, for he compelled posterity to create, to exalt forever that incomparable GOETHE we now observe rising again, after a century, to the highest zenith in the Heavens of the Mind.

In fact, on the world's gaming table, this great man is one of the happiest strokes the destiny of the human race has brought off.

But in the mysterious game of intelligence and chance, as in all games, we must examine the prospects of the players; and without flattering ourselves that we have discovered the answer and understood *what is*, by analyzing *what might be*, we can try at any rate to note the most obvious factors.

What I find more striking than anything else about Goethe

is his very long life. The apostle of development, the theorist of gradual action and stages of growth (oddly combined in him with the creator of Faust, who is impatience personified), lived as long as was necessary to test, time and again, each of the springs of his being; long enough to form several different ideas of himself, to extricate himself from each and find that he was still more vast. He succeeded in finding, losing, renewing, and re-forming himself; in being at different times the Same and Another; and in observing in himself the rhythm of change and growth. This development over the course of almost a century, by imperceptible changes in the tastes, desires, opinions, and powers of a human being, encourages us to imagine that a man who lived on obstinately enough would experience in turn every form of attraction and repulsion, would perhaps come to know all the virtues, certainly all the vices; would in the long run exhaust the whole gamut of reactions, both conflicting and harmonious, which everything he came in contact with was capable of provoking. After all, the Self responds to every appeal; and at bottom life is only potentiality.

The period of time that went into the making of Goethe was filled with events of the first magnitude, and during his prolonged presence in the world, it offered for his contemplation, his meditation, his acceptance, and sometimes for his rejection, a great number of important happenings, among them a general catastrophe, the end of an age, and the beginning of another.

He was born in a period which we now realize was delightful. He was brought up in that century of pleasure and encyclopedic knowledge when, for the last time, all the most exquisite ingredients that make a civilized life were present together. Elegance, sentiment, and cynicism were almost in-

terchangeable. Both what was sharpest and what was most tender in the human spirit developed together. The salons brought the geometers and the mystics together with the ladies. The liveliest and already the most liberal curiosity, the joyful stimulus of ideas, along with delicacy of form, were to be observed nearly everywhere. Goethe certainly had his share of the good things of life.

All this sparkled, flared up, and burned out. The sans-culottes were soon to romp through the capitals of Europe. Twenty-three years of war. An entirely new kind of war; no longer the war of Louis XV and Monsieur de Thorane, which taught French to young Goethe and introduced him to our tragic dramatists. It was a war that was going to change everything in the world; no longer a war of princes, but of principles; that is to say, of *disorder in depth*, in which the threatened dynasties, the nations awakening, growing conscious of the full resources of their strength, and finally an extraordinary genius, born and let loose with a will to refashion Europe in the image of his own mind, all together make up the noisy overture to the new age.

It was not perhaps this turmoil, which he had seen well up and subside, that affected Goethe most intimately. It is for some people a sort of problem to decide how much attention great minds ought to pay to the external events of history, whether they should become engaged, involved, or on the contrary, remain aloof as far as they can. As for Goethe, he obviously could not ignore the Revolution or the vicissitudes that followed it. He went to France with an invading army; he saw the French again in Germany. But it appears that his mind was less moved and disturbed by it all than by the ideal revolutions and battles at which he was present and in which he took part in the sphere of culture.

He witnessed the end of the reign of classicism and analytical thought, which had stemmed from the France of Louis XIV and Louis XV. The tyranny of clearly defined and carefully reasoned literary types, the completely abstract elegance, the subtle seduction by pure artifice, the noblest of rigors imposed by formal rules, all were condemned. Shakespeare, whom Voltaire had transformed into a European author, now killed tragedy, reducing Racine to a phantom, and annihilating Voltaire's own plays. Herder rescued the Germanic traditions from oblivion, proclaimed the exhaustion of French art, and brought Goethe to a halt on the threshold of the West.

At the same time, there was an extraordinary flowering of philosophical and musical works in the very heart of Germany. Those who were to become the august fathers of nineteenth-century thought, Kant, Fichte, and Hegel, and those who were to be the sublime fathers of music, lived and wrote not far from Goethe's home. And in the realm of the plastic arts, as in the realm of learning, the publications of the Egyptian Institute and the discoveries of Herculaneum renewed men's knowledge of antiquity. Pompeii was unearthed in the very year that Goethe was born.

Finally, during this same lifetime, and in the field of science, where Newton still reigned and even continued to increase that prodigious influence which, through the work of Laplace, penetrated to the tiniest inconsistencies in the World System, behold, electricity from Volta to Ampère was explored and recognized as the basic phenomenon of the universe. The science of chemistry was founded. Everything suggested that the power of man over energy was on the verge of a tremendous increase.

But natural science was no less eager to extend its domain. Metaphysics, banished from the heavens and from every field

in which experiment, measurement, and calculation could answer one another with accuracy, took hold of and attempted in a sense to merge with the mysterious phenomena of *life*. A great controversy broke out which in many points is still with us and is not unlikely to continue.

That, in a few words, is a picture of the events and of the most obvious external conditions which can have claimed Goethe's attention between adolescence and death.

To these must be added an infinite number of incidents and private circumstances, meetings, opportunities, friendship with his king, women, literary rivalries; and we must try to decide how this man, a very handsome man, a human being terribly alive, a wild voluptuary, but at the same time a mind continually discovering its own increasing vastness, came to terms with the complexities of life, discovered his own destiny, and ultimately won to immortality.

But how are we to avoid losing our way amid the versatility of this fantastic character?

As far as I can see, he seems to be endowed in the highest degree with precisely those qualities which he was the first to recognize in living beings in the course of his subtle and profound researches into biology.

Nothing struck him more forcibly than the ability of living things to adapt themselves and to assume the forms that are most appropriate to their environment.

Now I think we must recognize that he himself possessed this kind of genius. It was this gift that allowed him to react with such versatility, such a sense of occasion, such grace and sometimes with such energy against so many impressions, impulses, or books that attracted him; even against the consequences of his own actions, and at times against those resulting from his own personal charm.

Moreover, the genius for transformation is essentially

poetic, since it plays just as important a part in the creation of
the metaphors and images through which the poet achieves a
multiplicity of forms of expression, as it does in the creation
of characters and situations for the stage. But in the poet or in
the plant the same natural principle is at work: all living
things have an aptitude for adapting themselves, and that
aptitude, which is variable, is the measure of their aptitude
for living, that is to say, for remaining what they are by
possessing more than one manner of being what they are.

Goethe, Poet and Proteus, lived many lives in one. He as-
similated everything, and out of it formed his substance. He
transformed the very environment in which he was implanted
and where he flourished. Weimar owed him a cult and paid
its dues. He found it excellent soil, to which he adapted him-
self, and made it illustrious. What could have been more pro-
pitious than that small, cultivated territory, for growing and
putting forth the many branches that spread visibly through
the universe? There he was courtier, confidant, minister, a
diligent official, a poet, collector, and naturalist; he also had
the rather busy leisure to manage with zeal and enthusiasm
the Weimar theater while watching over the cuttings and
seeds of the rare plants that he studied, and perhaps a few
cocoons of silkworms whose hatching he tended. There too
he could observe at his ease, as though in a watch glass, a
miniature political and diplomatic life; and conforming with-
out the slightest difficulty to the demands of its protocol and
etiquette, he breathed an engaging atmosphere of freedom.
He was perhaps the last man to enjoy Europe in its perfection.

So many advantages are not everything. When we are too
much favored by circumstances, we may find that such favors
have their dangers. A life filled with ease and sweetness is a

life inwardly threatened. Proteus, if his heart is touched, is deprived of his resources. He must therefore be on guard against his heart; he must preserve what is unique beneath the many forms he assumes. And if the god, in pursuit of his pleasures, changes himself into a bull, a swan, or a shower of gold, he must not remain bound to one of them forever, caught in the trap of his own seductive disguises—in short, transformed forever into a beast.

Goethe, however, never let himself be caught. His genius for metamorphosis, by which he could assume so many forms at the prompting of his thought or of the passing moment, was necessarily accompanied by a genius for disengagement and flight. As soon as he felt that some attachment was exceeding that divinely allotted time when its duration is imperceptible, he at once felt himself besieged by all the forces of impatience, and there was no love, no habit, no interest that could keep him any more a prisoner than he should be. No man was more possessed than he by the instinct of freedom. He went through his life, passions, and circumstances *without ever feeling that anything was worth his whole being*. And I can guess what he took away with him when he fled and escaped as though carried off by his Demon. He snatched a priceless treasure from the sweetest moments of his life. He preserved in flight the mysterious casket in which all potentiality was enclosed, the whole invisible wealth of coming adventure and ulterior motive. He would suddenly pluck the future—his jealous future—from the hands of others. And what is more alive and more pressing in us? At bottom, our egoism is no more than an injunction and an unlimited draft on the future.

Goethe was possessed by an overwhelming sense that we live once for all. He had to have everything; he craved to

have known, felt, and created everything. And in that respect he was prodigal of all he was; he was prodigal of his modes of appearance, of the products of his variety; but he jealously held back *what he might yet be:* he was thrifty with his tomorrows. Is not life after all summed up in his paradoxical phrase: *the preservation of the future?*

Which sufficiently explains Goethe's freedom with love. It is well known that he displayed a curious magnificence in the independence of his heart. This great lyric poet was the least impulsive of men; the great lover was the least distraught of lovers. His highly lucid Demon bade him *love*; but for him, to love meant to extract from love all that it could offer to the mind, all that the intimate pleasures, with the emotions and personal energies they release, can contribute in the last resort to the faculty of comprehension, to the superior desire for enlightenment, to the power to produce, to act, and to eternalize. *He therefore sacrificed every woman to the Eternal Feminine.*

Love—a means to an end. The love of every woman must be sacrificed to the ideal of love. Love—a serpent you must defy in order to describe or to portray it. What is Don Juan, that simpleton who left nothing behind him, compared to a genius far more profoundly voluptuous and at the same time supremely free, who seems to seduce women and cast them aside only in order to extract from the different experiences of love the *unique essence that intoxicates the intellect?*

So Goethe had to have everything. *Everything*, and on top of that he *had to be saved*. For Faust *must* be saved. And in fact doesn't he deserve to be? The only people who are not and cannot be saved are those who, having nothing to lose, cannot even be lost.

But in the man who presents a contradictory combination

of the rarest gifts, nothing bears witness to his immortal destiny more clearly than the *abundance of his nature*, the multiplicity of his interests and his different gifts. The idea that he must necessarily have formed of himself was one of supreme detachment. It is as though he were compelled to set the level of absolute existence, his center of solitude and of inmost identity, so high that his reason, always sovereign mistress, his reason, which had to recognize and wanted to circumscribe the *Demonism* it observed in the many-faceted and elusive Goethe, had to come to terms with it and discover a new and universal meaning in this exceptional life. The pride of being such a brilliant success, a master of so many wonderful arts . . . that pride grew and was purified, rising to a metaphysical level that made it the equivalent of an in-finite modesty. It is not pride when the cedar recognizes that it is the tallest of all the trees; and the mysterious *Demonism* which enabled Goethe to ascribe to a principle of nature the merit or the apparent demerit of his attitudes, no doubt meant for him that every all-powerful impulse, *good or bad*, which is in us, which comes out and surprises us, must make us suspect some design of universal origin, since we find nothing in our hearts that can help us to foresee or understand their supposedly spontaneous impulses. And it was by this means that Goethe, having once recognized as the source of his pas-sions and his urge for independence and liberation a law created by nature herself, put his whole trust in it. He put all his good will—and it is one of the perfections of his greatness —in a complete submission to things that *are, in so far as they are*, that is to say, *in so far as they appear*. He professed absolute obedience and, as it were, abandonment to the teachings of the visible world. "I have always thought," he said, "that the world had more genius than I." He would not admit that

there was anything in the *subject* more significant or more important than was to be observed in the least *object*. The tiniest leaf had more meaning for him than any word; and on almost the last day of his life he was still saying to Eckermann that no speech was worth a drawing, even one tossed off casually. He was a poet who disparaged words.

But in Goethe's view, would not salvation, would not final redemption be purchased by this singular acceptance of appearances, this strange *mystique* of objectivity? An imaginary scene that I like to conjure up—or rather it occurs to me spontaneously—represents this attitude well enough by means of a simple comparison.

I am thinking of Shakespeare, who overflows with life and at the same time with despair. Hamlet (you will recall) holds a skull in his hands; he takes in the horror of its emptiness and his gorge rises. . . . He throws it down in disgust. But Faust calmly picks up the fearful object that can confound all thought. He is well aware that brooding leads nowhere; and that it is no part of the straightforward design of nature that our minds should lead us to lose ourselves in that future past, which is death. He therefore examines, he ponders over the meaning of the skull with meticulous attention; he himself draws a comparison between his present concentration and the effort he had made in the past to decipher ancient manuscripts. . . .

When he comes to the end of his examination, it is not a monologue inspired by the void that comes from his lips. But he says: "The head of mammals is composed of six vertebrae: three for the posterior part that encloses the treasure of the brain and the terminals of life, divided into slender networks that lead to the interior and to the surface of the whole. Three make up the anterior part, which opens onto the external

world, grasps it, embraces it, and *understands it.*" And he fortifies himself, he confirms himself in his being, by the perfectly clear and very unusual attitude that he adopts toward knowledge.

He brought all his powers of observation, all the mastery of his immense gift of imagination to the study and representation of the visible world. He lived like Lynceus, whose visual pleasures he celebrates so gracefully in the Second Part of *Faust*; he lived by his eyes, and his great eyes never grew weary of feasting themselves on shapes and colors. He became intoxicated with every object that brought him light; he lived by seeing.

What could be seen was for him so clearly set off against what existed in the shifting, indescribable world of the inner life, that he roundly declared he had never bothered to explore that dimension of our consciousness. "I have never thought about thought," he said. On another occasion he added: "What man observes and feels inside himself seems to me to constitute the least important part of his life. At such times he is much more aware of what he lacks than of what he possesses."

Goethe is the great apologist of the world of Appearances. He attributed to what is regarded as the surface of things an interest and a value in which I observe a frankness and a bias that seem to me of the utmost importance.

He understood that if we perceive an infinity of sensations that are useless in themselves, it is nevertheless from them, unimportant as they are, that we have extracted, through a curiosity which is entirely gratuitous and an attention which is a pure luxury, the whole of our science and our art. I sometimes think that there exists for some people, as there existed for him, an *external life* which has an intensity and a depth at

least equal to the intensity and depth that we ascribe to the inner darkness and the mysterious discoveries of the ascetics and the Sufis. What a revelation the first painful and marvelous flicker of daylight on the retina must be for the person who was born blind! And what solid progress, progress without any slipping back, he must feel he is gradually making toward the limits of knowledge—the sharpness of forms and of bodies!

The interior world, on the contrary, is always threatened by a medley of obscure sensations, memories, tensions, unspoken words, where what we wish to observe and to grasp changes and in a sense depraves the act of observation itself. ... We can barely conceive or give a hint of what is meant by thinking a thought, and as soon as we reach that second stage, as soon as we try to raise our consciousness to that *second power*, everything at once becomes blurred. ...

Goethe observes, contemplates and—sometimes in the plastic arts, sometimes in nature—pursues form, in an effort to decipher the motive of whatever it was that drew or modeled the work or object he happens to be examining. The same man who was capable of so much passion, of so much freedom, of all the caprices of feeling and the unexpected creations of the poetic mind, took delight in becoming an observer of inexhaustible patience; he devoted himself to the most meticulous of botanical and anatomical studies, the results of which he described in the simplest and most precise language.

That is one more proof of the diversity—and what might almost be called the ordinary incompatibility—of gifts which is essential to minds of the highest order.

But for Goethe, love of form was not confined to the delights

of contemplation; every living form is part of a process of transformation, and every part of any given form is perhaps a modification of some other form. Goethe was passionately attached to the idea of metamorphosis, which he caught a glimpse of in plant life and in the skeletons of vertebrates. He sought the *forces* at work beneath the *forms*; he uncovered morphological modulations; he became aware of the continuity of causes beneath the discontinuity of effects. He discovered that the leaf turns into a petal, a stamen, a pistil; that there is a profound identity between the seed and the shoot. He describes with the greatest accuracy the effects of adaptation, and some of the tropisms which regulate the growth of plants, the balance of forces which is established and re-established, hour by hour, between an inner law of development and the environment and accidental circumstances. He was one of the founders of the theory of evolution.

He says of the plant that "it combines with a fixity of origin, genus, and species a suppleness and a fortunate mobility which enable it, by modifying itself, to adapt to all the varied conditions that are found over the surface of the globe." He tried to conceive all the vegetable species as a single idea; he was convinced, he said, "that this conception can be made more concrete"—and the idea took shape before his eyes, "in the visible form of a single plant, the ideal type of all other plants." He had to *see*.

We have here a most remarkable combination of a botanical archetype and a theory of evolution.

It is not, perhaps, unduly bold to see in it one of the profound nodal points of this great mind. Everything holds together in a man's intelligence; the vaster it is the more it is unified: or rather, its breadth is only a sign of the high degree of its unity. This presentiment, this desire to discover and to

trace in living things a will to metamorphosis may have been derived from his early contact with certain doctrines, half poetic, half esoteric, which were highly esteemed by the ancients and which, at the end of the eighteenth century, initiates took to cultivating again. The rather seductive if extremely imprecise idea of Orphism, the magical idea of assuming the existence of some unknown hidden principle of life, some tendency toward a higher form of life, in every animate and inanimate thing; the idea that a spirit was fermenting in every particle of reality and that it was therefore not impossible to act by the ways of the spirit on everything and every being in so far as it contains a spirit, is among the ideas which bear witness to the persistence of a sort of primitive reasoning and at the same time of an impulse which of its nature generates poetry or personification.

Goethe appears to have been deeply imbued with the feeling of this power, which satisfied the poet in him and stimulated the naturalist. In short, he saw in the plant a sort of inspired phenomenon, a will to metamorphosis which, he said, "rises step by step, one form evolving from another, *as though ascending an ideal scale*, until it reaches the highest point in living nature, propagation by the two sexes."

The discovery of this kind of metamorphosis is one of his great claims to fame. It is one of the clearest examples of transition from poetic thought to scientific theory, or of a fact brought to light by way of a harmony discovered by intuition. Observation verifies what the inner artist has divined. The tree bears the fruits of knowledge.

In the same way, if Goethe discovered the intermaxillary bone, it was because he had already divined it. . . .

But his great gift of analogy came into conflict with his logical

faculties. It even aroused in him an aversion to the closed system of abstract metamorphosis. He was too much the genius of Appearances to be able to follow deductive reasoning, which has the precious and perilous effect of leading us often a long way from appearances into a world sometimes described as *imaginary* because it is impossible to imagine. That head, which was otherwise so well fashioned, was perhaps lacking in mathematical sense. Goethe was not a geometer. He said that he was "absolutely incapable of working in any way at all with signs and figures." He did not realize that algebra is also a *morphology* and in a sense an organic creation of number, of which it defines the species, transformations, and structure.

And yet I have caught him in the very act of trying his hand at geometry: I have found a strange appeal for mathematical help, and even help of quite a high order, in the very paper he wrote on the Metamorphosis of Plants: he thought that the transformations which are observable in plants could be explained by "combining" the elemental forces and the connections that function in vegetable growth, and he said it in so many words: "I am convinced that by following this procedure we should end by explaining the great variety of forms among flowers and fruits. Only it would be necessary for the ideas of extension, contraction, compression, and anastomosis to be properly defined and for us to be able to use them in the same way as algebraic formulas in order to apply them as they should be applied."

It would be impossible to wish for or to define more clearly a variety of symbolic calculus, analogous to those so frequently invented and used in modern dynamics and physics.

If I have insisted on the scientific cast of Goethe's mind, it

is because it seems to me to be of some importance to dwell on the favorite subjects of thought of a man whose work we are considering. Goethe put more of himself and perhaps more of his pride into research of this nature than into his purely literary works. He was delighted at the astonishment aroused when a poet (here are his own words) "usually occupied with those intellectual phenomena within the province of feeling and imagination, turned aside for a moment from his course and *en passant* made a discovery of such importance."

On the other hand, it is a remarkable instance of the characteristic ambiguity and of the very lofty ambitions of the great man.

With Rousseau, whose example prompted him to devote himself to the study of life, he reacted against the analytical method in fashion when he was a young man. Algebra was in the ascendant, like tragedy. Deductions from Newton's Law occupied the minds and aroused the admiration of the learned world. In the capable hands of Clairaut, d'Alembert, Lagrange, and Laplace, Newton was used to explain everything. Voltaire popularized him and sang his praises. Analytical mechanics was the queen of the sciences.

But the natural sciences were beginning to attract attention. Mathematics, which is an art of deduction and connection within a tightly closed system of properties, a sort of poetry of pure repetition, is not to everyone's taste. At this period there was a touch of romanticism in steering clear of it.

In short, Goethe presents an almost complete system of contraries, which is a rare and fruitful combination. He was *classic* and *romantic* by turns. He was a philosopher who was repelled by the method most generally in use in philosophy—the

analysis of the subject; he was a "savant" or "scientist" who could not or would not make use of the most powerful instrument of the positive sciences; he was also a *mystic*, but a mystic of an unusual kind, entirely devoted to the contemplation of the external world. He tried to arrive at a conception of nature which did not depend either on Newton or on God—or at least the God propounded by the different religions. He refused to accept the idea of creation because he regarded the evolution of organisms as an overwhelming refutation of it. On the other hand, he rejected the explanation of life based solely on physicochemical forces.

His ideas on this point are not so very far removed from our own. We have the advantage over him of a mass of facts discovered since his time. But our conception of life has gained only to the extent of being expressed in more precise contradictions and more numerous and complex enigmas.

In this respect the properties of life and the characteristics of Goethe's being were well suited to one another.

Goethe was hope itself; he rejected, he brushed aside everything that could weaken his will to live and to understand. He did not recoil before any apparent contradiction if the contradiction was likely to enrich his mind. He energetically smashed all bonds, even the tenderest of them; he was determined to ignore misfortunes, even those closest to him, if those bonds and those misfortunes made him feel that he was giving more life than he received from them. He constantly turned, like one of the plants he loved, to what was warmest and most luminous in the passing moment.

The ancients would perhaps have represented him in the ambiguous form of that monstrous god revered in Rome, the god of passage, of transition, who contemplated all possible things with his two faces looking in opposite direc-

tions: Janus. One of the faces of Goethe, Janus *bifrons*, was
turned toward the century which was drawing to a close;
the other looked toward us. And in the same way he could
show Germany a face classical in its beauty, and France an-
other entirely romantic.

But that same strange statue could contemplate as well a
hundred other forms of dualism; and gaze with its double
front at an astonishing number of opposite perspectives, com-
bined depths, complementary visions and considerations. For
all the Januses in Rome would not be enough to reflect all
the oppositions and all the contrasts or, if you prefer, all the
syntheses contained in Goethe. It becomes almost a game to
discover them in him, and the game even makes us wonder
whether he had not made a system of the cultivation of exact
contraries.

His lyrical moods alternated with the patient and tranquil
moods of the botanist. He was an amateur; he was a creator;
he was learned and gallant; his nobility and candor were al-
lied to a cynicism which Mephistopheles may have inherited
from Rameau's nephew; he was able to combine supreme
freedom with punctuality and zeal in his duties as a public
servant. Above all, he reconciled at will Apollo and Dionysus,
Gothic and Classic, Hell and Hades, God and the Devil; in
the same way that his mind reconciled Orphism and experi-
mental science, Kant and the demoniac, and everything in
general with something else which contradicted it.

All these contradictions uplifted him. Strong in his vital-
ity and in his poetic gift; completely in command of his
powers; free, as a strategist, in his own inner maneuvers—
free in the face of love, doctrine, tragedy, pure thought, and
thought about thought; free in the face of Hegel, Fichte,
Newton—Goethe takes his place, his unique and supreme

place, without effort and without rival in the world of the
spirit; and he so manifestly filled it, or rather created it, im-
posed its conditions by virtue of what he so obviously was,
that in 1808 it was inevitable, as though by some astrological
necessity, that he should receive a summons and have a meet-
ing—almost too desirable a meeting, too much in the nature
of a miracle and, as it were, too happily ordained by poetic
destiny—the summons and the meeting with Napoleon.

It must needs be—as the "Mothers," those "goddesses who
are unknown to mortals and whose name is only uttered with
reluctance," may have dreamed in their mysterious absence—
*it must needs be that these great lines should meet and that some
great event for the Spirit should emerge from their meeting. It is
necessary for these two unique beings to attract one another and to
have seen one another. It is important that the large and splendid eyes
of the Poet should have met the imperial glance, that the man who
disposes of so many lives and the man who disposes of so many
minds should know—or recognize—one another.*

Goethe never forgot that interview, which was certainly
his greatest memory and his crowning pride. . . .

The scene, however, was very simple; we observe with
interest the presence of Prince Talleyrand and the great care
taken by that personage, so highly thought of by Balzac, to
note and check its least details.

The ease with which literary capital can be made out of
such a subject makes me hesitate to dwell on it. Napoleon
himself warns us against constructing tableaux, as he puts it,
meaning those fanciful arrangements of circumstances which
seem to come into being of their own accord in the form of
illusions and situations that are oversignificant.

And yet how can we avoid meditating on it, and how can
we avoid giving their due to the romanticism and the rhetoric

of long ago? Besides, neither the Sorbonne nor the Academy had any such scruples. It may well be, after all, that the antithesis and the parallel correspond to some necessity of the spirit.

As I was saying, how can we fail to meditate on it?

The empire founded on intelligence in action and the empire of intelligence in its free state contemplated one another and conversed for *a moment*. What a moment! ... What a moment when the man who was the Hero of Organized Revolution, the Demon of the West, the Strong Man Armed, the Ravisher of Victory, the man whose coming, according to Joseph de Maistre, was foretold in the Apocalypse, summoned Goethe to Erfurt; summoned him and treated him as a *man*—that is to say, *as an equal!*

What a moment! It was 1808—the very hour, the priceless moment when the Star reached its zenith.

It was a moment which, of itself, might have said to the Emperor, using the fatal words of the pact: *Stop me ... I am so beautiful.* It was so beautiful that all the monarchs of Europe were at Erfurt, at the feet of Faust with a crown on his head. But he—he was not unmindful that in the great future his true destiny was not the destiny of battles. The fate of the world was certainly in his beautiful hands; but the fate of his Name was in the hands that hold the pen; and all the personal greatness of the man who thought only of posterity, of the man who feared above everything lampoon and irony—he knew that it all finally depended on the whim of a handful of talented men. He wanted the poets on his side; and with politic foresight he collected round himself, with the princes of the earth, the most illustrious writers of Germany.

They talked literature. Werther and French tragedy were used to fill in a seemly amount of time. But their minds were occupied with something very different. Although there was

nothing in what they actually said to make us feel the full weight of the coincidence—that conjunction of events which had brought together the Corsican Emperor and the Man who had led German thought back to the sunny source of classicism and guessed the sensual origins of pure form—the event was charged with a whole world of facts, ideas, and possibilities. . . . But coquetry was essential at such a meeting. Each wanted to appear at his ease, and carefully arranged his smile. They were two Magicians attempting to charm one another. Napoleon assumed the role of emperor of the mind and even of literature. Goethe appeared as the embodiment of mind itself. Did the Emperor perhaps have a clearer sense of the true nature of his power than Goethe imagined?

Napoleon knew better than anyone that his power, more than any other power in the world, was in the strictest sense *magic*—the power of mind over minds—a spell!

He said to Goethe: "You are a Man." (Or he said *of* Goethe: "There is a Man.") Goethe surrendered. Goethe was flattered to death. He was caught: a genius captured by another genius, and he would never go free. He was to be lukewarm in 1813, when the whole of Germany was boiling over and the empire was beginning to shrink.

"You're a Man." *A man?* . . . That is to say, *the measure of all things*; and that is to say, a man compared with whom all the rest are rough drafts, fragments of men, hardly men at all, because they are not the measure of all things as *we* are, *you and I*. You and I, Monsieur Goethe, possess the strange virtue of completeness, and some fury, some irresistible impulse that drives us to act, to become, to transform, and not to leave the world as it was before us. . . .

And Goethe (I am no longer imagining this), Goethe reflected, and remembered his strange theory of the Demonic.

And indeed, what an ideal figure Bonaparte would make for a Third Part of *Faust*.

The truth is that there exists between these two Augurs, these Prophets of the New Age, a curious analogy which can be seen only at a distance, a parallel that is apparent without my making the slightest effort to force it. I shall deduce from it perhaps a conception that is purely imaginary: but judge how it speaks for itself. You have only to look, to see it.

Both of them were minds of extraordinary power and freedom: Bonaparte, unleashed in the real world, led it by the nose, treated it violently, conducting the orchestra of events at a furious pace and giving to the march of human affairs the speed and uneasy appeal of a fantastic piece of fiction. . . . He was everywhere, and won all along the line; even misfortune contributed to his fame; he provided at every juncture for every contingency. Indeed, the ideal of *Complete Action*—that is to say, action that is imagined, *constructed* in the mind with incredible precision down to the least detail, then *executed* with the promptness and force of the spring of a wild beast—possessed him and showed exactly what manner of man he was. It was no doubt this Man's trait of being organized for Complete Action that gave him those features of a man of antiquity, so often remarked.

He strikes us as an ancient, just as Caesar strikes us as a modern, because they are both capable of living and acting in every age. A powerful and precise imagination recognizes no hampering tradition; and when it comes to innovations, it takes charge of them. Always and everywhere the exponent of complete action finds something to dominate. Napoleon was capable of understanding and manipulating all the peoples of the world. He would have commanded Arabs, Hindus, and Mongols as he led Neapolitans to Moscow, and Saxons

to Cádiz. And Goethe, in his own sphere, enlisted, assembled, and manipulated Euripides and Shakespeare, Voltaire and Trismegistus, Job and Diderot, God Himself and the Devil. He was capable of being Linnaeus and Don Juan, of admiring Jean Jacques and dealing with the problems of etiquette at the court of the Grand Duke. There were times when both Goethe and Napoleon yielded, each in his own way, to the seduction of the East. Bonaparte liked the simple and martial religion of Islam. Goethe was carried away by Hafiz; both admired Mohammed. But what is more European than to be attracted by the East?

Both had characteristics that belonged to the greatest epochs; they remind us at once of Mythical Antiquity and Classical Antiquity. This brings us to another remarkable similarity: *they both professed contempt for ideology*. Pure speculation made no appeal to either of them. Goethe did not want to think about thought. Bonaparte disdained mental constructions that did not demand sanction, verification, execution—positive and tangible results.

Finally, both adopted a more or less comparable attitude toward religions, an attitude in which we find a mixture of respect and contempt; they meant to exploit the political or dramatic value of religions without drawing any distinctions between them, and merely regarded them as springs of action in their respective theaters.

One of them no doubt was the wisest, the other perhaps the maddest of mortals; but for that very reason both of them were the most exciting characters in the world.

Napoleon, the adept of the lightning stroke, of concentrations of men and fire prepared in secret and launched with fury—Napoleon succeeded more by surprise even than by the force of the blow—in the manner of some natural disaster;

a sort of *volcanism* applied to the *art of war*, and even practiced in the realm of politics; for his aim was to remake the world in the space of ten years.

This brings us to the great difference between them! Goethe did not care for volcanoes. His geology, like his destiny, condemned them. He adopted the profound notion of imperceptible transformation. He believed in and was almost in love with the maternal slowness of nature. He was to live a long time. A long life, a full life, a lofty and voluptuous life. Neither men nor gods were unkind to him. There has never been a mortal man so successful in combining the voluptuousness that creates with the voluptuousness that *exceeds and consumes*. He was able to endow the trivial incidents of daily life, his distractions and even his minor irritations, with a universal interest. It is a great secret to be able to change everything into nectar for men's minds.

A Sage, they say. A Sage? *Yes*. With a dash of the devil for completeness' sake, and enough of what was absolute and inalienable in the freedom of the intellect to make use of the devil, and in the end to outwit him.

In the evening of his days, in the heart of Europe, himself the center of attraction and the admiration of all intelligent people, the center of the greatest curiosity, the subtlest and noblest Master of the Art of living and of deepening the taste for living, Genial Lover of All Things, *Pontifex Maximus*, which is to say, the great builder of bridges between the centuries and the forms of culture, Goethe grew to a luminous old age among his antiques, his herbals, his engravings, his books, his thoughts and his confidants. As the hour grew late, the least word he spoke became an oracle. He exercised a sort of supreme function, a magistracy of the European mind, even

174

more venerated and imposing than Voltaire's, since he was able to take advantage of many of the demolitions for which Voltaire was responsible, without inheriting the hate or rousing the fury that Voltaire had done.

He felt himself grow to be a supreme and lucid Jupiter of ivory and gold, a god of light who, under so many forms, had visited so many beauties and created so many enchantments; and he saw himself surrounded by a cortege of deities, some of whom were the creatures of his own poetry; others, his very dear and very faithful *Ideas*—his Metamorphosis, his Anti-Newtonian Colors, and his very familiar spirits, his demons, his genii. . . .

He could also make out a few equals in the purple vistas of this apotheosis. Napoleon, perhaps his greatest memory, whose look still lingered in his eyes?

Wolfgang von Goethe was to die a little more than ten years after the death of the Emperor, in that little Weimar which was a sort of delicious St. Helena for him, the eye of the world being fixed on it as it was on Longwood, and where he too had his Las Cases and his Montholon under the names of Müller and Eckermann.

What a noble sunset! What a view of the plenitude and glory of life when, in extreme old age, he contemplated, nay, *composed* his own twilight, from the splendor of the immense spiritual riches his labor had assembled, and the immense spiritual riches his genius had scattered abroad.

Faust could now say: "Moment, thou art so beautiful . . . I consent to die."

But when called by Helen he appears, *saved*, elevated by universal consent to the first place among the Fathers of Thought and the Doctors of Poetry: PATER AESTHETICUS IN AETERNUM.

Stendhal

I HAVE just reread *Lucien Leuwen*. It is not quite the same book I was so fond of thirty years ago. I have changed and it has changed. I hasten to add that the second *Leuwen*, which is a revised, enlarged, and improved version of the first, both brings back and heightens the delicious memories of that first reading. But I do not disown my pleasure of long ago.

Jean de Mitty, who first published *Leuwen* about 1894, has sometimes been harshly judged. I agree that for the future the text he gave us at that time will appear unfortunate—abridged and perhaps seriously tampered with; and I am not unaware that Mitty himself may have given cause for certain severe judgments not confined to this particular publication, but aimed at the man himself. I feel, however, that I am still in his debt, and I am going to risk putting in a good word for him here. We had met at Stéphane Mallarmé's, where he used to come quite frequently on Tuesdays. At the end of those delightful evenings we happened more than once to walk together the whole length of the Rue de Rome, which was half in darkness, chatting about Napoleon or Stendhal until we reached the brilliantly lighted center of the city.

At that time I was reading the *Vie de Henri Brulard* and the *Souvenirs d'égotisme* with passionate interest and preferred them to the famous novels, to the *Rouge* and even to the

Chartreuse. I cared little about plot or action. I was only in-
terested in the living system to which every event is related,
I mean the disposition and reactions of a particular man; so
far as *plot* was concerned, only his inner plot. In those days
Mitty was working on—putting together, if you like—his
little edition of *Lucien Leuwen*, which he sent me almost as
soon as it was published by Dentu. The book gave me im-
mense pleasure; I was among the first to read it and I went
round singing its praises.

Up till then I had read nothing about love which I had not
found excessively boring, or which had not appeared silly or
pointless. When I was young, I set love so high and so low
that I found nothing in the most famous works either power-
ful enough or true enough, either tough enough or tender
enough to satisfy me. But in *Leuwen* the extraordinary del-
icacy of the portrait of Madame de Chasteller, the nobility
and profundity of the hero's feelings, the progress of an at-
tachment which in a sort of silence becomes overwhelming;
the consummate art displayed by Stendhal in containing and
maintaining it in a state of uncertainty about its own nature
—all this appealed to me and had to be read again. I may have
had my own reasons for being so deeply moved by these in-
definable qualities; and what is more, I was amazed to be so,
because I could not and still can scarcely abide being deluded
by a literary work to the point where I can no longer dis-
tinguish clearly between my own feelings and those suggested
by the author's artifice. I see the pen and the person who is
holding it. I do not care for, I have no need of, his emotions.
I only ask him to let me into the secret of how it's done. But
Lucien Leuwen brought about in me this miracle of a con-
fusion which I detest. . . .

As for the picture of provincial, Parisian, military, political, and parliamentary or electoral life, a charming caricature of the first years of the reign of Louis Philippe, a vivid and brilliant piece of comedy verging at times on vaudeville—just as the *Chartreuse de Parme* at times suggests operetta—I found in that an entertainment glowing with wit and ideas.

My impressions of the first *Leuwen* were tender and vivid. So why not show a little gratitude to the shade of poor Mitty, to whom I owed some enchanting hours? I was charmed and moved by that primitive and imperfect version of *Leuwen* which he had given me; I shall never reread it in the faulty text that he provided. That is my reason for saying a few well-meant words of farewell to that early version and to the man who published it.

I had hardly written down the words "vaudeville" and "operetta" (a little earlier on) when I had a feeling that the reader would be shocked. He probably does not care for this mixing of the literary castes; he is astonished to find Stendhal, who was praised by Taine and Nietzsche, and who was almost a philosopher, placed so close to mere men of wit. But truth and life add up to disorder; connections and relationships which are not surprising are not real. . . .

Am I wrong in thinking that I can discern a path leading from Stendhal by way of Mérimée and the Musset of *Fantasio* to the little theaters of the Second Empire, to the princes and conspirators of the Meilhacs and Halévys? And this capricious track may have started quite a long way back. (But on the intellectual globe everything comes from everything and leads everywhere.)

Stendhal with his taste for *opera buffa* must have delighted in Voltaire's little novels, which will always remain marvels

of racy vigor and terrifying fantasy. May not a lively mind see in those nimble, cruel works, where satire, opera, ballet, pamphlet, and ideology are welded into a diabolical whole, in those fables which gave scandalous pleasure at the end of the reign of Louis XV, the elegant ancestors of the operettas that provided a pitiless entertainment during the last days of the reign of Napoleon III? I cannot reread the *Princess of Babylon*, *Zadig*, *Babouc*, and *Candide* without imagining that I am listening to a kind of music a thousand times wittier, more satirical, and more diabolical than the music of Offenbach and his like. . . .

In short, I am bold enough to think that *Ranuce-Ernest* might have had a success at the Variétés, and *Dr. Du Poirier* have practiced at the Palais-Royal.

Fortunately, Beyle inherited from the century into which he was born the inestimable gift of liveliness. The heavy-handed pundits and the bores never had an adversary quicker on the draw. Classics and romantics alike, in whose midst be moved and glittered, provoked his ready wit. He would have been amused (but decidedly flattered) if someone had shown him in a magic bowl his future swamped with doctoral theses. In the enchanted water he would have seen his sallies transformed into dogmas, his fancies turned into precepts, his quips developed into theories, doctrines extracted from his works, his brief maxims expanded into interminable homilies. His favorite subjects, *Napoleon*, *love*, *energy*, *happiness*, have produced volumes of exegesis. Philosophers have joined in the game. Scholarship has turned its magnifying glass on the least events of his life, on his scribbled notes, on his tradesmen's bills. The iconoclast's name and relics are venerated with a sort of naïve and mysterious idolatry. In accordance

with custom his eccentricities have encouraged imitators. All that is most contrary to the man, to his freedom, his whims, and his love of opposition has come out of him. There is a good deal that is unexpected in the growth of a reputation. A *mystique* attaches to fame, even the fame of atheists.

"To hell with this Stendhal!" the spirit of Stendhal must sometimes cry out in some nonconformist reader.

He had to put up with a great deal from his father and from the worthy, serious-minded people who kept him under their thumb, or who bored him; he was the slave—in whom there was so little of the slave—of those pompous individuals who worked in the Council of State, pillars of the Empire, counselors and consultants who were compelled unendingly to provide the hotheaded master of France, a France vastly expanded and in a continual state of crisis, with the required answers, the correct details, the figures, the decisions and specifications needed; he had seen at close quarters, noted, penetrated, and mocked the follies and virtues of people in official positions; had observed their occasional corruption, their invariable thirst for promotion, their profound and puerile schemes, their meticulous pettiness, their love of high-sounding language, their self-importance; the trouble they made for themselves and others; their incredible courage when confronted with mountains of files, columns of figures which crush the spirit without enriching the mind, the unending memoranda which give those in power the illusion of being alive, of knowing, foreseeing, and taking action. . . . Beyle always pits a pure young man, or a man of wit, against such gluttons for work, those monsters of silliness, greed, aridity, hypocrisy, or envy whose features, characters, and actions he portrayed on so many occasions. He learned from

his own disgust, and knew in himself that true value may be divorced from vanity, from mountains of paper, lies, solemnity, and automatism. He had observed that those self-important personages so inevitably associated with the smooth working of the State are speechless nonentities the moment they are faced with the unexpected. A State that fails to keep a few improvisers on hand is a State without sinews. Anything that moves quickly becomes a threat. Anything out of the blue annihilates it.

It is easy to see from his writings that Beyle would have loved to handle great affairs as though they were a game. He creates with loving care men of clear, quick judgment, whose reactions are *as sudden as events*, as brisk and breath-taking as a surprise—ministers or bankers who direct, settle, or cut their way through circumstances, who combine charm and profundity, finesse and good sense, in whose skins we are aware of the presence of Beyle himself; we feel that he is plotting or impertinently ruling under their masks, and besides, that by creating them he is taking his revenge for not being the sort of person they are. Every writer compensates himself as best he can for the injustices of fate.

What is valuable in many men of value depends on the variety of roles they feel capable of playing. Henri Beyle, who would have made a good prefect by the standards of 1810, was nonetheless a devil of a man, always on the warpath against respectability. A skeptic who believed in love. This unruly character was a patriot. This man always noting down abstract ideas was interested in painting (or strove or pretended to be interested). He claimed to be a positivist, and worked out a *mystique* of passion.

Perhaps the growth of self-awareness, constant self-scrutiny tend to make us discover or create our diversity?

The mind multiplies among its own possibilities, changes at every moment from what it was the moment before, listens to what it has just said, flies to the opposite, replies to itself, and watches the effect. I find in Stendhal the mobility and the fire, the rapid reflexes, the lightning retort, and the frank cynicism of that admirable pair of actors, Diderot and Beaumarchais. To know yourself is simply to predict yourself; to predict yourself ends in playing a part. Beyle's consciousness is a theater, and there is a good deal of the actor in the author. His work is full of sallies aimed at the audience. His prefaces stand down front and speak to it, wink at the reader, making signs of complicity, to convince him that he is the least foolish of the lot, that he is "in the know," that he alone gets the real subtlety. "No one but you and I," is what they say.

The effect on Stendhal's posthumous fame has been stupendous. He makes the reader proud to be his reader.

Beyle cannot help intervening directly in his works. He burns to be on the stage himself, to reappear on any pretext; he makes extravagant use of stage whispers, asides, and monologues. He manipulates his own puppets, and they form a very complete social group where the roles are clearly defined, as they were in the early theater. He creates lovers, old fogies, prelates, diplomats, savants, republicans, and ex-guardsmen. His types are more stylized than Balzac's and therefore more sharply drawn. He sees their ideas rather than their thought, their feelings rather than their motivation and their function in the world. For Stendhal, Napoleon (for example) is a *hero*; he is a model of energy, imagination, and will power, a great soul endowed with a prodigiously clear intellect, a lover of ideal greatness who loves power and glory with a passionate love in the manner of Stendhal himself. But Balzac sees the administrator and the Empire, the Civil Code,

the Revolution fulfilled, consolidated, mastered, society re-established, the legend emerging from history and, through the popularity of myths, invading the domain of politics.

Beyle perceives the traits Napoleon inherited from antiquity, his Italian features, the powerful personality in whom he recognizes Rome and Florence, Caesar and the *condottiere*. Balzac is primarily concerned with the Emperor of the French.

It will be seen that, for anyone who enjoys such exercises, a parallel between Balzac and Stendhal is possible and could quite reasonably be pursued further. They both dealt with the same period and the same social data. They are both imaginative observers of the same object. . . .

All Stendhal's characters have one thing, which may be a vice or a virtue, in common: it is impossible for them not to display, on every occasion, and according to their nature or their condition, some primary reaction of *antipathy* or *sympathy*.

The artist sometimes appears to cherish his pet aversions. Without realizing it, we are fond of a person whom we enjoy tormenting. The artist falls on them with glee, marks them, transfixes them, tears them to pieces. He returns to his prey, takes infinite pleasure in jeering at their stupidity, their baseness, their schemes. There is nobody who escapes his mockery completely; no one who does not deceive or is not deceived; or both at once, which is what usually happens. Even his favorites are the victims of their own tender hearts, the dupes of the Beautiful.

It is hard to see why Stendhal did not go in for the theater, for which he was clearly so well equipped. We might reflect on the gap if we had the time. The period was probably not yet one in which plays and comedies by Henri Beyle would have had much chance of success.

But he—the writer who in his heart is an actor—he con-

structs a stage in his own mind—or in his soul or his brain (the word matters little; we are simply trying to suggest a sort of place-and-time where what happens is seen by each of us alone—where what is seen is not easy to distinguish from what one wants and what one does).

On this private stage he puts on a continuous performance of Himself; he turns his life, his career, his loves, his multifarious ambitions into an unending play; he performs his own gestures, speaks his own replies, reacts to his own impulses, his own naïveté, his "fiascos" of various kinds.

Among the characters in this morality play, with its continuous performance and its unbroken run, constantly enlivened by topical inserts, we recognize a few allegorical beings or familiar spirits: the Beau Ideal, Happiness, Logic, Money, the Noble Style . . . the ghost of Bonaparte, the silhouette of the Jesuit, the puppet called "the greatest rogue among Kings," etc., who take it in turns to get themselves applauded or hissed off the stage.

This mime play even has a kind of *music* in it. We sometimes hear, breaking through the text like highly personal themes, certain turns of speech, almost interjections, actually no more than *nervous signals* to sound the rallying call of energy, the resurrection of the "sweetest of memories," the awakening of the will to be again what one was, to desire what one once desired. . . .

These short sharp incantations break the spell of the present, banish the gray day, and surge up from the depths of the personality like a call to arms; as though in the midst of dismal and depressing surroundings, against an overpowering feeling of boredom or melancholy, against the sense of shabby and unlucky circumstances, the all-powerful drumbeat of personal value, the warning cry of the *one and only self* is heard

like the clear trumpet whose voice once upon a time made the young cavalryman, sprawling over his animal's neck, sit bolt upright in his saddle as the recruits of his regiment were crossing the Alps to join the reserve army of Year VIII.*

Alors comme alors! . . . this is the theme of egotistical egoism, as it resounds in his writings.

Another theme: *Nets strung too high*.

Pride holds them so high that nothing real is ever caught in them. Vanity keeps the trammel-net right at the bottom and always manages to fish up, here and there, some pleasing advantage.

Questions of pride and vanity are always of the first importance in dealing with a man who performs in public; they are oddly mixed up with talent, stimulate and sometimes create it, corrupt it or constantly help it to find its bearings. In the case of Stendhal we must therefore pause for a moment to consider them. The comparative amounts of vanity or pride to be found in a work are *characteristic quantities* which the chemists of criticism should always strive to assess. They are never negligible.

The least foolish of great authors, yet always fretting about being read forever and found moving, Stendhal, for all his wit, for all the pleasure he took in catching himself out, correcting himself, recognizing his absurdities, laughing at himself (as we pinch ourselves to come to our senses and remember who we are), was nevertheless divided between his immense desire to please and to become famous, and the opposite mania, his delight in being himself, in his own eyes,

*Stendhal was a cavalryman, not a hussar. Moreover, when he crossed the Alps he was not yet mobilized. (Comment by M. Arbelet.) [P. V.]

in his own way. He felt, deeply embedded in his flesh, the spur of literary vanity; but he also felt a little deeper down the strange sharp pricking of an absolute pride determined to depend on nothing but itself.

Our talents drive us to use them; the vivid, the continual generation of ideas provokes a strange impatience to give expression to them. The future work ferments in its future author. But this furious urge is determined to sell our soul to other people; and the power within us, once it overflows and takes its course, nearly always sweeps us away from ourselves; it carries our Ego where it did not expect to go, involving it in a world of display, comparison, and counter-evaluation where the Ego becomes somehow, for itself, *an effect of the effect it creates on a large number of unknown people.* . . . Once a man is *known*, he tends to be no more than an emanation of an indistinguishable number of unknowns, that is to say, a creature formed by opinion, an absurd public monster to whom the real man gradually yields and conforms.

That is what happens to the blessed who have been up-lifted by their humility and set upon altars, where their poverty is rewarded with gilt and their humility with incense.

We listen to the tempting voice of our own powers at the expense, perhaps, of what is most precious in our hearts; of what is jealous, fierce, and incommunicable, and wishes to remain so. This naïvely insular being and the lover of fame (who is no less so) adapt themselves as best they can to one and the same fate. . . .

How are we to extricate ourselves from the conflict between two fundamental impulses of the mind? One of them inspires us to seek favor, to force and win men's minds at random.

The other jealously reminds us of our unalterable solitude and strangeness. One urges us to seem, the other rouses us to be, and to confirm ourselves in what we are. It is a conflict between what is too human in man and what has nothing human about it and feels no kinship with anything. Every pure, strong being feels that he is something other than a man; he refuses and in a naïve way fears to recognize in himself one of the innumerable examples of a species or a type that repeats itself. In all profound minds some hidden virtue is perpetually at work creating a recluse. When brought into contact with or reminded from time to time of other people, they become conscious of a peculiar sensation that pierces with a sudden sharp pain, making them withdraw at once into some indefinable inward island. This is an attack of inhumanity, a reflex of invincible antipathy that may end in madness, as befell the emperor who wished that the human race had only one head which could be cut off at a single blow. But with people who are less brutal by nature and more contemplative, this violent feeling, this obsession of the man with himself, can give birth to ideas and works. The man who feels himself a victim of the evil of not being unique wears himself out in inventing something that will distinguish him from his fellow men. The desire to be different becomes an obsession. And it may well be that it is not so much the desire to set himself above other people as to set himself entirely apart from and, as it were, beyond comparison with them which gnaws at him and drives him on. "Great men" provoke a smile on the part of men who are "immeasurable."

Perhaps the great "sin"—the metaphysical sin par excellence which the theologians have called by the fine name of *pride*—has its roots in the irritability that springs from the need to

be unique? But again, if we pushed this line of argument further, carried it a little too far along the path of the simplest feelings, we might discover at the bottom of pride merely the horror of death, because we only know death through other people who die, and if we are really like them, we too shall die. And so the horror of death produces out of its darkness some insane will to be *unlike*, to be independence itself and the absolutely singular being, that is to say, a god. The refusal to be like other people, to have fellow beings, the refusal to recognize the attributes of being in those who are apparently and from any reasonable point of view our like, is to refuse to be mortal, and to will blindly not to be of the same substance as those people who pass by and melt away, one after another, around us. The syllogism that leads Socrates to his death more surely than the hemlock, the inference that forms its major premise, the deduction that concludes it, all awaken a protest and an obscure revolt of which the cult of the self is an effect that can easily be deduced.

That is where egotism leads when we track it to its source in order to discover its nature. I may have pursued my inquiry rather further than was appropriate in discussing Stendhal; what I have just written would be more applicable to Nietzsche, and more to the point as a marginal comment on *Ecce Homo* than on *Henri Brulard*. But the greater includes the less, and illuminates it. And a *Self* so contaminated only exaggerates and makes acutely sensitive the secret tendencies and the innermost temptations that are not lacking in the more or less normal Self.

As for egotism à la Stendhal, it implies a faith, the faith in a *natural Self*; and education, manners, and *morals* are its enemies. This natural Self is known to us, and can only be

known to us, by those of our reactions which we consider or imagine to be primal and truly spontaneous. The more these reactions seem independent of social environment and the habits or training we have acquired from it, the more precious and authentic they are for the Egotist.

What strikes me, what amuses and even delights me in the Egotist's determination to be natural is that it requires and is necessarily based on a *convention*. In order to distinguish the natural from the conventional, a convention is indispensable. How otherwise can we decide what belongs to *nature* and what belongs to *culture*? The natural disposition is variable; the causes of spontaneity differ very considerably in each of us. Can we believe that even love itself is not imbued with things we have learned, that there is not something traditional in the very fury, the excitement, the complications of thought and feeling it may provoke in us? If I even say that in the make-up and moods of any of us, the *natural* is what emanates directly from our *organism*, I mean that there are as many ways of being natural as there are different complexions, that is to say, individuals, each of whom considers the words and actions of any other person very far from what he finds natural—*in himself.*

Comment: to be an *egotist*, and to make use of the works of other writers with the effrontery we all know, is a combination well calculated to astonish.

We can easily see, too, how entertaining it is to proclaim, to profess "nature" and the "natural" as a doctrine and in the form of a theory.

This naïve and attractive system, associated with Rousseau, which reappears whenever the fact of being civilized

makes someone more conscious of the rules and constraints of such a condition than of its advantages, is liable to fill those who reinvent it, and their followers, with pride. It is at once a form of private morality, a rule of conduct to be observed in society, a religion of the personality, a literary bias, and an expression of that temperament of a born actor which I find in Stendhal and in all those who indulge in self-confession. Nothing could be more interesting and nothing, perhaps, more comic; nothing more exciting, nothing more ingenuous than to adopt the line of being one's *self*, of being *true*. This great and simple decision is by no means uncommon in literature. There are plenty of examples because the attractions are so great. A short cut to being original—a kindred superstition—and to being original simply by being what one *is*; the certainty of finding ample facilities once the first bold step has been taken; the license to make use of the least incident of one's life, the insignificant details that create the impression of *truth*; the freedom to use plain language and to create values out of trifles that are usually passed over in books; the undoubted fascination of showing one's own habits and behavior in a light that reveals clearly what is normally hidden or kept in the background—all these are great advantages.

Cynicism in literature is usually the sign of a degree of desperate ambition. When we can no longer think what to do in order to create a stir and survive, we prostitute ourselves, we expose our private parts in public.

After all it must be rather fun, by the mere fact of unbuttoning one's fly, to give oneself and other people the impression of discovering America. We all know perfectly well what we shall see; but at the first move everybody is excited. Such is the magic of literature.

Literary Egotism consists, in the last analysis, of playing the part of one's *self*; of being a little more *natural* than nature; a little more oneself than one was a moment or two before the idea came into one's head. When we furnish our impulses or our impressions with a conscious *agent* who, by deferring, by waiting expectantly upon ourself, and above all by *taking notes*, draws his own portrait more and more clearly, *perfects* himself from work to work *as his talent for writing develops*, we substitute an imaginary character for ourself and finish imperceptibly by using him as a model. We must never forget that the observation of ourselves involves a great deal that is highly arbitrary.

I should not be surprised if Stendhal fortified himself in his egotism by mixing with some of those Englishmen who deliberately set out to be original and who were to be found at that time in Italy, where they were very busy being eccentric, having the wherewithal for the job: the physical constitution, the boredom, the chilly wit, the guineas, the indispensable insolence, the prestige of their country which they purported to scandalize, knowing perfectly well that it did not in the least object to being shocked. The effect on him of those *milords* may well have been exciting enough. Remember what he disliked most in the world—small-mindedness, thrift, the lack of whims, any stupid or sordid habit, all the anti-passionate virtues (fear of public opinion, fear of spending money, fear of liking what one likes) which he had observed at close quarters, suffered from and blasphemed against in childhood, and which had made Grenoble and the whole of French provincial life odious to him. He abhorred tradition, the small town, local pride, inescapable mediocrity. When he thought of it, he bristled and became an isolated inhabitant of the Isle of Ego.

The belated love for little old villages, country churches, and useless "antiques," which nowadays mingles strangely with an excess of novelties, had not yet been invented. The cult of place and ancestor worship had not yet been revived, since railways and the chaotic effects of modern economy had not yet made certain people feel that more or less profound need of more or less real roots, and that longing for a quasi-vegetable state which those who have experienced it have not always found particularly enjoyable.

Stendhal is one of those people whose characters are plainly molded, armed, and indelibly marked by the experiences of childhood. All his life he will judge things according to the memories of the young Beyle, and his opinion will be directly based on them. His father, his Aunt Séraphie, his grandparents, the charming phantom of his mother, his first friends, his teachers never ceased to provide him with types—criteria of sensibility, wickedness, silliness, or boredom. He will compare everybody he meets later on with them. He entered maturity with a full cast of characters.

On one of his birthdays, Henri Brulard unbuttons his trousers and writes inside the belt: "I have just passed my fiftieth birthday."

Every admirer of Brulard must have spent a few minutes puzzling over this disclosure. What on earth can have prompted it? What was the point of this uncommon act? And what is the sense of the act that followed—that of writing it down? Did Beyle really record it on so personal a flyleaf? If it was a piece of sheer invention, what was the object of such a curious fabrication? What future reader did he think would be impressed by it? Was he hoping to make himself

appear a "living and singular figure," or to emphasize the sincerity of his diary by the almost indecent intimacy of this detail? *Hypotheses non fingo*. . . .

But apart from this, what was the point of his linguistic fantasies, the numerous notes in which he uses English or Italian words that have nothing particularly mysterious about them?

Why write: "Lettre *of the author of the** Cenci"? Or "C'est à *forthy* (sic) *seven* que Dominique," etc.?

On other occasions he indulges in unusual permutations of syllables: the *trespres*, the *ligionre*. . . .

I hope with all my heart that he did not flatter himself that this would put inquisitive people off the scent.

These habits seem to me to be nothing but a piece of cryptographic comedy. He pretends to write in code, in much the same way that an actor pretends to eat or drink; and perhaps he does so in order to create the illusion that he is in league with himself, *that he is on rather more intimate terms with himself than the common run of Egos.*

Did he imagine vaguely that his native language—the language of the inner word—might secretly suggest to him, by being written down, some manner of feeling which was absolutely his own and independent of his country? The liberated Ego lives in Cosmopolis and thinks in all languages.

It is true that everyone who is jealously and strongly individual works out a secret language. What takes place in a family, or in a very tiny secret society like a couple of friends or lovers, also takes place in a single head. The immediate invention of a special vocabulary sets the seal on every form of complicity. Every form of private understanding is created at

*English in the French text. [J. M.]

the expense of public conventions. Stendhal conspires with Stendhal under a variety of names—(Léautaud counted 129 pseudonyms)—conspires sometimes against Stendhal, always against fools, the self-important, the insensitive.

Stendhal, the inventor of the *happy few*, had such a marked taste for secrecy in matters of opinion, and for cliques who share the same likes and dislikes, that he makes me think of the spontaneous generation of those very small, very ardent, and vigorously uncompromising groups which have been responsible for all the innovations and ideas that on two or three occasions during the past fifty or sixty years have transformed our literature and our art. He is in a sense the forerunner of the "esotericism" which was the source of Naturalism, the Parnassians, and Symbolism. Experience has shown that coteries have their virtues. The "general public" is entitled to the normal and well-tried products of the industry. But the reconditioning of the industry itself calls for many tests, daring experiments that can only take place in laboratories, and only in laboratories is it possible to obtain the very high temperatures, the exceptionally rare reactions, the degrees of enthusiasm and the extremes of analysis without which science and art would follow an all too beaten track.

The characteristics of Beyle that I have just recalled are interesting because they are not easy to explain. They are no doubt the result of his theories and eccentricities: I think I detect in them an element of calculation, a tendency to gamble on the reader of the future, a marked determination to attract by carelessness and apparent improvisation—which imply and suggest a "just between you and me" relationship between the author and the unknown reader who is to be won over. . . .

Stendhal was an "ideologist" in his way, and liked precepts and principles. He formulated rules of conduct and aesthetics for his own guidance; he claimed to be a reasoner. It is not impossible that he did a good deal of reasoning where reason scarcely applies.

As for his eccentricities, they are plainly visible. But what is an eccentricity?

What is most striking about a page of Stendhal, what gives him away at once and attracts or irritates the reader—is the *tone*. He possesses, and for that matter affects, the most individual tone to be found in literature. This tone is so pronounced, it makes us so strongly aware of the man as a presence, that in the eyes of Stendhalians it excuses (1) his carelessness, his willful carelessness, and his contempt for all the formal qualities of style; (2) a good deal of pillaging and a great many plagiarisms. In all criminal cases the essential thing for the accused is to make himself appear infinitely more interesting than his victims. What do we care about Beyle's victims? He transforms their sorry goods into books that are readable because he has introduced a certain *tone*.

What does the tone consist of? I may perhaps already have given the answer: be lively at all costs; write as you speak when you are a man of wit, with plenty of allusions even if they happen to be obscure, with gaps and leaps and lots of parentheses; write almost as though you were talking to yourself; keep up the pace of free and lively conversation; push it occasionally to the point where it becomes pure monologue; avoid the poetic style like the plague, and let the reader know that you are avoiding it, that you are breaking up the sentence per se which, because of its rhythm and

length, would sound too pure and grand, would turn into the sustained style which Stendhal ridiculed and detested and in which he saw nothing but affectation, attitudinizing, and ulterior motives not in the least disinterested.

But it is a law of nature that you can only protect yourself against one form of affectation by using another.

The plans and prohibitions he prescribes for himself have one aim, to make us hear a real voice; his own pretension leads him to cram into a book all the symptoms most expressive of *sincerity*. His originality, so far as style is concerned, was to be bold enough to write in accordance with his own *character*, which he knew—and could even *imitate* to perfection.

I do not dislike the tone he created. There are times when I find it enchanting, and it never fails to entertain me; but contrary to the intention of the author, it does so by the comic effect that so much sincerity coupled with a little too much *life* invariably has on me. I confess to finding his accent three or four times too sincere; I sense a determination to be himself, to be genuine to the point of falsity. The genuineness he strives to promote changes imperceptibly under his pen into a tone designed to appear genuine. Truth and the will to truth together form an unstable mixture in which there is a ferment of contradiction and from which, without fail, a falsified product emerges.

How can we avoid selecting what is best out of the *true* we are working on? How we can avoid underlining, rounding off, touching up, adding color, trying to make it clearer, stronger, more disturbing, more intimate, more brutal than the model? *In literature the true is inconceivable.* Sometimes by simplicity, sometimes by oddity, sometimes by an exactness carried too far, sometimes by carelessness, sometimes by the confession of things that are more or less shameful, but al-

ways *selected*—as carefully selected as possible—always and by every means in the author's power, whether he is Pascal, Diderot, Rousseau, or Beyle, and whether the nakedness exhibited is that of a sinner, a cynic, a moralist, or a libertine, it is inevitably lighted, painted, and made up according to all the rules of the mind's theater. We know very well that people only expose themselves for an effect. A great saint who undressed in the market place knew it too. Everything that is contrary to custom is contrary to nature; it implies an effort, a conscious effort, an intention and therefore artifice. A woman undresses as though she were about to go onto the stage.

It follows therefore that there are two methods of falsification: the first is by *embellishment*, the second by the effort to *appear true*.

The second case is perhaps the one that reveals the most urgent pretensions. It is also a sign of despair of arousing public interest by purely literary means. Eroticism is never far from the minds of the utterly frank.

Moreover, the authors of confessions or memoirs or private diaries are invariably taken in by their own desire to shock; and we ourselves are the dupes of such dupes. It is never one's self that anyone wants to present; we know perfectly well that a real person has very little to tell us about what he is. He therefore writes the confessions of somebody else who is more impressive, purer, blacker, livelier, more sensitive, and even more himself than is permissible, for the self has its degrees. Anyone who confesses is a liar and is running away from what is really true, which is something null or shapeless and, in general, blurred. But every confession has an ulterior motive: fame, scandal, an excuse, or propaganda.

Beyle plays a dozen parts in his private theater—the dandy,

the coolly rational man, the connoisseur of the fine arts, the soldier of 1812, the man in love with love, the politician, the historian. He gives himself a hundred pseudonyms, less as a disguise than to have the sensation of living a number of different lives. Like an actor on tour with his wigs, beards, and costumes, he carries round in his suitcase his Bombets, his Brulards, his Dominiques, his ironmongers. . . . In the *Mémoires d'un touriste*, made up as a prosperous traveling salesman, he talks as people do in a public conveyance, plays the economist, gives his views on administration, criticizes and suggests improvements in the plans for the layout of the railways of the future. He enjoys frightening himself about the espionage system of the police, is suspicious of the postal service, uses codes and signs so transparent that they would be comic if his fears were not fictitious and if he didn't want to be frightened. He populated his own life as best he could; and the pretense of being afraid helped him to feel that he was alive. Sometimes his exaggerated taste for mystification and the parade of secrecy reminds us vaguely of Punch. . . .

His temperament, which transformed his life into a perpetual scenario, made him in turn treat all human affairs as comedy. He was supremely sensitive to hypocrisy, and could smell a hundred miles off any suggestion of pretense or deceit in the social sphere. His belief in universal falsehood was unshakable and almost constitutional. He went so far as to seek out and to define the things it is impossible for a man to simulate (personal courage and absolute pleasure).

This highly "conscious" being attached immense value to the "natural." This painter of the double life was always creating types delicious in their simplicity—the Fabrices and the Luciens, people still pure, brave, young, and fresh, caught

at the moment when they enter the world and begin acting in all innocence in the midst of a conspiratorial charade.

He himself acted his own person, and put on his own sincerity. What does being sincere mean? There is practically no difficulty when you are dealing with the relations between individuals; but what about one's relations with oneself? As I have said and repeated here, as soon as the "will" comes into the matter, the *will to be sincere with oneself* is inevitably a principle of falsification.

External sincerity is a pact between the two faces of man, one visible, the other a deduction or a probability. But to give a meaning to the idea of inner sincerity, there must be some sort of operation, some sort of division of the subject in order to introduce an absolute observer of our recent states of mind almost at the moment of their formation. . . . Now the function of this observer is to inform *us* whether the thought we have just had is in conformity or not with the persistent idea that we have, or should have, of ourselves. This crude analysis is sufficient to make explicit some of the conventions at work in the illusion of sincerity. Nor is that all. These very conventions are necessarily borrowed from the external world—for example, from acquired morality (to judge or blame oneself is play-acting).

Comedy and convention consist in substituting *what one knows* for *what one is*—and one does not know what one is.

In short, Stendhal's own sincerity—like all forms of willed sincerity, without exception—was part of the comedy of sincerity he played for himself. To be sincere means ignoring the observer who is the judge in the case, or imagining that he is *off duty*. In this way and in accordance with the promptings of his heart, Stendhal assessed the pretenses of others and felt that he was somehow infinitely *sensitized* to this kind of

"truth" at one remove which can be attributed to anyone; and which anyone would reveal to a witness sufficiently withdrawn into his own reflective consciousness.

Almost every word he heard sounded like a lie in his ears. He could read people like an open book, or imagined he could.

The period was eminently suited to this form of intellectual activity.

Never were circumstances more propitious to every form of social masquerade. Ten different regimes in fifty years. People had lived as best they could under governments whose life was short and rough, all anxious to probe people's hearts and none of them inimical to fraud. People were used to the extraordinary suddenness with which the gravest personalities molted and renewed their plumage, to the abruptness with which badges changed, to the phantasmagoria of power, to the exits and re-entrances of legitimacy, freedom, eagles— of God Himself; to the astonishing spectacle of men reduced to distraction by the different oaths they had taken, divided between their memories, their emotions, their interests, their rancors, and their prognostications. . . . Some of them brought confusion on their heads by wearing a whole scaffolding of different hats and hair styles: wigs, skullcaps, red caps, hats with tricolor plumes, cocked hats, bourgeois hats. They were sometimes surprised, sometimes justified by events; now by the restoration of the fleur-de-lis, now by the backlash of 1815, now by the trickery of 1830, they were kept hanging on the moment, all set to change overnight from proscribers into proscribed, from suspects into magistrates, from ministers into fugitives; they lived through a more or less dangerous farce, and most of them, of all parties and under all sorts

of masks, finished up by no longer believing in anything but money. This *positive* attitude emerged under Louis Philippe, when finally the acquisition of wealth was put forward shamelessly and nakedly as the supreme moral lesson, the ultimate truth, the definitive ethic of half a century of political and social experiment. Stendhal saw the new world established on the ruins of the different regimes. He was in a position to observe the beginning of the reign of talk and business. The parliamentary system was being given a trial—a system which is by nature dramatic, rigorously subordinated to the laws of the theater, entirely made up of harangues and retorts, sudden reversals of opinion; a system based on words, on the emotional approach to events, on the outcome of meetings, and on stage idols. The parties were in the process of formation. It was the moment of the monstrous advent of statistical values, *public opinion*, averages, confused and fluctuating majorities; and the rigging of majorities led to the immediate creation of the art of vitiating and poisoning the sources of power, already far from pure, and of interpreting their unconscious utterances; the reign of abstract myths and their battles, the apparition and antics of black specters and red specters, conjured up, exhibited, and controlled by skillful showmen. . . .

The same period witnessed the loudly trumpeted entry into the political sphere of the twin forces of finance and publicity. The era of big business had dawned. The hour had struck for the vast industrial transformation of the world. But not all the sciences together could have succeeded without the power of the spoken word. On all sides commercial eloquence created the vocation of "gulls" in innumerable varieties. As the campaigns for the issue of shares, prospectuses, and the irresistible publicity multiplied their crude

blandishments, wealth of all sorts was mobilized at the appeal of the jobbers and the joint-stock companies. Public credulity exceeded the wildest expectations.

Even in literature there was a sort of revolution which initiated the Muses into the behavior, violence, and charlatanism of electoral campaigns. Among the poets, factions came into being which adopted the rough and ruthless methods of the political parties. Manifestoes were drawn up. The first night of *Hernani* was a real "public meeting," with partisans and their adversaries well organized, their stations and roles worked out in advance.

This sort of thing did not encourage general frankness. Everyone who counted lied, exaggerated, pretended. How could it have been otherwise?

It was a time when all the highest posts were filled with "turncoats"; decorated with handsome "weathercocks."

The most august tongues had been heard to lie on the most sacred occasions. Swearing either by their swords, on the Gospels, or by the Charter, everybody in turn found themselves compelled to sacrifice solemnly to falsehood. The promises of peace, freedom, and pardon—the pledges of the Allies—all lies. The dispatches of the Grand Army, the proclamations of a succession of authorities, the newspapers of all political shades had lied, were lying, and were to go on lying. People lied on the rostrum, in the pulpit, on the stock exchange, at the Institute; even philosophy lied, even the arts, even style! Chateaubriand and the poetic style lied. Monsieur Victor Hugo and his friends disfigured and inflated the truth every time they opened their mouths.

This brief review of the functions of lying between 1800 and 1840 could be duplicated by any reader with a little

patience simply by choosing sentences from the books, letters, and notes of "Dominique."

His suspicions and his contempt were not confined to his charge of charlatanism against the whole of the politics and almost the whole of the literature of his time. Even the scholars did not always escape. He tells a plausible story somewhere or other of two learned brethren. The ingenious pair agreed to spread the tale that they knew one of those obscure languages —Etruscan or prehistoric Mexican—which are easier to teach than to understand. The powers that be, only too delighted to give the impression of honoring Science and encouraging the talents of those who gave no trouble, loaded them with decorations, pensions, and university chairs.

Nevertheless, Beyle had preserved a somewhat remarkable reverence for mathematics. He had studied briefly for the Polytechnique and had appreciated the beauties of the equation of the second degree. He had hoped, too, that his algebra would enable him to make his escape from Grenoble. He got away by other means; but his brief study had left him with the precious and redoubtable habit of mind which consists of treating *everything vague* as equally null and void— along with all the other unprovable propositions that occupy men's minds.

I observe in passing that the illustrious Lagrange was perhaps the only one of his contemporaries of whom he never spoke except in terms of the utmost respect.

As for the clergy. . . .

The clergy was one of Stendhal's favorite irritants. Sometimes a sly Stendhal describes a bishop looking at himself in a glass, a mitered Narcissus who practices his blessing with

unctuous nobility in front of a mirror in the sacristy; at other times a brutal Stendhal denounces the idiocy or jeers at the silliness of the ecclesiastic. Not even Voltaire spoke in such crude terms of the priesthood; he never went so far as to look into the heart of a priest in search of what he already knew— the lying or the stupid credulity, one or the other of which Beyle is always sure to find there. Apart from the kindly Blanès, the astrologer-abbé, who was a liberal, something of a magician, and slightly heretical, there is not a single priest in Beyle who is not a hypocrite or a fool, or who can possibly be anything else.* There are no exceptions. There is no middle course. It is impossible to imagine a third alternative, a not unfavorable combination, neither immoral nor absurd, of the man and the Order.

The problem is real. In the eyes of people who are indifferent in matters of religion there is a mystery about the priest. The problem exists and precisely because those people who observe religion from outside also exist. The intelligent unbeliever necessarily regards the priest as something of a puzzle, a monster—part man, part angel—who surprises him, makes him smile, and quite often disturbs him. He says to himself: *How is it possible to be a priest?*

The delicate and very real problem of the possibility of the priest deserves a few moments' thought.

It is impossible to think of Stendhal without the question of sincerity coming to mind in one form or another. The problem of the priest—that is to say, of the professional believer—is simply one aspect of the problem of belief. In the

*M. Paul Arbelet has drawn my attention to the fact that the Abbé Chélan in the *Rouge* and the Abbé Pirard must rank with Blanès among the priests in Stendhal who are not without faith or brains. [P. V.]

eyes of the unbeliever the sincerity or intelligence of the be-
liever is always suspect; and the converse is sometimes true.
To the unbeliever it is almost inconceivable that an educated
man, who applies his mind calmly to the subject and is capa-
ble of looking beyond his wishes or his vague fears (or who
sees in them only something personal, organic, and almost
morbid), who is also capable of speaking frankly to himself
and of establishing a proper distinction between the different
spheres and values, does not dismiss as legends or fairy tales
those strange accounts of immemorial or improbable events
which are essential to maintain the authority of all religions,
that he does not realize the brittleness of the proofs and argu-
ments on which dogmas are founded, is not amazed to the
point of denial when he perceives that revelations and decla-
rations literally of infinite importance to man are presented
to him as dangerous riddles, in the manner of the Sphinx,
with such feeble guarantees and in a form so far removed
from what he requires in the case of things that are true.
Nothing is more difficult than to admit all this without reser-
vation, when it concerns someone like ourselves. There is no
doubt that faith exists; but we find ourselves asking with
what it coexists in those in whom it exists. An unbeliever
regards it as a peculiarity, although contagious, and is con-
vinced that the believer with a distinguished or superior
mind, a man like Faraday, who was head of a sect called the
Sandemanians, or Pasteur, must really be a dual personality.

The problem becomes graver still when we turn to the
question of the continuity of faith and its permanent effects.
The unbeliever finds it difficult to accept the fact that sincere
belief can coexist with behavior which is not irreproachable,
just as he finds it difficult to conceive that it can be reconciled
with intellectual rigor and clarity of mind. If therefore he dis-

covers weakness or vice in a believer, he will always be tempted to conclude that the faith of the sinner is mere pretense. The sins of the believer are a sort of *temptation* for the unbeliever—a form of trap which the "psychology" of the one sets for the psychology of the other.

Stendhal *visse, scrisse, e amó* at a time when religious belief was at a low ebb. He witnessed the publication of the *Génie du Christianisme*, and I can well imagine the effect on him of such a dull book and one that had such vast repercussions. With that book Chateaubriand inaugurated the picturesque, romantic mysticism whose literary and even religious effects can still be felt today. But Stendhal possessed in himself everything that was necessary to avoid being taken in by this refurbishing of the beauty and emotional values of faith and worship. He had disagreeable memories of the pious folk he had found so irksome in his childhood. He retained a remarkable confidence in the Encyclopedic spirit and may not have abandoned the high hopes that had been nurtured, in the second half of the eighteenth century, of reducing our knowledge of man to a finite system governed by precise laws, clearly written and capable of being logically construed, built on the model of the elegant and purely analytical constructions by which the Clairauts, the d'Alemberts, and the Lagranges had represented the physical world as it was conceived in their time. He was a very fair incarnation, abstract sensualist that he was, of the protest of the year 1760 against the year 1820 with its dreary sermonizing.

Moreover, as the poet of personal energy, the avowed admirer of the proud and violent deeds of the Convention, and a worshiper of the Bonaparte of the first period, he was not much impressed by past history. He only wanted to preserve its individual traits, the characters of distinguished

persons who were immoderate and strong in themselves alone. It followed necessarily that for everything traditional he had the feelings of all those who take it ill that someone else should have thought, judged, and chosen for them.

For men of this stamp, tradition and religion are by definition antipathetic and even odious. They see them as power founded on *imitation*, and this imitation reinforced, if need be, as Pascal well pointed out and recommended, by *play-acting*: "Follow the practice with which they began; that is, by *behaving exactly as though they were believers*, taking holy water," etc.

(Imagine the expression on Beyle's face when he read that sentence, if he ever did.)

No doubt such men cannot find anything in their hardened hearts which commits them to all these sacrifices of intellect and pride, and which orders the body to go through with its play-acting so that little by little it may bring the soul to truth. They have no insight into that *substance of things hoped for* which, combined with the accepted teachings, the externally prescribed rules, and regular practice, ends by constructing religious belief in a man. All they saw at life's extreme was a highly unpleasant quarter of an hour. *No tomorrow*, they thought, and death only represented for them one of the essential properties of life—that of losing all the others.

We can see that for such minds there exists what I have called the problem of the priest. Stendhal, as I remarked a few moments ago, disposes of it summarily. His intellectual make-up, and the way in which it had inevitably developed his earliest impressions, the vivacity that led him to push his antipathies to extremes and express them in formulas too simple to be true, too clear to be applicable to men, easily

betrayed him into a serious confusion of method. He bases his argument on priests of his own creation. He puts himself in their place, and naturally feels either a faker or feeble-minded. As he was incapable of imagining their faith, he endows them with nothing but credulity. As he knew perfectly well that they were not all foolishly credulous, he brings charges of lying, fraud, and pretense against any who were not.

But though very common, it is manifestly an error to claim to solve by pure reason problems whose elements cannot be enumerated or defined. Only problems of pure algebra can be solved inside oneself and by the mind alone. When we are dealing with real things the point can only be settled by observation. I know from my own experience that there are priests who are genuine and whose intellectual endowment is impressive. I know some of them, and that is sufficient for me. I am not saying that I understand it: I am saying that Stendhal's opinion was based on the mere *accident* that he did not happen to know any priests like mine.

That is how people deceive themselves through the desire for clarity. The example of Stendhal's way of judging priests leads at once to a general observation. The majority of those who flatter themselves that they are experts on the human heart do not distinguish between the insight of which they are so proud and an unfavorable attitude toward mankind. They look at it with a jaundiced or an ironic eye. Nothing, to be sure, is better calculated to give the impression of being a *psychologist* than a persistent attitude of *denigration*. By this often convenient rule, to be clear-sighted means to look on the dark side of things.

In this respect (a charming notion for those who like odd juxtapositions) Beyle can be ranged with those Fathers and Doctors of the Church who have shown least indulgence for

mankind and were the most rigorous masters of moral
theology. The form and intention are very different in the
two cases, but the look of suspicion and the almost guilty
wish to believe the worst are the same. The worst is the food
of critical minds. Evil is their prey. So for them it has to be
the rule. A "psychologist" à la Stendhal, thoroughgoing
sensualist though he be, needs the badness of our human
nature. What would become of men of wit if there were no
original sin?

In order to create a deeper, or what one might call a more
hard-bitten, idea of society, Balzac, who was even gloomier
in outlook, collected round him all those whose job it was to
be observers and discoverers of wickedness and shame: the
confessor, the doctor, the lawyer, the judge, the undercover
man, all of them trained to find, to describe, and in a sense to
minister to the dregs of society. Sometimes when I read Bal-
zac I have *second sight*, and, as it were, a lateral vision of a vast
and crowded opera house—all a mass of shoulders, light,
glitter, velvet, men and women from the smartest society,
exposed to some hypersensitive eye. A dark gentleman with
a sinister look, and very much alone, looks on and reads the
minds of the dazzling throng. All those groups gilded with
light, throwing rich shadows, the faces, the flesh, the jewels,
the seductive whispers, the fixed smiles are nothing in his
eyes, turned on the splendid gathering, mercilessly transform-
ing it into a hideous collection of vices, wretchedness, and
secret crimes. Wherever he looks, he sees nothing but evil,
shameful lives, failures; he sees adultery, debts, abortions,
syphilis and cancer, imbecility and lust.

But however searching a look of this kind may be, it is
to my mind too simple and systematic. Every time we accuse
and judge . . . we miss the heart of the matter.

Someone ought to do "Stendhal's Soliloquy." It would consist of sentences taken from every part of his work and joined together. We should see all his problems at once.

"To live. To please. To be loved. To love. To write. Not to be fooled. To be oneself—and nevertheless *arrive*. How to get oneself read? How to get on, when you hate or despise all factions.

"Where to live? Italy is under the thumb of princes and priests. The climate of Paris is ghastly, and everybody there a schemer. Too little passion, too much vanity. You can be a man of wit there.

"All that is left is the future. (He managed to keep the illusion of posterity.) I must work out a policy of future fame. In fifty years everyone will like what I like now. What makes me what I am will then appeal to the minds that determine ultimate fame. They will despise what is admired today. They will laugh at Maistre and Bonald. Chateaubriand and the poetic style will have become impossible. And then too, people will be bored. We shall have two Chambers and the American style of republicanism will have triumphed everywhere. Hypocrisy will have changed masks.

"Nevertheless, I do have to hold on, get through half a century. How can I get through forty years of Romanticism without perishing in the process, so as to arrive at literary immortality? There will have to be a chain of admirers, a sect of the *happy few* (to see him through to the period of Taine and Paul Bourget, to the time when that nervous poet Nietzsche, a German-speaking Slav, taking to the idea of energy as to a drug, will transmute Stendhal's type of cosmopolitan into the Good European)."

This Beyle was a highly entertaining person, possessed by a

great desire to scandalize, along with more refined ambitions. He seldom failed to point out that his reader ought to take offense at what he said. He was by no means without the desired effect. He provoked artists by his style, the powers that be by his disrespect, women by his cynicism and his strategy. The loquacity, the opinions, the "cheek" of this man of so much wit sometimes remind us of those prehistoric commercial travelers who dazzled and exasperated their corner of the inn table in the days of the last stagecoaches and the first railways. But this Gaudissart who puts up at the *Grand Hôtel de l'Europe et de l'Amour* is an *original* of the first order. What he deals out is alive; it will live and he will live. His stock of singular and glittering goods will excite many a philosophical mind. Serious men will do their utmost to make themselves brisk and sharp like him.

In my view, Henri Beyle is much more a type of mind than a man of letters. He is too radically himself to be reducible to a writer. That is why he rouses strong likes and dislikes, and why I like him.

I have seen Pierre Louÿs heap insults on his intolerable prose, fling *Le Rouge et le Noir* on the floor and stamp on it with a strange and perhaps justifiable fury. . . .

But Stendhal, such as he is and whatever he is, has become, in spite of the Muses, in spite of his pen and almost in spite of himself, one of the demigods of our literature, a master of that ardent and abstract style which is drier and lighter than any other, and characteristic of the French. His work is of a kind that deals only in actions and ideas, disdains ornament, laughs at harmony and formal balance. It is concentrated in the flash, the phrase, the tone, the sting; it multiplies the short cuts and the lightning reactions of the mind. It is always fast-moving, quick to be insolent; it seems ageless and in a sense

without substance; it is personal to the extreme, directly *centered* in the author, as disconcerting as a retort, avoiding both the dogmatic and the poetic, which it finds about equally detestable.

We should never have done with Stendhal. I can think of no higher praise.

Gérard de Nerval

I CAN SEE myself—no, I only remember—sitting on a pale wicker chair with tapering coral-colored legs, my heels hooked over the rail and my head between my fists, always reading the same books: a fat volume published in 1840 which had the cheek to call itself *The Complete Works of Victor Hugo* (a pirated edition from Belgium); and a "Michel-Lévy" with a sickly green cover, *La Bohème Galante*, that delicious, that inexhaustible collection of tales in which I found all the charm and remoteness from reality which a twelve-year-old craves.

The mention of Nerval's name brings back to me the memory of the faded green of that copy, and moved by the color, I relive those absurd and exciting moments snatched from boredom, from homework, from the everyday world by the magic of words. I passed from the appalling *Bug-Jargal* and the dreadful *Han d'Islande* to medieval Paris and back again: to the Pont Neuf when it was still new, to all the sinister, moving, fantastic, and irrefutable things suggested by the marvelous story of that "Enchanted Hand" which, freshly severed by the executioner and fallen from the corpse of the hanged man, began to run on its five fingers like a scurrying crab, vanishing between the feet of curious onlookers. I could draw it. . . . I can imagine the etching that a master could make of it. I like to dream of the liberation of that organ of doing and

grasping, the delight of a hand finally set free and boldly seeking action in the great world. I must confess that this strange indulgence of the mind (which sometimes carries me quite far) takes hold of me often when, listening not at all, I gaze at the fingers of a virtuoso careering across a keyboard.

But in that beloved *Bohème Galante* I was also particularly fond of one truly delightful chapter which was my introduction to the most exquisitely poetic region of France, the Valois country, and at the same time to a kind of literature that must be called "popular"—a horrible word for so refined a work. Does anyone realize that those few pages devoted to the old French ballads have not been without their influence on certain poets who were in their twenties when I was twelve years old? Moréas knew them well; others, too.

Nerval was the first to bring these delicious things to light. Needless to say, not one of our anthologies of poetry has found a corner for these spontaneous products of the love of singing. There are among them some which give me the impression of a thing that is perfect in its own essence. I find in them the impulsive freshness of a completely natural and joyous burst of life, which, by force of contrast, defines and almost predicts the advent of those expertly wrought poems of ours which cannot do without meditation and abstract thought on the part of their authors, nor cultivation and lively attention on the part of the reader. How can it be that a stream of poetry so pure and so graciously fluent should have dried up, and that our people should appear to be condemned forever to poetic sterility, helplessly exposed to what is basest, and becoming even baser, in the ignoble storehouse of trash and vulgarity?

There was also among the handful of books that brought me such excitement in those days a little volume in very poor condition about which I must say a word or two because, for reasons which are not purely chronological, it is often associated in my memory with the work of Nerval. This frayed pamphlet was called *Almanach Prophétique*. It was illustrated by a few delightfully bewitching woodcuts. It contained certain lucubrations meant to be frightening, a few recipes for exorcism and arithmomancy, some anecdotes in which the devil played a part, and finally the disturbingly arresting tale —I am unable to say in how far it was "historical"—about the King of Prussia in a Masonic lodge at Verdun, where someone called up the ghost of Frederick the Great before his eyes and made it speak to him. . . .

All the foggy and intoxicating stuff in that poor almanac was sublimed in Nerval's mind.

In that mind racked with doubts and fears, light and shadow were curiously distributed. I have already spoken of his exquisite taste for the more naïve voices among French poets. He loved with the same love the woods and streams which surround Senlis, and the noble Forest of Compiègne, where one night I saw in a marshy clearing the full moon weaving in veils of mist a rainbow whose cold colors were shot with silver. The wonder of that icy specter would no doubt have delighted Nerval, a great lover of those legendary scenes usually situated on the banks of the Rhine. The tales and *lieder* which that river has inspired were all the more familiar to him because he possessed an excellent knowledge of the German language. We know what high praise he received from Goethe for his translation of the First Part of *Faust*. He was perhaps the only French Romantic who really knew the

Germany of the lyric poets and philosophers from which our own Romantic Movement sprang. His compounded erudition, overflowing all the critical limits, added little by little to his exact linguistic knowledge *a realm of uncertainty* where the most curious and most seductive products of world thought were mingled in a sort of *spectral learning* tinged with theurgy, gnosis, the cabala, deciphered myths, and every kind of mystery that could be absorbed by a mind longing too avidly for light. Neither magic nor the blandishments of the arcane sciences and the perspectives opened up by the boldest speculations escaped his craving for the marvelous.

For a mind of this nature, in which curiosity is only a form of anxiety, anything that is hidden, veiled, sealed, has a special attraction, and such people cannot help thinking that the value of a particular piece of knowledge is directly dependent on its difficulty of access. They pore over hermetic writings and believe in the secrets of secret societies. At the supposed source of such traditions, Nerval could imagine a hieratic Egypt where the priests who ruled in the shadow of the Pharaohs must have possessed a storehouse of profound and fearful power. Yet very nearly in his own day, and not at all buried in the fabulous mists of time, the idea of a science of the initiatory sciences and of a truth hidden from the eyes of the vulgar, handed on from one of the elect to another, and revived or rediscovered from time to time by some unexpected revelation, had been if not originated, at any rate developed, preserved, and elaborated with extraordinary fervor. This cult of mystery reached its peak no more than a few years before his birth. If we played the game of affinity of minds, and tried to establish similar tendencies in the men of the first half of the nineteenth century and those of the preceding century, it would be easy to pick out in Nerval more than one trait relating him to the contemporaries of Swedenborg, Saint-

Martin, the theosophists and the mystics over whose works he had perhaps brooded too much, and some of whom appear in his book *Les Illuminés*. He was not the only man between 1830 and 1850 to seek light in the contemplation of darkness. At that time, while Stendhal continued in his own way a certain free, lively, positive vein of lucidity, which may perhaps have derived from Diderot or Beaumarchais, Balzac, in more than one portion of his vast work, displays a curiosity that does not always seem purely literary. He is interested in strange experiments; he believes in talismans; he creates in *Louis Lambert* a sort of hero of the unauthorized contemplative life, and invents or borrows the magical, highly disagreeable story of the *Peau de Chagrin*.

At this point a most delicate question arises. Must we regard a taste for the occult, a belief in extraordinary but hidden phenomena, a belief in beings beyond nature, and in their manifestations, as a symptom of mental debility or derangement? Good sense no doubt demands that the problem should be treated statistically. How many genuine madmen have been found among the large number of people who apply themselves seriously to the study of the invisible world? Until the end of a very long life, Swedenborg lived in a way which was completely normal: a member of various academies, a scholar, an engineer of repute, a high official, a man of the world, his visions were as separate from his behavior in society as our dreams are from our own. Nerval, on the other hand, appears in middle life to have lost from time to time all control over his inner activity. But he would recover and was aware that he had been raving. In these matters, I think that we should be very circumspect in applying the fallacious principle of causality. Can certain ideas lead to a permanent dislocation of normal functions, or can certain pathological

states generate certain ideas (not confused, but quite lucid ideas)? It is impossible to treat these problems with the necessary intellectual rigor; *we do not even know how to state them.*

Moreover, the case of Nerval is complicated by "literary factors." Gérard was a writer. *He was therefore acutely sensitive* to everything which, whether coming to him in the form of insight or thought, derived its value from being a product of the resources of language. *Homo Scriptor*, the *man with a pen*, cannot help thinking about the effect on his reader of what he puts down on paper. He gambles, unconsciously or otherwise, on the power of words. But the certainty that such a calculation must have taken place inevitably awakens in the critical reader a certain presumption of *qualified sincerity*: he senses, alike in the mystic, mystagogue, initiate, leader of men, or director of souls *who writes*, a desire, whether avowed or hidden, to misuse their powers of expression: he knows that the intention or the vocation to influence others makes us other than ourselves. . . .

I am not at all suggesting that Gérard transmitted to us rather more of the invisible world than he actually saw; but I cannot forget that literature corrupts everything it deals with, since it is in its essence an unnatural development of the powers of language, and that there is no form of sincerity, good faith, or good will that it can express which may not leave us with the thought that they are the most deliberate, the most cunning of artifices. It does not seem impossible that the beautiful and "inspired" pages to be found in *Aurélia* and the *Filles du feu* were the result of pure talent. Literature has shown itself marvelously able in all ages to play with the accepted idea of madness. Many writers today cultivate in themselves a carefully limited form of dementia: they invest it with the value of *second sight*, and with little trouble acquire the reputation or dignity of "seers." The "state of song" is

today less sought after by poets than the "state of frenzy." It is one of the most interesting of literary fashions: it demonstrates the possibility of inducing *artificial paranoia* and crystallizing it in dazzling quasi-poems difficult to distinguish one from another. Some writers have taken the Book of Enoch and the Apocalypse as their models—a choice more than sufficiently explained by our demented era.

The present state of our literary sensibility has endowed Nerval with a belated celebrity which is likely to prove lasting. For far too long his unhappy end, and the legend associated with it, were just enough to preserve his name from oblivion. But during the past thirty or forty years he has begun to be read, and to be reprinted, and his best lines are learned by heart; he is loved.

His work is small in bulk. And we have to admit that the little there is of it is contained in a few dozen stanzas. The rest is very weak indeed; it will not stand up to scrutiny and dissolves into facile lyrics, or merely arouses pity for a romantic content and rhetoric which all Hugo's genius was scarcely sufficient to sustain, and which Baudelaire had the wit to do without. Under the title of *La Tête armée*, which with Nerval remains no more than an exciting announcement, Hugo would no doubt have produced something extraordinary. I must, however, extract from that poem these strange lines, in which a certain incoherence tempts us to re-read in spite of ourselves:

Alors on vit sortir du fond du Purgatoire
Un jeune homme inondé des pleurs de la Victoire
Qui tendit sa main pure aux monarques des Cieux.

It is possible to like this mythical concoction.

But what survives, and will survive, of Nerval as a poet is concentrated in the famous *Desdichado*, in *Artémis*, and in the *Vers dorés*.

That charming "Neapolitan saint with her hands full of fire" (rays of gilded wood), and the skillful symmetry which brings into contrast "the sighs of the saint and the cries of the fairy," these will not be forgotten; and we could go on meditating forever on "the pure spirit which grows under the skin of stones."

The undoubted charm of these few sonnets, which are like nothing else that I know in our literature, lies perhaps in the impression they create of a personality at once weak and violent, learned and naïve, rebellious and masked, whose undefined yet genuine and profound despair mingles in his lamentations every form of symbolic expression suggested by his imaginary memories of vanished lives. He commands the whole chaotic treasure house of occult erudition shining out of the darkness: the esoterics of antiquity, Christian allegory, the magic and the fairy tales of the Middle Ages, the poetry of pantheism. This composite learning, whose elements are all dubious and suspect when considered individually, nevertheless constitutes a very rich and heady vein of lyricism. The Saint, the Fairy, the Knight of Death, the Siren and the Sibyl, Christ and the god Kneph—all those names brought together in a few lines of verse, and the poet, identifying himself by a word with each of them, gives a confused, mysterious, and poignant sensation of metempsychosis, of the syncretic evocation of dead men or legendary beings coming vaguely to life on the borderline between faked memory and poetic creation. We are reminded of a phase in the dissociation of acquired ideas, in which they all separate or combine or substitute one for another, according to the highly flexible laws of a dream at whose whim Philosophy turns into

Fable as easily as Fable becomes Philosophy, while if the Muses take a hand, Rhythm, Number, and Rhyme prepare, like a carrying wave, to sustain upon the forms of prosody —which are instances of complete harmony between the Voice, which is an act, and Hearing, which is a sensation— the modulations of the soul, absorbing into their pattern the surprise of the play of wit and chance.

But an appalling distress is the common theme of these poems, whose phantasmagoria and strange naturalistic mysticism reveal far more than they hide of the sorry state of a sensibility subjected to the rigors of destitution and the terrible promptings of morbid anxiety. The painful impression left upon us from reading them is only aggravated by what we know of Nerval's gruesome death.

When as a child I used to read the *Bohème Galante*, I was unaware of the fate of the author of that delightful book. Méryon, another great artist whose mind was haunted by visions and fearful shadows, has done a powerful etching of the surroundings of the Mortuary where the scene of January 26, 1855, took place. "Death by hanging," runs the entry in the Mortuary register. It was terribly cold—below freezing. The corpse had no overcoat. It was in *evening dress*. It was found to be wearing two flannel vests under two calico shirts. These are cruel details. One thinks of Edgar Poe when, on an equally cold day, he followed his wife's coffin, wearing the shawl in which she died. He had nothing else to wear.

Lithography is, perhaps, of all the methods of illustrating a book, the one best suited to poetry. Wood and copper have their virtues: they are very good for prose. But poetry is not thought; it is the divinization of the Voice. It will therefore show its preference for an art which operates by just touching the surface of stone, an art whose vivid and flexible line,

thanks to the tender nature of the pencil that draws it, can be inflected like the speaking voice, may fade away at times like a murmur in the shadows, and at other times, by using blanks, deepen them to the pure black of absolute silence.

Luc Albert Moreau answered the appeal of poetry as a man whose artist's heart was divided between two powers of enchantment: Voice, Line, Fiction, and Form clash and harmonize within him. He has his own way of loving his poets, which is to bring them before his inner eye, while his hand, in expectation of the coming insight, suspended above the fine grain of the stone, awaits the command of the dream their works create.

Just as he has done with Rimbaud, he is now interpreting Nerval, surrounding him with invented figures, and with a respect, a discretion, a rightness of feeling which I find moving, but on which I hardly dare to compliment him. I know only too well that in our time it is not permissible to talk about *taste*. That kind of praise, which was once regarded as the supreme compliment, is now treated as a sort of insult. But what does an age matter, when after all one's only aim is to get away from it, and when the act of taking up a pen or pencil has meaning and serious value only when it is directed against what exists in the present, and is dedicated to some century in the indefinite future. . . .

As Goethe enjoyed his *Faust* transposed into the language of Nerval, Nerval no doubt would gaze with an enchanted eye on the images from his *Chimères* filtered through the mind and pencil of Luc Albert Moreau.

The Temptation of (St.) Flaubert

I confess to a weakness for *The Temptation of St. Anthony*. I may as well admit straight away that I have never cared for either *Salammbô* or *Bovary*, the one with its learned, gruesome, and extravagant imagery, or the other with its "truth" of a minutely reconstructed mediocrity.

Flaubert shared with his age a belief in the value of the "historical document" and in the raw observation of the present. But such things are vain idols. The only thing that is real in art is the art.

The best fellow in the world and a very tolerable artist, but without much grace or profundity of mind, Flaubert was defenseless against the very simple formulas propounded by Realism and against the naïve sense of authority which imagines that it can base itself on vast reading and "textual criticism."

The Realism fashionable in the 1850s saw little or no distinction between the precise observation practiced by scientists and the crude unselective view of things as they appear to the ordinary eye; it confused the two, and its policy was to treat them as though they were identical, to use them as a weapon against the passion for embellishment and exaggeration it had discovered and condemned in Romanticism. But

"scientific" observation requires accurate working methods capable of transforming phenomena into usable intellectual products; it is a matter of changing things into numbers, and numbers into laws. Literature, on the other hand, which aims at immediate, instantaneous effects, seeks an entirely different "truth," one that is true for everybody and therefore cannot diverge from the common view of things—from what can be expressed in ordinary language. But the writer's ambition must necessarily be to distinguish himself from the common run, whereas ordinary language is in everybody's mouth and the common view of things is as worthless as the air that everybody breathes. This conflict between the fundamental tenet of Realism—preoccupation with the common-place—and the will of every writer to turn himself into an exceptional being, a specially endowed personality, drove the realists to an interest in the refinements of style. They created the artistic style. They lavished a care and industry, a subtlety and virtuosity, quite admirable in themselves, on the description of the most ordinary and sometimes the most trivial of objects; but they did so without realizing that in this way they were striving for something which lay outside their principles, that they were inventing another version of "the true," a truth of their own manufacture which was completely fictitious. In fact, they placed the crudest of characters, who were incapable of taking the slightest interest in color or enjoying the shapes of things, in settings whose description required a painter's eye, a capacity for feeling which belongs to the sensitive individual who responds to precisely those things that escape the ordinary man. Thus their peasants and their *petits bourgeois* lived and moved in a world which they were as incapable of seeing as an illiterate man is of deciphering a page of print. If they spoke, their fatuous remarks and

clichés were encased in a highly elaborate style composed of rare terms and studied rhythms whose every word was carefully weighed, betraying its self-regard and its desire to be noticed. Realism ended curiously enough by giving an impression of deliberate artifice.

One of its most disconcerting manifestations was the one to which I referred a few moments ago and which lies in mistaking for "reality" the data that we find in "historical documents" belonging to some more or less remote period of history, and trying to reconstruct, with their help, a work which would give the impression of conveying "the truth" about that period. I find nothing more distressing than to imagine the amount of work that went into building a story on the illusory foundations of an erudition always more pointless than any fantasy. All pure fantasy arises from what is most authentic in human nature—the desire to be happy—and takes its course through the hidden propensities of the diverse modes of sensibility of which we are made up. We invent only what can and wants to be invented. But the forced products of erudition are necessarily impure, since the hazards which provide or withhold the documents, the conjectures which go to their interpretation, the translation which falsifies them, all become mixed up with the aims, interests, and passions of the scholar, to say nothing of those of the scribe, the evangelist, or the copyist. This brand of production is the paradise of the middleman. . . .

That is the trouble with *Salammbô*, which worries me when I read it. I get far more pleasure from tales of a quite frankly fabulous antiquity, like *The Princess of Babylon*, or Villiers' "Akëdysséril," books that do not make us think of other books.

(What I have said about truth in literature is equally applicable to works that lay claim to the "truth" of inner observation. Stendhal flattered himself on knowing the human heart, that is, on not merely inventing it. But the things that interest us in him are the things that Stendhal does in fact invent. As for fitting them into an organic system of knowledge of mankind, such an aim presupposes either extremely modest requirements with respect to that knowledge, or a confusion such as we might make between our actual enjoyment of a delicious dish exquisitely prepared by an expert cook and the definite knowledge that comes from an exact and impersonal chemical analysis of the ingredients.)

It is not impossible that some inkling of the difficulties created by the desire for realism in art, and the contradictions which emerge as soon as this desire becomes imperative, encouraged Flaubert in his idea of writing a *Temptation of St. Anthony*. The "Temptation"—a temptation that lasted all his life—was like a personal antidote against the boredom (which he admits) of writing his novels of contemporary manners, erecting stylistic monuments to the banality of provincial bourgeois life.

There was one other thing that may have spurred him on. I am not thinking of Brueghel's picture, which he saw at the Balbi Palace at Genoa in 1845. That naïve and complicated painting, with its conglomeration of monstrous details—horned devils, hideous animals, amorous ladies, the whole of that superficial and sometimes amusing phantasmagoria—may have awakened in him a taste for *diableries* and descriptions of impossible beings: incarnate sins, all the aberrations of fear, desire, remorse; but the real impulse that led him

to conceive and to embark on the work seems to me to have come from reading Goethe's *Faust*. There is a similarity of origin and an obvious kinship between the subjects of *Faust* and the *Temptation*: the popular and primitive origin, the itinerant life of the two legends, which might be arranged in the form of "pendants" under the common rubric: Man and the Devil. In the *Temptation* the devil attacks the faith of the hermit and swamps his night with despairing visions, with contradictory doctrines and beliefs, with lewd and corrupting promises. But Faust has already read and experienced everything, already burned everything that can be worshiped. He has exhausted in himself everything the devil suggests or reveals by means of images to Anthony, so that, to begin with, the only thing left which can attract him is love in its most juvenile form (which seems to me rather surprising). In the end, he manages to work up, as a final excuse for his love of life, a sort of aesthetic passion, a supreme thirst for Beauty, once the emptiness of political power and the conjuring tricks of finance have been revealed by his Mephistophelian experience of them. Faust is reduced to hunting for something that could really tempt him; Anthony would much rather not be tempted at all.

Flaubert seems to me to have had no more than a glimpse of what the subject of the *Temptation* had to offer in the way of themes, possibilities, and opportunities for producing a really great work. His scrupulous concern for accuracy and verifying references alone shows how lacking he was in the decisive spirit and the constructive will which were essential for the invention and manufacture of a literary machine of great power.

A too obvious desire to impress by the number of episodes, apparitions, transformation scenes, arguments, and conflicting voices creates in the reader the growing sensation that he is trapped in a library where all the books, suddenly let loose in a wild uproar, bellow their billions of words at the same moment, and the rebellious portfolios fly open and, all together, disgorge their engravings and drawings. "He's read too much," we say of the author, as we say of the tipsy man that he's drunk too much.

But Goethe, speaking in *Eckermann*, said of his "Walpurgis Night": "An infinite number of mythological figures are jostling one another to get in, but I keep a sharp watch on myself. And I only admit those who provide the eye with the images I am looking for."

Such wisdom is not to be found in the *Temptation*. Flaubert was always haunted by the Demon of encyclopedic knowledge, which he tried to exorcise by writing *Bouvard and Pécuchet*. In order to make Anthony impressive, it was not sufficient to turn over the pages of the great secondhand authorities, the thick dictionaries of the kind produced by Bayle, Moreri, Trévoux, and the like; he had to scrutinize as many original texts as he could lay hands on. He made himself positively drunk with notes and memoranda. But all the work he put in on the hordes of faces and formulas which spread desolation over the hermit's night; all the mental energy he expended on the innumerable entries of the demoniac ballet, the themes of gods and deities, heresiarchs and allegorical monsters, he deducted from or denied to the hero himself, who remains a poor and pitiable victim in the midst of the infernal turmoil of phantasms and errors.

We have to admit that Anthony hardly exists.

His reactions are disconcerting in their feebleness. We are astonished that he is not more attracted or more dazzled by the spectacle, or more irritated or indignant at what he sees and hears; that he finds neither invective, mockery, nor violently ejaculated prayers to hurl at the obscene masquerade, at the elegant phrases pursuing him with a revolting stream of blasphemy. His passiveness is deadly; he neither yields nor resists; he waits for the end of the nightmare, during which he simply makes a few feeble exclamations from time to time. Everyone of his retorts is a defeat, and like the Queen of Sheba, we feel a fearful urge to pinch him.

(Perhaps this makes him more "real," that is to say, more like the average man? Are we not living in a rather horrible and entirely absurd dream? And what are we doing about it?)

Flaubert gives the impression of being carried away by the accessories at the expense of the main point. He was diverted by the décors, the contrasts, the "amusing" accents of detail, which he had picked up here and there in books he had seldom or only carelessly read. Thus, like Anthony himself (but an Anthony who succumbs), he lost his soul—I mean the soul of his subject, which was its capacity to develop into a masterpiece. He spoiled one of the finest possible dramas, a work of the first order which was crying out to be written. By not making up his mind above all else to endow his hero with real vitality, he neglected the very substance of his theme; he failed to respond to the depth of its appeal. What was the real problem? Nothing less than to communicate what might be called the physiology of temptation, the whole fundamental machinery in which colors, flavors, heat and cold, silence and

noise, truth and falsity, good and evil, play the part of forces and take root in us in the form of constantly impending conflicts. Clearly, all "temptation" is the result of seeing or thinking of something that arouses in us the sensation of craving it. It creates a need which previously either did not exist or was dormant, and so we are changed at a single point, solicited by one of our faculties, and all the rest of our being is carried away by the part that has been excited. In Breughel the glutton's neck stretches out long and thin toward the pudding that draws his eye, lures his nostrils, and we feel that the whole of his vast body will follow his head, which will already have connected with the object of his gaze. In nature, the roots of plants thrust down toward moisture, their tops rise toward the sun, and the plant grows from one imbalance to another, from one appetite to another. The amoeba changes shape, lengthening toward its tiny prey, obeying the thing it is about to transmute, then draws up to its outstretched pseudopod and gathers itself together again. This mechanism is the same for the whole of living nature; the Devil, alas, is nature herself, and temptation is the most obvious, the most constant, and the most inescapable of the conditions of life! To live means at every moment to be in need of something—to change ourselves in order to get it—and thus once more to place ourselves in the position of needing something. We live on instability, by instability, through instability; that is the whole business of Sensibility, which is the diabolical mainspring of life in organized beings. What could be more extraordinary to try to conceive, what more "poetic" material could be found, than this irreducible force which is everything for every one of us, which coincides exactly with ourselves, which sets us in motion, which speaks to us, and to itself in us, which assumes the forms of pleasure, pain, need,

disgust, hope, strength or weakness, determines our scale of values, and makes us into angels or beasts according to the time of day? I am thinking of the variety, the intensity, the versatility of our sensitive substance, of its infinite possibilities, of its innumerable *relays*, by whose interplay it divides against itself, deceives itself, multiplies the forms of its desire or rejection, transforms itself into intelligence, language, symbolism, which it develops and combines to create strange abstract worlds. I do not doubt that Flaubert was aware of the depth of his subject, but you might almost say that he was afraid to plunge into it, down to that depth at which everything that can be learned ceases to count. He therefore lost his way among too many books and too many myths; and that is where he lost sight of his strategy—I mean the unity of his composition which could only reside in an Anthony in whom Satan would have been one of the souls. . . . This work of his remains a diverse collection of moments and fragments; but among them there are some which were written to last forever. Such as it is, I regard it with reverence, and I never open it without finding reasons for admiring the author more than his book.

Villon and Verlaine

NOTHING IS SIMPLER, and until recently nothing would have appeared more natural, than to compare François Villon and Paul Verlaine. It is child's play to the connoisseur of historical parallels, that is to say, imaginary parallels, to show that these two literary figures resemble one another. Both are admirable poets; both were rascals; the work of both is a mixture of the most pious feelings with descriptions or observations which are exceedingly frank; and both pass from one to the other tone with extraordinary ease. Both are truly masters of their art and of the language of their time, which they use like men in whom culture is combined with an instinctive sense of the living language, of the very speech of the people among whom they lived, which creates, modifies, and blends words and forms to its own fancy. Both have an adequate knowledge of Latin and an excellent command of slang; both haunt church or tavern according to their mood; and both, for very different reasons, found themselves condemned to harsh confinement, where they managed not so much to make amends for their faults as to extract from them their poetic essence of remorse, regret, and fear. Both fall, repent, fall again, and rise up great poets! The parallel suggests itself and works out quite well.

But what can be brought together and superposed so eas-

ily and so speciously can be separated and dissociated without great difficulty. It would be a mistake to attach any great importance to it. Villon and Verlaine no doubt balance each other quite neatly in some fanciful edifice of French literature where we might amuse ourselves by the symmetrical arrangement of our great men, carefully chosen and coupled, sometimes on account of their supposed contrasts: Corneille and Racine, Bossuet and Fénelon, Hugo and Lamartine; at other times on account of their resemblances, like the two whom we are discussing. It is pleasing to the eye, until a moment of reflection reveals how ill these neat arrangements hold together and how pointless they are. I am of course simply making these observations to put you on your guard against the temptation and the danger of confusing a purely . . . decorative rhetorical device with any genuine critical method that may produce positive results.

I must add that the Villon-Verlaine parallel, this obvious and attractive conjunction of the two exceptional beings I am to talk about, though it holds together reasonably well and can be reinforced by certain biographical details, weakens or collapses as soon as we compare their works in the same way that we have compared the men—as I shall try to show you in a few moments.

In short, the idea of juxtaposing them comes from partial resemblances between their lives, and has led me to do something here of which I am usually rather critical. I consider— and it is one of my paradoxes—that a knowledge of the lives of poets is irrelevant, if not actually detrimental, to the proper use of their work, which lies either in enjoyment or in what we may learn about the problems of art. What do I care about Racine's love affairs? It is *Phèdre* that matters. What do I care about his raw materials, which can be found more or

less anywhere? It is his talent and his power of transforming his material which moves me and makes me envy him. All the passion in the world, all the incidents, even the most moving, of a man's life are incapable of producing a single fine line. Even in the most favorable circumstances, it is not the extent to which the authors are human that gives their work its value and its enduring qualities; *it is the extent to which they are a little more than human*. And if I have said that curiosity about their lives may be harmful, it is because it is too often an opportunity or an excuse or a device for not making a detailed and functional study of their poems. We think we have done justice to these when in fact all that we have done is to avoid them, to refuse contact with them, and by the devious route of tracking down an author's ancestors and friends, or dealing with his troubles or his profession, to dodge the main issue in pursuit of the trivial. We know nothing about Homer the man. The *Odyssey* loses nothing of its marine beauty on that account. . . . What do we know of the poets of the Bible; of the author of Ecclesiastes or the Song of Songs? The venerable texts lose none of their beauty for that. And what do we know of Shakespeare? Not even whether he wrote *Hamlet*.

But this time the biographical problem is inescapable. It forces itself upon us, and I have to do the very thing I have just been condemning.

For the double case of Verlaine-Villon is a singular case. It has a rare and remarkable character. A very important part of their respective works is concerned with their biography, and the works of both are no doubt autobiographical at more than one point. They both make definite confessions. We are not certain that these admissions are always accurate. If they tell

the truth, they do not tell the whole truth, and they do not tell nothing but the truth. An artist selects even when he makes a confession. Perhaps most of all when he makes a confession. Here and there he lightens or darkens the colors. . . .

I have said that the case is rare. The majority of poets, to be sure, talk about themselves a great deal; while those among them who are lyric poets never talk about anything else. If it comes to that, about whom and about what could they talk? Lyric poetry is the voice of the *Ego* speaking in the purest if not the loftiest tones. But such poets speak of themselves in the same way as musicians, that is to say, by condensing the emotions roused by all the particular events in their lives into an intimate substance of universal experience. To read them, it is enough to have delighted in the light of day, to have been happy, and, still more, unhappy; to have desired and possessed, lost and regretted—to have felt the few very simple sensations of life, which are common to all men and each of which corresponds to one chord of the lyre. . . .

That is enough in general, but it is not enough for Villon. The fact was noticed long ago, indeed more than four centuries ago, for Clément Marot had already observed that, in order to "know and understand" a large part of Villon's work, "it would have been necessary to live in Paris in his time and to have known the places, things, and men of whom he speaks; the more these are forgotten the less the skill of the lays will be appreciated. For this reason, anyone who wishes to write a work that will last a long time should not take as his subject such base and particular things."

This means that we are bound to concern ourselves with the life and adventures of François Villon, and to try to reconstruct them in the light of the details that he gives, or to

unravel the allusions that he is continually making. He cites the actual names of people who fortunately, or unfortunately, were involved in his checkered career; he thanks some of them, curses or pokes fun at others; names the taverns he haunted, and in a few words always marvelously well chosen, describes the different parts and the appearance of the city. All this is intimately incorporated in his poetry, inseparable from it, and often makes it almost unintelligible to anyone who cannot imagine the Paris of the period, with its picturesque and its sinister qualities. I think that to read a few chapters of *Notre Dame de Paris* might not be a bad introduction to reading Villon. Hugo seems to me to have seen clearly, or clearly imagined, with his customary power and precision in the realm of the fantastic, the Paris of the end of the fifteenth century. But I must send you first and foremost to the admirable work of M. Pierre Champion, where you will find everything that is known about Villon and the Paris of his time.

The difficulties that face us in Villon's text are not due merely to the difference of the times or the altered aspect of things, but also belong to the particular character of the author. For this witty Parisian was a redoubtable individual. He is no student or bourgeois who writes verse, gets into a few scrapes, and confines the risks to that, as he confines his impressions to those of a man of his time and condition. Maître Villon was an exceptional person, for it is exceptional among writers (though we are highly adventurous in ideas) for a poet to be a kind of brigand, an acknowledged criminal, strongly suspected of a deviant sort of vagrancy, a member of terrifying gangs, living by theft, forcing strongboxes, a murderer on occasion, always on the alert, and with the feel of the rope round his neck, meanwhile writing magnificent poetry. The result was that this hunted poet, this gallows bird

(whose end we do not know and may rightly fear to learn) introduced into his poetry many a turn of speech and numerous words belonging to the fugitive and private language of the world of ill fame. He sometimes wrote whole poems in it, which are virtually incomprehensible to us. The inhabitants of the world where this language is spoken are a people who prefer night to day, even in their language, which they handle in their own way, keeping it in a sort of *twilight zone* —I mean keeping the syntax of the common language while using a mysterious and rapidly changing vocabulary transmitted by initiation. This vocabulary, which is sometimes hideous and has a base ring to it, is sometimes horribly expressive. Even when the sense escapes us we dimly perceive, beneath the brutal or caricatural appearance of the terms, wonderful meanings and images powerfully suggested by the very form of the words.

This is true poetic creation of a primitive type because the first and most remarkable of poetic creations is language. Although grafted on to the speech of decent people, slang, jargon, or *jobelin* is an original linguistic form, continually elaborated and refashioned in the dens, jails, and darkest corners of the great city, by a whole world which is the enemy of the world—both frightening and frightened, violent and wretched, its cares divided between the planning of crimes, the urge to debauchery, or the thirst for vengeance, and the vision of the inevitable torments and tortures (so often atrocious at that time) which is perpetually present or imminent to a mind always uneasy and turning like a wild beast in a cage, back and forth between crime and punishment.

The life of François Villon, like his work, is somewhat murky in every sense of that term. There are great obscurities in both, and in the character of the man himself.

All we know about him tells us very little about his true nature because everything, or nearly everything, comes from his poetry or from the records of Justice—two sources which are more or less in agreement on the facts, and which, when combined, present us with a picture of a very bad and vindictive man, capable of the most dreadful exploits, but who suddenly startles us by a pious or tender accent, like the one we catch in the famous and beautiful poem where we overhear the prayer of his mother, the poor woman who one day about 1435 handed over that child destined for evil, fame, bondage, and poetry, François de Montcorbier, to Maître Guillaume de Villon, chaplain of the chapel of St. John in the church of Saint-Benoît-le-Bétourné.

You will remember that ballad, one of the ornaments of French poetry:

> *Femme je suys povrette et ancienne,*
> *Ne rien ne sçay; oncques lettre ne leuz,*
> *Au moustier voy dont je suis paroissienne*
> *Paradis painct où sont harpes et luz. . . .*

In spite of a few slightly altered words, the language is still our language; and it will soon be five hundred years since it was written: we can still enjoy it and are still moved by it. We can also marvel at the art which produced this masterpiece of highly wrought form, the construction of the stanza, at once clear and musically perfect, in which a remarkably varied syntax, a natural richness in the sequence of images, easily fits into the mold of ten lines of ten syllables with four rhymes. I admire the enduring quality of these values, created under Louis XI. I regard it as a living proof of the continuity of our literature and of the essential qualities of our language through the ages. There is scarcely a European country except

France and England which can pride itself on such continuity; since the fifteenth century these two nations have not ceased to produce works and writers of the first order from generation to generation.

In short, hanged or not, Villon lives: he is as much alive as any living writer; he lives because we understand his poetry and because it works on us—more still, it can stand up to any comparison with what is most powerful and most perfect in the four centuries of great poets who succeeded him. For form itself is solid gold.

But I must turn from the story of his work to that of the man. I have said that it is only known to us in fragments. It is a Rembrandt, largely enveloped in shadow, of which certain parts emerge with extraordinary clarity and certain details with a terrifying distinctness.

These details, as you will see, have come down to us in documents used in criminal proceedings, and we owe our knowledge of these documents, which contain the sum total of our reliable information about Villon, to the magnificent work of three or four men who were scholars of the highest order. Here we must pay tribute to Longnon, Marcel Schwob, and Pierre Champion. For until they came we knew nothing about our poet which was not highly conjectural. They explored in turn the National Archives and unearthed the essential documents among the bundles of papers and files of the Parliament of Paris.

I did not know Auguste Longnon personally, but I knew Marcel Schwob very well, and I recall with deep feeling our long twilight conversations, in which this strangely intelligent and passionately clear-sighted man told me about his research, his intuitions, his discoveries, in pursuit of his quarry—which was the truth about the Villon case. He brought to his task the

inductive imagination of an Edgar Poe and the sagacity, in matters of minute detail, of a philologist inured to analyzing texts, as well as that peculiar interest in exceptional people, in lives that diverged widely from the norm, which led him to discover a number of books and establish many literary reputations.

Following the example of Longnon—and the police too, in practice, go about it in the same way—in order to catch and apprehend Villon, Schwob employed the dragnet method. He would cast his net over the suspected whereabouts of the delinquent whom he hoped to capture by arresting—I mean by identifying—the whole band. He would amaze me by showing how carefully criminal affairs were followed up at that time. One evening he related the disastrous adventures of a group of criminals who were Villon's associates. Schwob picked up their trail at Dijon, where they committed hundreds of crimes. When they were on the point of arrest, they scattered and fled. But the magistrate of the Court of Dijon did not lose sight of them. He sent a report to one of his colleagues which tells us in the greatest detail about the fate of the fugitives. Three of them, who were in possession of the spoils, hid in a forest. There, two of the three leagued together, killed their companion by stabbing him in the back with a broad, short sword, divided the booty he had with him, and parted. One of them, I believe, got himself hanged at Orléans; the other was boiled alive at Montargis for circulating counterfeit money. We can see that the police authorities of the time, without telegraph or telephone, photographs, fingerprints, or other anthropometric aids, were pretty good at their job!

Villon is most strongly suspected of belonging to a gang known as "The Companions of the Cockleshell," or "Coquil-

lards." His regrettable and productive life was no doubt quite a short one, and it is highly unlikely that he lived to the age of forty. I will summarize it in a few words, or rather I will summarize what has been established with certainty by the learned men whom I have mentioned and whose writings should be read, as much to help us better understand the work of the great poet as to admire the achievements of exact historical research, and to realize that there is a genius for *seeking* as there is a genius for *finding*—a genius for *reading* as there is a genius for *writing*.

Villon, who was originally called François de Montcorbier, was born in Paris in 1431. His mother, who was too poor to bring him up herself, placed him in the care of a learned priest, Guillaume de Villon, who was a member of the community of Saint-Benoît-le-Bétourné, where he lived. It was there that Villon grew up and was given his first schooling. His adopted father seems always to have treated him with kindness and even with affection. At the age of eighteen the young man took his bachelor's degree. In the summer of 1452, when he was twenty-one, the degree of master of arts (the *licence*) was conferred on him. How much did he know? No doubt what was to be learned by attending the courses at the Faculty of Arts, more or less regularly: grammar (Latin), formal logic and rhetoric (both according to Aristotle, as he was known and interpreted at the time); later there would be the rudiments of metaphysics and a smattering of the moral, physical, and natural sciences of the period.

But the word *licence* has a double meaning. As soon as he had taken his degree, Villon began to lead a more and more irregular and soon a dangerous life. The society of clerks was a strangely mixed one. The status of clerk was much sought

after by those who felt that they might one day be called upon to account to justice for their actions. Anyone who was a clerk could demand, as of right, to be tried by an ecclesiastical court, and in that way escape the jurisdiction of the ordinary courts, whose hand was much heavier. A good many clerks were people of appalling morals. A large number of sorry specimens mixed with them and pretended to be clerks; and sometimes a very peculiar sort of Latin lessons were given in prisons to enable some accused person to claim that he was a clerk in order to change judges.

In this ill-assorted world Villon made acquaintances of the worst sort. The ladies who frequented it were probably not without their charms. They played, as might be expected, an important role in the thoughts and adventures of the poet. But none of them could have dreamed that the lad would give them a certain immortality. Not Blanche the Shoemaker, nor Grosse Margot, nor the Fair Armorer, nor Jehanneton the Hoodmaker, nor Katherine the Pursemaker. Note all these corporative names. . . . Anyone would think that all the trade guilds must have sacrificed their womenfolk to the goddess, and that to be an artisan in the Middle Ages led infallibly to marital mishaps.

Now comes the moment when vice and debauchery turn into violence. On June 5, 1455, Villon killed a man. We are quite well informed about the case because it is set out in the act of remission granted by Charles VII to "Maître François des Loges, *alias* de Villon, aged twenty-six or thereabouts, who on the day of the Feast of Our Lord was sitting on a stone situated under the face of the clock of Saint-Benoît-le-Bien-Tourné in the Grande Rue Saint-Jacques in our Town Paris, and with him were a certain Gilles, a priest, and a cer-

tain Ysabeau, and it was about nine of the clock or thereabouts."

Then comes a certain Philippe Sermoise, or Chermoye, a priest, and Maître Jehan le Mardi. According to the act, which follows Villon's account without in any way impugning its veracity, the priest Sermoise tried to pick a quarrel with the poet, who began by giving him a soft answer and got up to make room for him. . . . But Sermoise pulled a large dagger from under his habit and struck Villon a blow in the face "which caused copious bleeding. Villon, who for the evening was wearing a coat and had a dagger under it hanging from his belt," drew it and stabbed Sermoise in the groin, "not thinking he had struck him." (Such an excuse is highly suspect.) As the other apparently had not had enough and came at him again, Villon knocked him down with a stone, hitting him full in the face. All the witnesses fled.

Villon hurried away to have his wound dressed at a barber's. The barber, who had to make a report, asked the customer's name. Villon gave the false name of Michel Mouton. As for Sermoise, he was taken first to a convent, then to the Hôtel-Dieu, where he died two days later, for lack of proper care. The killer thought it prudent to disappear.

A few months later the letter of remission, from which I have quoted, was granted. It is a remarkable thing that this express act of clemency should have been based entirely on Villon's version of the affair. There was no investigation. The excuse of self-defense was accepted without challenge. When the interested party asserted that ever since the unfortunate incident his behavior had been irreproachable, they took his word for it. But we cannot help feeling that his account is decidedly suspect: the unexplained attack by the priest Sermoise, the false name given by Villon to the barber Fouquet,

his flight, the disappearance of the witnesses—all very disturbing factors in the case. Many have been sent to the gallows on slenderer evidence. But let us not be more severe than the king who, "wishing to put mercy above stringency," acquitted and pardoned both the act and the case, "and thereupon," runs the text, "we impose perpetual silence on our procurator." The silence was soon to be broken.

There is not the slightest doubt about the second of Villon's known crimes, and every possible condition laid down by the penal code was present. Nothing was missing; it was a robbery committed by night in an occupied house, complete with housebreaking, burglary, the use of passkeys and a whole outfit of burglary tools.

Villon, who was the finger man, accompanied by professional lock pickers and other accomplices, carried off in this manner five hundred gold *écus* belonging to the College of Navarre and contained in a chest deposited in the sacristy of the college chapel. The theft was not discovered until two months later. Nothing is more curious than the details of the inquiry carried out by the king's investigators at the Châtelet. I will only quote one.

The investigators summoned and swore in, as expert witnesses, *nine* locksmiths who took a special oath and whose names and addresses have been preserved in the files of the proceedings. They reconstructed with great accuracy the thieves' maneuvers. But the latter had made their escape. Unfortunately for them, they were given away by the imprudent remarks of a chatterer, their accomplice, who was overheard by a *curé* in some tavern talking about the case of the College of Navarre. The priest, who would seem to have been better qualified for police intelligence than for the priesthood, embarked on a remarkably thorough investigation that led

straight to François Villon. Villon hastily made for the provinces.

Heaven knows what his life must have been like during this period! . . . We meet him sometimes in prison, at other times in contact with the prince and poet, Charles of Orléans, and no doubt from time to time he took part in the operations of the Coquillards. In any case, he seems to have tasted the rigors of the extremely harsh episcopal prison at Meung-sur-Loire, perhaps as a result of the theft of a chalice from a sacristy. The Bishop of Orléans, Thibaud d'Auxigny, treated him with a severity that left Villon with bitter memories; he was put to the water-torture, and chained up in a dungeon. Louis XI released him and he returned to Paris, but not, alas, to lead a decent life! He discovered some old acquaintances there, and made some new and far from reputable ones, whose contact involved him in the most distressing affair of his whole life. As a result of a scuffle in which a pontifical notary was wounded, Villon was condemned by the Court of the Châtelet to be hanged and throttled on the Paris gallows. Judging by the joy he displayed when the Parliament of Paris allowed his appeal and reduced to ten years' banishment from Paris the sentence he had always dreaded, of which he had had horrible dreams, and which he had sung with such raw realism, he must have lived through days of great anguish, between torture and the ghastly thought of his body swinging on the gibbet. The relief that he felt on learning that his life was to be spared made him write two poems, one after the other: one addressed to the turnkey, congratulating himself for having appealed, and the other to the court to express his gratitude. He pledges all his senses, all his limbs and organs:

Foie, poumon, et rate qui respire,

to celebrate the praises of the court!

So he left Paris, delighted to have got off so lightly. After that . . . But after that we know nothing more. When and how did Villon's life come to an end?

Dictes-moy où, n'en quel pays?

We know absolutely nothing about it.

That life, in which there was no lack of shadows, vanished into the darkness. But already in the sixteenth century this criminal's work began to be printed; this vagabond, this thief, this man condemned to death, took high rank among French poets, from which no one has dislodged him. When he was dead, our poetry turned to antiquity; settled into a formal style in which fastidiousness became the absolute rule. It felt more at home in the salons than in the dens and back streets. Villon, however, was still read, even by Boileau. Today his fame is greater than ever; and if his ill-fame, proved or corroborated by authentic documents, is more clearly apparent than it was in the past, it must be admitted that it adds more than it decently should to the interest of his poetry. A study of the literature and the theater of all periods shows that crime has great attractions, and that vice is not altogether without interest even for virtuous or semi-virtuous people. In the case of Villon it is a guilty man who speaks, and he speaks with the voice of a major poet. And so we find ourselves confronted by a problem that I should feel inclined to describe as psychological if I knew precisely what that term means.

How can the conceiving and planning of crimes, and the very definite intention to commit them, coexist in the same head with the sensibility that certain poems reveal and art itself demands, along with that powerful element of self-knowledge which is not only present but explicit and ex-

pressed with such precision in the celebrated *Débat du coeur et du corps*? How does this ruffian, who trembles at the thought of being hanged, have the courage to put a song—in admirable verse—into the mouths of the unfortunate puppets that swing and disintegrate in the wind, at the end of a rope? His terror does not prevent him from choosing his rhymes; his appalling vision is used in the service of poetry; it *serves a purpose*, which is not at all the one that justice anticipates when it attempts to justify itself and its severity by what it terms the exemplary nature of its penalties. But it is in vain that it hangs some, draws and quarters others, or has them boiled— it cannot prevent a great criminal who is a still greater poet from turning his bad deeds, his vices, his fears, his remorse, and his repentance into poetry, and extracting from the horrible and pitiful mixture the masterpieces we all know.

The status of poet—if it is a status—is not necessarily incompatible with a completely regular social life. The majority, the great majority of poets, I can assure you, were or are the most honorable men in the world, and sometimes the most honored. And yet . . .

Anyone who gives a little thought to the matter of deciding the poet's proper place in the world, soon finds himself embarrassed by this indefinable species. Let us imagine a well-ordered society, that is, a society in which every member receives the exact equivalent of what he gives. Such perfect justice would eliminate everyone whose contribution was not of the kind that can be measured. The contribution of the poet or the artist cannot be measured. It is nil for some and enormous for others. It is impossible to establish any system of equivalences. Such beings can thus only survive in a social system defective enough to allow the most beautiful things man has made—which, in return, make him truly man—to

be produced. Such a society accepts inequality of exchange, resourcefulness, almsgiving, and all those things which enabled a Verlaine to live without having to rely, as Villon did, on the shares distributed by associations of criminals, and which had been collected in the night, by housebreaking and burglary, from the well-filled coffers of sacristies.

I do not propose to dwell on Verlaine's life: it is too close to us; and I shall not now reopen the dossier which was sent by the record office at the Court of Mons to slumber (not without occasional awakenings) at the Royal Library in Brussels, just as Villon's dossiers passed from the cabinets of Parliament into those of the National Archives. Villon is far enough from us to be spoken of as a legendary figure. But Verlaine! . . . How many times I have seen him pass my door, angry, laughing, swearing, banging on the ground with the heavy stick of a cripple or a threatening tramp. How difficult to imagine that this vagrant, sometimes so brutal and squalid in his behavior and language, so alarming and at the same time so pitiable, was nevertheless the author of the most delicate and musical of poems, of the most original and touching verbal melodies that exist in our language? Every possible vice had spared in him, had perhaps planted or developed in him, that power of graceful invention, of expressing gentleness, fervor, pensive tenderness, which no one else possessed as he did, for no one was able, as he was, to disguise or submerge the resources of a consummate art, practiced with all the subtlety of the most skillful of poets, in works facile in appearance and naïve, almost childish, in tone. Think of:

> *Calmes dans le demi-jour*
> *Que les branches hautes font . . .*

Sometimes his poems remind us of prayers murmured to the rhythms of the catechism; sometimes they are astonishingly careless and written in the most colloquial language. Sometimes he experiments with prosody, as in that strange poem, *Crimen amoris*, written in eleven-syllable lines. What is more, he tried almost every possible meter, from five syllables to thirteen. He used strange combinations, some of them not heard since the sixteenth century; he wrote poems wholly in masculine or wholly in feminine rhymes.

If we insist on comparing him with Villon, not as a criminal character with a police record but as a poet, we shall find —or at any rate I find, for it is only a personal impression—I find to my surprise that Villon (vocabulary apart) is in certain ways more "modern" than Verlaine. He is more precise and more pictorial. His language is markedly firmer: *Le Débat du cœur et du corps* is constructed out of dialogue as clear and crisp as a passage from Corneille. And his work is full of unforgettable phrases, each of which is a *trouvaille* of the *classical* type. . . . But first and foremost, to Villon belongs the glory of a truly great work—the famous *Testament*, a work unique in conception, complete, a *Last Judgment* pronounced on men and things by a man who, at the age of thirty, had already lived too much. This collection of poems, in a form like the provisions of a will, has about it something of the *Danse Macabre* and the *Comédie Humaine*. Bishops, princes, executioners, bandits, strumpets, companions in debauchery— each receives his or her legacy. All those who have befriended the poet, all those who have treated him harshly, are there, fixed in a single stroke, in a line that is always definitive. And in this curious composition, between the extremely accurate portraits where real names, nicknames, even addresses are mentioned, we find, in more generalized forms, the loveli-

est ballads ever written. The familiar monologue breaks off in their presence. The confession turns into an ode and takes wing. The apostrophe, a habit with Villon, serves a lyric purpose, and the interrogative form, which is so common in his work—

> *Mais où sont les neiges d'antan?*
>
> *Le lesserez-la, le povre Villon?*
>
> *Dictes-moy où, n'en quel pays?*
>
> *Qu'est devenu ce front poly*
> *Ces cheveulx blons, sourcils voultiz?*

—becomes through repetition, and still more by the tone, a powerful source of pathos. He is the only French poet who has been capable of using the "refrain" to get powerful effects that increase in power to the end.

As for Verlaine, if I tell you (at my own risk) that he seems to me to be less literary than Villon, I do not mean *more naïve*: neither of them is more naïve than the other, nor more naïve than La Fontaine; poets are only naïve when they do not exist. I mean that the poetry which is special to Verlaine, like *La Bonne Chanson, Sagesse*, and so on, suggests at a first glance a shorter literary tradition behind it than the poetry of Villon; but this is only apparent: the impression can be explained by the remark that the latter wrote at the beginning of a new era in our poetry, and at the end of the poetic tradition of the Middle Ages—that of allegories, moralities, romances, and pious stories. Villon is, in a way, oriented toward the period soon to follow, when poetry will be written in full consciousness of itself and for itself. The Renaissance was the birth of art for art's sake. Verlaine is completely the reverse: he came out of, departed from, and escaped the Parnassian Movement;

he was, or thought he was, at the end of an aesthetic paganism. He reacted against Hugo, against Leconte de Lisle, against Banville; he was on good terms with Mallarmé, but Mallarmé and Verlaine represented two extremes which approached each other only in the fact that they had more or less the same admirers, and the same enemies.

Well! Verlaine's reaction led him to create a form the complete opposite of the one whose perfections had become irksome to him. . . . We sometimes have the impression that he is fumbling among syllables and rhymes, that he is seeking the most musical form of expression of the moment. But he knew very well what he was doing, and even proclaimed it: he decreed an *art poétique: de la musique avant toute chose* ("music before everything"), and for that he chose freedom. . . . This pronouncement was significant.

For this apparently *ingenuous* individual was a highly organized primitive, a primitive of a kind never seen before, evolved out of a highly skilled and very conscious artist. None of the authentic primitives is like Verlaine. He may perhaps have been more accurately classified when, about 1885, he was called a "decadent." Never was there a more subtle art than this, which assumed that it was leaving another behind, and not that it had a precedent.

Verlaine, like Villon, compels us to admit that dubious behavior, the struggle against a hard and uncertain life, a state of insecurity, periods spent in prisons and workhouses, continual drunkenness, mixing with the dregs of society, and crime itself are by no means incompatible with the most exquisite refinements of poetic production. If I were going to philosophize on the matter, I should stress at this point that the poet is not a particularly social being. In so far as he is a poet he does not fit into any utilitarian organization. Respect

for civil law expires at the entrance to the den where his verse is forged. The greatest poets, like Shakespeare and Hugo, preferred to imagine and to breathe life into characters whose conduct is irregular, rebels against all authority, adulterous lovers, transforming them into heroes and "sympathetic personalities." They are much less at their ease when they try to exalt virtue. Virtuous people, alas, are poor material! Contempt for the bourgeois, which was introduced by the Romantics and which has not been without certain political consequences, is at bottom a contempt for a regulated life.

It follows that the poet carries a kind of "bad conscience." But the moral instinct always finds a niche somewhere. We can see among the worst of scoundrels, in the most appalling environments, the reappearance of rules and the proclamation of laws of the jungle. In the case of poets, the legal code contains only one clause, which shall be my last word:

"Under pain of poetic death," says our law, "see that you have talent, and even . . . a little more than that."

Verlaine Passes By

A FEELING I was unable to overcome always prevented me from going and introducing myself to Verlaine.

I was living close by the Luxembourg, and a few steps would have brought me to the marble-topped table where he used to hold court from eleven in the morning until midday in the back room of a café, which for some unknown reason ended in a rockery grotto. Verlaine, who was never alone, could be seen through the window. The glasses on the marble table contained a greenish liquid which looked as though it had been drawn from the emerald pool of a billiard table, the "pond" of this nymphean grot.

 Neither the magic of his fame, which at that time was at its height, nor the curiosity I felt about a poet whose work had meant so much to me for its innumerable musical discoveries, its delicacy, and its depth; nor even the fascination of a career with such appalling ups and downs, and of a mind so gifted and so wretched, were ever able to overcome some obscure resistance to my own inclinations and a sort of sacred awe.

 But I used to watch him go by nearly every day when he emerged from his grotesque cavern and, gesticulating as he

went, made for some cookshop near the Polytechnique. Blessed and accursed by fate, he limped along, thumping the ground with a heavy walking stick of the kind used by tramps and cripples. Although he was a lamentable sight, there was a spark of fire in the eyes under their shaggy eyebrows, while a sort of brute majesty and the outrageous remarks delivered at the top of his voice made people turn round in astonishment. Flanked by friends and leaning on the arm of a woman, he talked, as he stumped his way along the street, to his devoted little bodyguard. There were sudden halts marked by a furious stream of full-throated invective. Then a quarrel would begin. And Verlaine, with his supporters, would move on to the accompaniment of a painful banging of clogs and a stick, working himself up into a magnificent rage which sometimes changed, as by magic, into a burst of laughter almost as fresh as the laughter of a child.

A few minutes before Verlaine, I rarely failed to see another passing figure of a very different stamp. He walked with a stoop, wore a short beard, was soberly and unobtrusively dressed, with a rosette in his lapel. Behind the crystal glint of his spectacles his look was fixed and vacant. He went along as though vaguely following his own large bowed forehead. He seemed to leave the guidance of his faltering steps to the lower faculties of his being. All the way along the wall, as it receded behind him, this illustrious passer-by described curves in the air with an absent-minded forefinger, unconsciously revealing the profound concentration of the geometer's mind; and the body that housed the mind would progress as best it could in our world, which, after all, is no more than a particular world among the various possible worlds. Henri Poincaré was completely absorbed in the ceaseless mental activity which

leads thinkers to their own particular form of light, or to fame, or sometimes, and just as likely, to their death under the wheels of a wagon.

Poincaré, being moved by the same laws as Verlaine to sit down to eat at regular intervals, would walk ahead of Verlaine along the same strip of pavement, going home. He seemed to me to predict the appearance of the poet—to the nearest ten minutes. I was amused by this meridian transit of two such different stars. . . . I thought of the immensity of the spiritual distances between them. How different the images forming in those two heads must have been! What utterly dissimilar effects the sight of the same street must have created in these two systems, following one another so closely! In order to think about it, I was obliged to choose between two admirable orders of things which in appearance were mutually exclusive, but which resembled one another in the purity and profundity of their aims. . . .

Yet in the end the only thing I found in common to both passers-by was the same obedience to the secret injunctions of noon.

That part of Paris was rather well populated with gods and demigods who showed themselves at fixed times, some in their professorial chairs, others at tables with a mounting pile of saucers in front of them.* They were quite unaware of each other. I need not mention the goddesses and nymphs; they were to be seen more or less everywhere. About two o'clock Leconte de Lisle appeared among the trees in the Luxembourg gardens. He would proceed with an air of dignity from the École des Mines to the library of the Senate,

*An allusion to the former practice, in French cafés, of serving with each drink a saucer with the price stamped on it. [M. T.]

passing the very spot where today his statue can be seen. . . .
I am not saying that anyone looks at it; it can be seen.

At that time Leconte de Lisle, alive and venerable though
he was, was already for many people no more than an empty
shadow. At any rate he was no longer talked about, which
was unjust and in keeping with the natural law. The young
and the proud were hunting for new poetic systems which
some of them thought should be more complex and others
entirely different from Leconte de Lisle's. These multifarious
tendencies had nothing in common except the one essential
thing: a passion for poetry. It is permissible, at this point in
time, to divide them into two broad classes: the followers of
Verlaine and the disciples of Mallarmé. The distinction is a
rough-and-ready one; it leaves out of account the finer shades,
the mixtures, the vacillations and reactions, which is to say,
the individuals.

Leconte de Lisle might have observed, with a philosoph-
ical and contented eye, that his rebellious posterity had as
their guides, if not as their creators, two prodigal sons of the
Parnassians. I am very much afraid that he did nothing but
curse, and curse with a certain bitter vigor, his children and
his grandchildren.

Poetry springs from the desire to create a form of speech
charged with more meaning and filled with more music than
ordinary language has, or can bear. Nothing is easier to un-
derstand than the desire to continue indefinitely the accumu-
lation of beauties to be imposed on or substituted for the
purely utilitarian content of language. But the extent to which
the load can be increased has a limit, soon reached; the
balance which must be preserved in the reader between the
effort demanded of him and the power conveyed to him is

always ready to be upset. Obscurity on the one hand, empti-
ness on the other; excessive vagueness, absurdity, exaggerated
personal peculiarities—all these dangers, which never cease
to hover round the works of the mind, are a special danger
for poetry and lure it toward the abyss of oblivion. Poems
often enough succumb beneath the weight of beauty the
poet has tried to put into them, and under the noble burden
of meanings and ornaments. Readers of the future will some-
times stumble upon the remains of incomparable beauty
among the rubbish. The loveliest lines in the world will be
rescued from such ruins, where some will be found so pure
that the rest of the edifice surrounding them was bound to
perish. . . .

Poetry therefore involves great risks, but without them
it could not exist. These risks become enormous when art
has just experienced a period of dazzling triumphs, a too long
series of great successes and lucky finds, which seem to ex-
haust its good fortune and to impoverish in advance any
generation that follows immediately on a generation too
much favored by fortune. It is a great misfortune to be born
in the midst of recent masterpieces and to be driven by
desperation to try something completely different.

It was at such a moment that Verlaine and Mallarmé ap-
peared. Arriving on the heels of so many masters, when
Victor Hugo and Baudelaire were still alive, and coming
from the Parnassian group who formed, as it were, a sort of
great poet with several heads, they had to carry on the game
and sit in the very places which had been occupied by the
luckiest of the players. They were driven in their different
ways, one to renew, the other to perfect, the work of all the
poets who had gone before them.

Stéphane Mallarmé, whose genius was essentially a genius

for form, gradually reached an abstract conception of all the combinations of figures and turns of speech and made himself the first writer who dared to envisage the literary problem in its universality. I will only say that he conceived as algebra what all other writers had thought of only in terms of arithmetical detail. . . .

Verlaine was the exact opposite. Never was there a more genuine contrast. His verse does not aim at describing another, a purer, and more incorruptible world than ours and, as it were, a world complete in itself, but finds a place in poetry for all the varied phases of the soul as it really is. Verlaine wanted his poetry to be as intimate as possible; he is full of inequalities which bring him extremely close to the reader. His verse, as free and flexible as it can be within the limits of language, does not hesitate to descend from the most delicately musical tone to prose, and sometimes the worst sort of prose, which he borrows and adopts deliberately. Nothing separates him more clearly from Mallarmé, whose verse never raises the slightest doubt about its quality as verse; it is always transparently something which cannot be prose.

As for the ingenuousness of Verlaine and his art, there is no doubt that it never existed. His poetry is far from being naïve, since naïveté is an impossibility for a genuine poet. We forget too easily that by the nature of his case the poet is necessarily the last person in the world to be satisfied with mere words.

Four Letters on Nietzsche

I THINK it must have happened to very few people to dis-
cover here, there, and everywhere, letters they have written
to one person, and with no thought of the future, never imag-
ining that they would one day become objects of curiosity and
barter, that they would circulate under the protection of the
law, whose reluctance to protect anything of no material
value is well known, just as we all know how unwillingly
and with what distaste it deigns to consider the interests of
the heart and mind. Every day I find old friends of many
years ago, selling what I had written to them in confidence
—some of them not even withholding the notes and messages
relating the vicissitudes of their private lives. These papers,
in my handwriting, are hawked around, offered for sale
privately, appear in shop windows, are reproduced in cata-
logues; and all this because of the laws, or rather the legisla-
tors, who have not yet had the good sense to put letters be-
yond the reach of commerce, as they once did human beings.

I now mention this abuse (for which the general baseness
of the spirit of our laws, as well as the high cost of living and
the lowered resistance it involves, along with the increase in
unworthy forms of curiosity, are responsible) only to ac-
knowledge publicly the polite and considerate request made

to me by the *Cahiers de la Quinzaine* for permission to publish four letters which I wrote many years ago to Henri Albert about his translations of Nietzsche. I am delighted to have an opportunity of paying tribute to the deserving and remarkable work of Albert, who devoted so many years of his life to making the thought of the poet-philosopher of *Zarathustra* known to the French public.

As for my letters, they do not amount to much: a few words of thanks, a few lines scribbled in great haste in which my impressions of what I had read are barely discernible. I have no very clear recollection of the views I held about Nietzsche's theories in those days: but when I re-read these brief notes as though they had been written by someone else, I still find something of myself in them. Nietzsche aroused my mind's fighting spirit and the exhilarating pleasure of making lightning *retorts*, which I have always enjoyed rather too much. I also liked him for that intellectual vertigo arising from excesses of consciousness and intuitions of relationship, for pushing the mind *to the extreme*, for the sense of a superior will intervening to create the obstacles and arbitrary rules without which thought can only escape. I found in him a mysterious alliance between the lyric poet and the analytical thinker, which no one else had yet achieved with quite the same deliberation. Lastly, in the free play of an ideology fed on music, I greatly enjoyed the mixture and the brilliant use of ideas and data scientific in origin; Nietzsche was, so to speak, armed with a combination of philology and physiology, adapted or applied in a remarkable way to his own mental machinery.

But there were other parts of his work that shocked me. He offended my sense of intellectual rigor. I could never conceive why this vast and violent mind could never leave the unprovable alone. . . .

I find also in my letters a few words touching on politics. There is a reference to the German question.

We may wonder what the author of *Untimely Reflexions* would think today?

When I re-read my note to Henri Albert of October 1907, there is nothing in it that I would wish to change. Nevertheless, some things have happened during the intervening years.

> Monsieur Henri Albert
> c/o Le Mercure de France
> 15 rue de l'Echaudé
> Paris
> Sunday [postmarked Nov. 11, 1901]

My dear Albert,

I devoured a fragment of *Aurora* with all the bad feelings required when reading Nietzsche, and from time to time I threw in a feeling of gratitude to the translator.

At a time when the best work being published consists of translations, you have achieved a high and certain place. Believe me, I admire you for bringing your protracted labors to a conclusion, and for battling so long and unceasingly with the entire series of works in which a genius—the most tiring and strident genius—abounds.

Do you ever go to the *Mercure*?

I am a long way from it—in several senses—because if I get over the difficulty of distance, I find an absence of friends and a decline in the quality of the talk which make me sorry that I bothered to go.

The result is that I don't know how to get in touch with you, except on this inadequate scrap of paper.

> Yours,
> P. Valéry

P.S. And Bonnières? Do you still go to his Mondays?

Monsieur Henri Albert
c/o Le Mercure de France
15, rue de l'Echaudé
Paris [postmarked Dec. 10, 1902]

My dear Albert,

What a traveler, and what a Shade follows him! This Nietzsche is a scandal—a prodigious display of human strength that is itself certainly prodigious.

But what a lot of weaklings will imagine they are strong merely because they've read him!

Yet if each of us questions himself and realizes the immeasurable within—then Nietzsche is justified; he rules—if only among us. . . .

To you belongs the extraordinary cunning of having brought into the France of today someone who was very inquisitive about and almost greedy for . . . an earlier France.

The reader may blush over some of the praise he no longer deserves.

At any rate—let us praise the excellence of the translation. I was glad to read several reviews that showed a proper appreciation of the continuous perfection of your vast labor. I echo the praise and add my own long-standing thanks and good wishes.

P. VALÉRY

Monsieur Henri Albert
11, rue Mazarine
Paris
40 rue de Villejust—
Tuesday [postmarked Aug. 4, 1903]

My dear Albert,

I have read as best I could the volumes you sent me—less finished, more important—well worth a thorough study.

But at present I have neither the tranquillity nor the ferocious leisure I need, to weigh and mull over these few innumerable ideas.

In spite of worries that are far from speculative, I recognize that I do not care for the Eternal Return, nor the Author's many offenses against that "propriety" which he so rightly defined and praised. For example, his criticism of Christianity is sketchy—conjuring up a sketchy sort of Christian—the reality is the variety among the billions of Christians; every possible type can be found with the greatest ease—even the doctrinal ones. Napoleon learned his catechism like Louis XVI.

So the criticism is only valid on paper, if that!

It's the same for morality—— There are at least three things—morality as *written* prescriptions—morality as an odd, unwritable form of deliberation (which is cooked up in the mind), and lastly—what you do. It's impossible to argue about the last, which is the important one. The second is a hieroglyph, *halfway* indecipherable—The first is a fantasy, an approximation—(whatever can be said about the productions of the pen, etc.).

As for the parts you mentioned in our conversation—it seems to me that N. came a little too soon to make proper use of the theories of energetics. Moreover, he seems unaware of certain results already achieved in his own time, which might either have confirmed him in his views, or led him to abandon them——Everything is possible. But, unless I am mistaken, the *odious* Spencer also propounded an Eternal Return with the help of the same theories and in spite of Clausius' theorem, which would seem to rule it out.

Excuse this hasty judgment—to which I won't add in detail the favorable—admiring—"qualifications" which would be necessary.

My mind is elsewhere—occupied with eternal return!
With best wishes, my dear Albert, and all my thanks.

P. VALÉRY

October 1907

My dear Albert,

These points certainly appear to me pertinent for the predatory reader (which one has to be)—considering that the author never wrote anything more Germanic; considering that everything Germanic and the future of this central European cloud are now a riddle of capital importance for everybody, including the Germanic peoples.

It is for the rest of us, at any rate, to think about it, to circumscribe it with complete lucidity, as the philosopher does his pain.

Nothing is stranger in all history than France listening with a keen ear in that direction—anxiously in 1905—with more curiosity today, trying to make out something true, clinging to contradictory rumors, shamefacedly undecided.

One very striking thing (unless I'm mistaken). It seems that Nietzsche was no better informed: he knew everything about the Germany of his own day; but he tells us nothing about what was to follow.

After all—it is perhaps enough to look at a globe and glance through a few statistics. . . .

Yours very cordially,

P. VALÉRY

Recollections of J. K. Huysmans

DURING THE PERIOD he spent at Ligugé, in the shadow of the abbey where he was a regular attendant at the offices, Huysmans published *La Cathédrale*. I was fond of him. He had always treated me as a friend. Indeed, I was indebted to him for some good advice and a certain recommendation for a government position. During the years between the publication of *Là-Bas* and his departure for Ligugé, I used to call on him fairly often at his home in the Rue de Sèvres, or pick him up about five o'clock at his office at the Sûreté Générale in the Rue des Saussaies. I enjoyed his well-turned and ribald remarks, the extraordinary stories, the droll recipes and precepts with which he peppered his conversation. He was extremely high strung, quick to develop violent antipathies, prompt to deliver appalling judgments, prolific in disgust, predisposed to the worst, with an appetite for extremes, unbelievably credulous, swallowing with no trouble every horror that can be imagined about human nature, with a relish for peculiar behavior and the sort of tales you might hear from hell's concierge; yet his hands were unstained and he was sometimes as open-handed as a man on the verge of poverty can be; actively charitable, loyal to friends who had fallen on bad times, steadfast in his admirations, even of men whose persons had become unbearable or repellent to him.

I remember him so clearly that I could draw his enormous spherical skull, bristling with stiff, cropped silver hair, his forehead too broad, the aquiline and curiously twisted nose, the bushy eyebrows which shot up devilishly toward his temples, and that awkward mouth which fired off a stream of bitter and entertaining observations from a turned-up corner under the thick mustache. I can still hear him saying: "The idiocy of the thing!" . . . He rolled cigarettes in his fine feminine hands and lit and consumed them rapidly, just lightly clipped in the middle between his thin fingers; he inhaled deeply, swaying in his armchair, with his skinny thighs tightly crossed, a boot suspended in mid-air impatiently beating empty space. We chatted away. His gray eyes shot out cold flashes.

There hung about him an emanation of strange learning, seasoned with a medley of all the combined superstitions of the writers of his time and group, those of government employees, of the *petits bourgeois*, and of ladies far gone in piety, hovering between heresy and dementia. He laughed at them and took them up. He had a nose for every brand of dirt, evil, and shame in all the affairs of this world; and he may have been right. He nosed out lost souls among the clergy, he discovered formidable scholars and all-powerful magicians in poor devils who wore heavy rings and smelt abominably, and ghosts and evil spirits all over the place. When he went in for mysticism, he took a delight in combining his minute and indulgent knowledge of tangible and visible filth with a keen, inventive, and uneasy curiosity about supernatural filth and suprasensible dirt. He went to an extreme in his contempt for men of the world, his hatred of the rich, tradespeople, soldiers, politicians, and lovers of abstractions. He was accused of not

being a philosopher, but there is nothing to prove that one ought to be or that one can avoid being a philosopher. He more or less admitted that he lived in terror of charms and spells. It was a matter in which he was easily influenced; his natural skepticism, which was great and always on the alert, let down its guard only when it came to the dangerous nonsense that certain people recounted to him, some with conviction, and others to make a fool of him.

Art, Woman, the Devil, and God were the great interests of his intellectual life, which was constantly both attracted and exasperated by the endless catalogue of the evils of existence. He sought out all its pain and ugliness. His strange, palpitating nostrils smelled out everything that was nauseating in the world. The disgusting stench of cookshops, the acrid smell of cheap incense, the stale or poisonous aromas of low dives and flophouses—everything that revolted his senses excited his genius. You might have thought that in every sphere of life he was driven to dwell on the horrible and the repugnant, and that the effect of abominations of every description was to produce, in a man specially created to suffer from them, an artist specially equipped to describe them.

He forged a style that was peculiarly suited to his nerves: a language that was always striving after the unexpected and the extreme, overloaded with adjectives perverted from their usual meaning; an elaborate monologue, a curious mixture of rare words, peculiar overtones, trivialities, and poetic *trouvailles*. He liked doing violence to the order of words, separating the adjective from the noun it qualifies, the complement from the verb, and the preposition from the word expected to follow. He systematically used and abused epithets not implicit in the object but suggested by circum-

stance: a device that he used constantly, a very seductive, a very powerful device—but a dangerous and short-lived one, like all artistic devices that are easy to analyze.

But how avoid affectation, continual figures of speech, deliberate violations of syntax, technical vocabularies, tricks of punctuation, when you are a late-comer and adopt a literary tradition already rich and mature; and when you must still go on trying to describe, after a century of description—after Gautier, after Flaubert, after the Goncourts? On pain of appearing insipid, he was forced into overloading, transposing, and the monstrous coupling of words. Even if his work seems barbarous, shocks people of taste, bewilders the simple-minded, annoys reasonable people, and contains within it the seeds of death and the certainty of neglect arising from its peculiarities, it was nevertheless a work of obstinate will and an event in the world of Letters; for it has changed the direction of more than one writer, revealed the limitations of naturalism, brought to the knowledge of many readers the existence of an exceptional, a hidden art, and extracted from mysticism, from occultism, from the lives of contemporary priests and monks, a decidedly valuable literary substance. The state of religious feeling and of troubled minds between 1880 and 1900 is defined and in part described in Huysmans' three main works.

Durtal

[1898]

Introduction (1937)

When La Cathédrale *was published, although it was a very un-
even book and rather overloaded with erudition, I decided to take
the opportunity of expressing my feelings for the author. So I began
to write this essay on* Durtal. . . . *But I had scarcely begun work
when I realized the great difficulty I should face in trying to give
pleasure without ceasing to be myself. I was doing it for Huysmans,
and not for some dimly perceived reader; but I was at the opposite
pole from his temperament and ideas. Many things which he con-
sidered real did not seem to me even possible, or of any interest. The
oddities and peculiarities left me cold; and when it came to the
strange or the extraordinary, I found these qualities, in a form more
in keeping with my tastes at that time, in certain speculations and
abstract theories rather than in mysteries, sorcery or, indeed, any-
thing that seemed externally, necessarily, and, as it were, essentially
marvelous.*

*What I found most difficult of all was to speak of the author
personally, and of the great and admirable spiritual changes which
he had undergone. I was no better than a blind man who is called
upon to give an exact description of colors. What is more, I was re-
luctant to write anything likely to shock or wound even in the
slightest degree the man to whom I wished to pay tribute. I did not*

269

know what style to adopt; I hovered between his and mine. The result was what could have been expected: neither he nor I was satisfied with it.

I had not re-read this essay since the time it was written. I find the style barbarous, the movement awkward, as though hesitating between the picturesque and the abstract, and in fact all the signs of uncertain execution. And I was reminded of the circumstances in which I undertook this Durtal *as a duty.*

THE CHARACTER of Durtal gives unity to three books which alone have brought something generally new to the contemporary novel.

The novel form, as developed by the Naturalists, consisted of a series of poems, between which the action and dialogue simply served as links. Once a writer had learned to produce one of these poems, there was nothing to prevent him from producing a great many of them: and the writers' problem was to pass from one poem to the next and to choose the subjects most suitable for this sort of transition. They soon reached the point of suppressing all action. Their dialogue, ruthlessly simplified, was reduced to a mere exchange of words, remembered or invented by the author; and only in exceptional cases did it reproduce the give-and-take of real conversation—that sort of ensemble of several different minds in several different voices. At that period neither the construction of the work nor characterization went very deep. Construction was limited to pure chronology, to the expansion of a simple function of time. The novelists avoided the creation of character, either by no more than juxtaposing genuine speech and arbitrary descriptions of types, or by

confining themselves scrupulously to recording the trivial story of some contemporary person. All the characters formed in this way remain creatures of circumstance: they are amusing, unconvincing, and leave us indifferent. Besides, there is no mistaking the inadequacy of a psychology that remains silent in face of the most elementary facts, and only recovers its voice in order to go wrong on really complex questions. Finally, their language, though extended by the use and abuse of the systematic joining of words as far removed and as different from one another as they could be—in fact, purely poetic combinations of words—nevertheless allowed its former abstract qualities to fall into disuse, since writers gradually gave up studying the various modes of transition from one proposition to another, and used detailed enumeration instead of pursuing generality of expression—instead of seeking the instantaneous law of all that one wants to say.

Huysmans wrote *Là-Bas* after he had discovered the limitations of the system I have just described. It was then, I think, that the novel first built up a striking multiple vision and revealed more than one dimension of a state of mind. A triple existence runs through the book; is situated at one and the same time in several milieux which are irreconcilable and yet coincide; disrupts the normal time-sequence; places us in the presence of forces of darkness common to people widely separated, to the living and the dead, to closed epochs which still keep their distinctive secret. In the heart of this rich territory, people who cannot be compared and yet are similar communicate with one another, zones of time become linked, different stages are brought abruptly face to face and unified; making a combination of pious interiors, a revived

Middle Ages, a dour love affair à la Degas, a flattering gust of kitchen steam which carries up to heaven the aroma of a well-filled stockpot. From a distance, each memory of the book is composed, like a bouquet, of several different scents. The least breath given off by it has a complex flavor as it dies away.

En Route is a work of innovation which discards all the trappings of the old novel. It is a long and faithful transcription; the flow of unbroken time; thought itself, whose utterance involves the sum total of internal and external impressions, the whole of one form of reality. More effective than the customary arrangements of human time in books, this factual succession is nevertheless sufficiently purified and sufficiently different from simple sequences of ideas to be not easily changeable at will.

Nothing is closer to the very form of thought than the general structure of this frank and fluid book; yet it describes an exceptional case; it enumerates rare states of mind. The reader's mind, whatever its direction, could scarcely be more simply constrained to follow by the most natural path the supernatural direction which the author magnetizes, and which Durtal is bound to follow. This strength and purity of method involves the renunciation of ordinary calculations, the apparent absence of any choice of ideas—in order the better to represent, and in consequence to grasp, the modulation of that precise interior phenomenon which joins the author to his book and the book to its reader.

In the course of the independent wandering of his thought which transfers ideas, images, or nothing at all to his indifferent page, each writer preserves for literary purposes certain remnants: those which appear to him likely to move and impress other people most vividly, those which will be iso-

lated, fixed, and given a certain position, in order to serve his designs against that indispensable victim, the reader. He throws out the rest, the unused, and it flows away or just remains in a fluid state. Thus, when compared to our language, our habits, our reality, the function of our thought seems irregular and changeable, since thought indiscriminately assumes clear or obscure, absurd or beautiful forms, and others that are inexpressible, useless, irrational—monstrous combinations. We classify these forms, as I have just been doing, we choose those which suit us—that is to say, those which correspond to a small number of conventional and ready-made concepts—and we then write them down in an order very different from that in which they came to us. The act of writing obviously makes this choice inevitable at the same time that it makes it possible, since it gives it finality.

But in this strange book *En Route*, where we often overhear the soundless, unceasing voice, the voice that falls silent when we speak, the flow of the sentences is so similar to that of our ideas that the inevitable choice, the work of creation, becomes imperceptible and allows the reader to believe that he is thinking rather than reading. This form of imitation attains its end, reaches its climax, when the reader, who has discovered in it an interior monologue similar to his own, and who in the process has identified himself with this reconstruction of the thinking man, suddenly finds that he has gone beyond this point, that he has already absorbed an idea not familiar to him, that all unawares he has swallowed an unknown and active emotion; that he is reproducing for, or inside, himself novel representations of reality and marvelous happenings.

For, little by little, in the bare text, which is the same for everybody, there begins and is brought to a conclusion, by

way of the ordinary happenings of life, that immense or that conventional transformation which is the very subject of the book. The reader has touched on every aspect of a conversion. He has dreamed of being someone else and, in the end, he has experienced that complete operation of the mind which is the greatest imaginable example of innovation in the realm of knowledge, and which nevertheless does not alter the basic laws or the concrete elements of thought.

I now notice that in one continuous stroke I have been able to pass from the form to the subject of the book.

But what is the depth and wherein lies the strangeness of the transformation? We are continually changing, converted by the simple movement of our ideas, by the flow of our being, in which we cannot prevent changes from taking place. The new certitudes that we acquire do not have the slightest effect on our possibilities of change; they are a part of what changes: they are not creations or exceptions so extraordinary that the laws of the mind are affected by them. This fact may seem to reduce Durtal's conversion to nothing more than a sort of translation, the use of a new dictionary, or else the mere substitution of one set of psychological terms for another, which would leave his fundamental outlook untouched. And, in fact, we know perfectly well that a preoccupation with God can be forgotten like anything else; we go to sleep and it fades away; we hear a noise, become inattentive, and it leaves us; we add up a few figures, and it is no longer, can no longer be there. Durtal himself, in the new dimension in which he has slowly remade himself, retains his former tastes, his creative eye, his previous tone of voice. What has changed? In what way does this great, this general conversion differ from the hundreds of tiny conversions which are taking place in the mind at every second of the day?

At this point I am going to take a chance. . . . I do not think one can discuss mysticism without being either a mystic or absurd. On the other hand, a mystic who writes and is anxious to explain himself can scarcely be understood by anyone except his fellow mystics, and I could tell you why. I intend, however, to venture on certain suppositions while emphasizing the fact that I am in no sense attempting to examine belief as such. No one can decide the point except for himself. I suspect, too, that purely logical arguments will turn out to be fruitless in an analysis of faith: they are limited, in the last resort, to demonstrating the conformity or nonconformity of a given proposition with certain postulates, such as the principle of identity or the principle of contradiction. Now these postulates themselves postulate certain accepted definitions, and the definitions end by demanding objects which are perceptible to the senses. It follows therefore that logic can teach us nothing if we set up against it a direct belief in objects not perceptible to the senses. Logic may well be nonexistent for the recluse.

Standing, as I do, outside, and being without any understanding of mysticism or the special knowledge that the mystic alone is really capable of acquiring, I begin by seeing in his way of life only a fresh arrangement of the values of things, a new, a personal dictionary.

We liked an object or an action, that is to say, the thought of it was pleasant to us. We disliked some other object or action. All objects and actions were classified in this way. Something happens; time marches on. The thing we liked, the thing that attracted us, undergoes a change of value. From now on, it repels us. Conversely, something which was previously a matter of indifference to us, or which we found odious, becomes dear to us, arouses our warmest feelings.

That is the simplest example of the facts of this order. It

should be observed that the thing which was liked and became repugnant is, in general, liked: often, indeed, we ourselves only liked it out of imitation, because we were taught to do so.

At a higher level, the object of repulsion which we transform into a source of desire may be physically intolerable; that is physical pain, a thing which everyone does his utmost to avoid, and which is the first degree of reality, the sharpest point of our world; it is the thing-in-itself which for the time being is irrefutable; like the penetrating fringe of an alien environment. The mystic reaches the stage when he welcomes pain, when he causes himself pain. So that the elementary fact assumes enormous proportions.

For such a thing to be conceivable—and it is—the mystic must have substituted a new idea for his previous interpretation of his physical sensations. It is essential that the new situation, which combines an act that has not changed with an idea that is new, should be able to resist not merely immediate appearances or the most ingrained of mental habits, but the very objurgations of pain. It must be that, in relation to the new spiritual combinations which have formed in the mystic, reality in its harshest or its most blistering form becomes as soft and fleeting as our habitual thinking is shown to be if a cannon suddenly goes off under our nose.

What takes place in such a mind is the formation of an altogether personal kind of reality; and this new world may be so solid that the first thing to be observed about all mystics is the presence in them of alien elements that put up a long resistance. They hear voices telling them things that are absolutely new, fighting against their opinions, coming as a shock to the ideas they have acquired. They carry on prolonged dialogues in which the unforeseen maintains its position and may resist indefinitely.

276

That is why, if we return to the example of the dictionary, if we equate conversion with a change of signs—which from an abstract point of view is accurate—if we recall that every system of signs is founded on something regarded as unchanging and capable of being repeated indefinitely, we have to admit not merely that the mystic has provided himself with a solid base, we must also realize that it is more solid than anything known to us. In the dictionary of his mind every impression corresponds to a value such that ordinary suffering, when added to a certain interior state, will become a source of delight, and ordinary pleasures, viewed in a different conjunction, will arouse horror, disgust, and pain.

In this region of new relationships the mystic, like a first-class physicist, will henceforth be able to create huge figures: God and the Devil, their retinues and their habitations, and vast systems endowed with coherence and powerful properties which, like enormous and accurate diagrams, will represent the measure and the mode of operation of his love.

The psychology of the mystics remains to be worked out, like all the other psychologies. I imagine that if somebody managed, by means of a double analysis, to follow out the extraordinary procedures of this species, to retranslate the barely intelligible personal vocabulary of the particular authors, the result would be impressive. Mysticism makes me think of an individual form of pure science. It concentrates on producing feelings and visions which are utterly divorced from ordinary reality; it creates for its own use a language of pure convention, which, because it uses the same words as our own, appears to be full of contradictions. In the same way that the geometer, moving in a sphere beyond any possible image and in the special realm of the purely conceivable, the purely verbal, where writing is stripped of all but its own in-

herent powers, can give existence to imaginary quantities and to metageometric space, so the mystic in the realm of the imaginary pushes back the apparent frontiers and attains the limits of interior change. Perhaps, if the laws of representation were already discovered, if we could appreciate the results of the imagination's work and of the transformations of a given object presented to consciousness; if, on the other hand, we knew how to decipher their vocabulary, which is at once loose and specialized, strict and indeterminate, then perhaps we might find that the literature of mysticism was the most precious of documents on a whole region of the mind.

The truth is that in seeking to translate in this way certain terms which long ago were used in a technical sense and have now become commonplace, or which designate known objects, in seeking periphrases corresponding to words like prayer or ecstasy, we have the feeling that we are in the presence of one of the profoundest forms of research, one of the most astonishing forms of psychological discovery.

Religion is a continuing event, resulting from the widest experience; in the eyes of the nonbeliever, it is an incomparable achievement which has never been attacked except by incomplete arguments; which form its beginnings has provided itself with the true and only instruments of all science; but they are applied to a special end. If someone with a taste for analysis, and like myself an unbeliever, examines the fact of prayer, strips it of its name and its superhuman direction, and tries to find a definition of it, he will observe that in the man who is praying, a sort of adaptation takes place: a definite and total naïveté, the presence of all that is continually disturbed by the flow of the world of movement, an exhibition of those shamefaced or vague creatures of the mind which the most clear-sighted of men—Pascal, Stendhal, Baudelaire —tear out of themselves with great effort. The subject looks

at himself as a whole, reduces himself to that gust of memories arising in him; detaches himself from them, and sums himself up as a unique speck of unrest in the world; he is no longer his own flesh; he is no longer what he has seen with his eyes or smelled with his nose; he feels different from his thought at every moment. He blots out necessary thoughts by pitting one against another with the aid of an insatiable sense of guilt —the perfect mechanism. After that, nothing gives him any difficulty; neither the act of describing this résumé aloud, exactly as he sees it in himself, to another person, part of an arbitrary, vanquished reality; nor the act of associating with the feathery wafer of the host, the whole of the immense new reality which he has made his own: he says that he believes in the Real Presence and there is no difficulty. It is easy. . . .

I am filled with wonder. For I know, on the other hand, that the highest and most concentrated form of speculation lies exclusively in the painful labor of making and unmaking associations of ideas, whether methodically for a particular purpose or in order to be in a position to contemplate the whole scheme of possible transformations, which is the reign and the realm of the thinking man. We arrive at the same position through the deeper understanding of art.

But mysticism is not for everybody. It is the act of a soul on the offensive, flinging itself upon the external world, while ordinary religion is only a mediocre and hesitating form of the defensive.

Now the step has been taken and the day has been won; Durtal returns to things, and they too have changed. He must be able to find again, at every moment of the day, the path that leads to the great moments of his life.

On the threshold of the mystical life and under the initial

shock, detail is obliterated; petty ideas vanish along with the scraps of morality, the completely simple acts, the moments of vegetation. Everything seems either worthless or immensely important while the new man is emerging. Next, when habit has been refashioned, the tiniest objects come back to life in the new environment, and they tell of new things. The Middle Ages, which thought of everything, had already provided for the necessity and the weakness of the attention. To every corner of the universe the Symbolism of the Church ascribed an agreed meaning. Huysmans has simply grouped this extraordinary, artificial nature round a Cathedral.

This time we watch the action of a universal vocabulary: a church that is always present, whether as an intense feeling or an enormous pile of stone rising, unique in the sky, or an infinitely expanding interior, a greatness that can be breathed in, a lungful of the darkness always at hand; then myriads of abstract beings, brought into existence at a certain point in an empty, wind-swept town, by the central figure of a man who broods, puts out his hand, then rejects, and rises—such is the immediate impression left by this latest book.

A pacified Durtal—but his mind still wants something—now seeks out for himself a place both tranquil and ardent, a place of gentle and glowing embers, still pensive, where a breath would be sufficient to bring back to life the vanished ages and their certitudes which have gradually been submerged in sleep.

And so he comes to Chartres, with pious and living people, confronting the purest revelation of French architecture, among the thousands of the blessed there, coloring the sunlight, clustered in the stone of the porches; other, more fluid

beings, emanating from books, come and go in the memory of the visitor.

And all the material means of a return to God are made manifest.

First and foremost there is the church itself—a mass of stone whose objective is strictly spiritual, an almost perfect mechanism.

To begin with, the darkness of the interior cuts off the individual life, suddenly swamps its senses, and as they come flowing back, allows them to empty into a vault of darkness. The spirit alone seems permitted to enter. The individual adapts himself. Sight returns; he is caught up in a series of vast lines which flow with a whole system of obscure geometry. Everything there resembles the darkness and the tints of the self-questioning mind. Strange patches of color vibrate; jeweled crescents form; we feel we have closed our eyes in order to think about something. But what? And we haven't closed our eyes. The church has artfully lowered our eyelids; it constructs an inner darkness.

Then the windows blaze with light like visions we have discovered. Their coloring is imaginary. We meet them suddenly as we walk toward them; they are startling, symmetrical, deliberate, and distinct. We haven't gone out of ourselves after all.

Then we feel drained by the absence of noise and movement, by the continuity of simple, massive objects. We become conscious of the effort of all those stones which above our heads enclose a vast space in which there is only a stray remnant of daylight; we are prepared. . . . We find ourselves in a mood of pure, sad cynicism.

The account of the astonishing sunrise in *La Cathédrale*,

with the light plunging downward into the church, must be read. The whole of this tremendous store of erudition, this chart of the world of mysticism, is opened then with the first blaze of the rose windows of Chartres. The host of saints come to life and mingle strangely with the vague misfits of the town, with the somnolent priests and the timid scholars. A servant girl, at once ecstatic and disturbing, wanders round, and the little group of real people, friendly and charming, brings a sense of reassurance in the midst of the symbolical vegetation and the bestiaries.

In the course of the book we come across most of the author's favorite themes, like familiar memories. We are suddenly reminded, by some cryptic allusion, of *A Rebours* and *A Vau-l'eau*. Or we hear a few peals of Carhaix's bells, and his excellent cuisine can be faintly discerned in the steaming dishes that Madame Bavoil produces. The Bièvre itself, the ancient Bièvre, is almost tempted to flow as far as Chartres, with all its smells perfuming the wind! And pages already famous recover their glow in the sudden appearance of a magnificent Solomon with his Queen of Sheba, "who had come from so far to propound her conundrums and to bring turmoil to a king's bed."

Durtal comes finally to a halt, casts a glance over the whole of his life and his spiritual crisis, then turns toward a hard and enviable spot, the calmest in the world—the cloisters.

With this pure line the three books fade away together. *Là-Bas*, bitter and complex in the distance; *En Route*, smooth and full like polished stone, and finally this last volume, an extraordinary network of modern metaphors in which we catch, as though in its entirety, the tremor of the vast and exact alphabet of symbols willed by the Middle Ages. The sequence of the three books is not simple. It sets up in us some-

thing that ripens, changes its intensity, and is suffused in a golden light, a sentient being leading away, through the world of hieroglyphics, the man and the milieux he traverses.

The whole of this work of Huysmans belongs to the realm of poetry by its ferocious coupling of images, the accumulated snatches of vision, the demand of every created thing to become a symbol of every other, by the systematic transformation of whole groups of impressions into other groups. At other times it seems to hold itself in, penetrates to the bottom of reality and, at the last, comes face to face with itself, rising again to the freest possible interplay of words. Elsewhere, after plumbing the depths of every sensation, distilling the life of the man of habit, it appears changed and somber. At such moments it goes straight to the point, posing the most direct and most elementary questions. It confronts boredom, death, sickness, impotence. It describes a being who can no longer turn aside. He has reached an age at which everything is clearly calculated in terms of patience and suffering; he hovers round the peculiar moment when there is no longer anything to hope for. That is the point at which the final changes in man are possible, and he knows it. But in the individual, who is thus induced by the operation of time and thought to feel his own feeble but clear significance, everything is writ large. Finding in everything the sour and precious taste of what is definitive, Durtal, molded by the sadness of life and ready for the most meticulous weighing of alternatives, the deepest and most patient of sentiments, concentrates on the past which is certain, and on the faith which is surer still; he is ripe for expressing, amid the utmost literary exuberance and with all the newly discovered resources of the contemporary novel, the strange and opulent thought of his creator.

At the Grave of Pierre Louÿs

How can I possibly talk about Pierre Louÿs? Don't imagine that I have the heart to paint a portrait at a time like this. How could I deliver a eulogy, produce a study of his work, collect my memories, in my present shocked and shattered state, or distinguish between what interests the public and what has overwhelmed me with such confusion and grief? How could I give voice to the foolish monologue, the senseless lament that goes on of itself inside us over a man who has just died; a man dead yet so close, so well known to me, so alive, so present still, still thinking and speaking, but in a world now horribly brought to an end? . . .

Yesterday, under the impact of a few words, it seemed as though a huge fragment of life had fallen away from me, uncovering some great gaping, smarting wound, where hundreds of memories appeared suddenly exposed and as though maddened by the sudden light of death, rushing in unimaginable disorder, as if trying to repair the loss suffered by my heart and grasping despairingly at the past. In place of the unthinkable event, there came this swarm of memories which would not accept the fact of death.

For my friendship with Pierre Louÿs was an event of capital importance in my life. One chance in a thousand brought me to know him, and my life was completely

changed. How often we used to talk about our first meeting! The result, so far as I was concerned, was that almost at once I felt impelled to write. My new friend insisted that I should take as a duty, as a sort of virtuous exercise, what I had sometimes practiced for pleasure without allowing it to become a burden. Most of my early verse was simply written to be exchanged for his, or to fill up space in the little review which he had founded and which only published verse. It was he who sent to Heredia and Henri de Régnier my first efforts, written a long way from Paris. And it was he who one evening introduced me to Stéphane Mallarmé.

At that time he was the shyest, the most imperious, the most tactful, and the most obstinate of young men, with a seductiveness and an elegance which I have never come across in anyone else. At first he was very reserved, with an almost diplomatic air of mystery about him, and exquisite manners, infinitely careful over forms and nuances, stuttering in a very low and very gentle voice those gracious words which hold us and reveal nothing to indiscreet listeners. But once trust had been established, the real Pierre emerged. His great gifts, his endless curiosity, his vast and astonishing culture which he constantly nourished, his enthusiasms which sometimes verged on the fanatical, his devastating and irresistible whims, the charming surprises he arranged, and all the characteristics of a person who was absolute in his friendships, his admirations, and in their opposites, dominated by the unswerving, unconditional, truly mystical devotion that he felt for the perfection of our art, were displayed with such vivacity that the rest of us, by comparison, always seemed in some degree less young, less ardent, less determined, less versatile; and we felt ourselves under the sway of his passion.

He was a charming tyrant, and being himself the slave of

what he found most beautiful in art and in things, he had a marvelous gift for imposing his own gods and his own idols.

Who among those of us who were his friends does not owe much to him?

The most famous of them all, Claude Debussy, found in Pierre Louÿs support, counsel, even instruction or essential insights into literature—in short, the invaluable mainstay of his career in all its aspects, at all times, in all its difficulties, even those of fame.

I could mention other names, call on the living and the dead.... Let it suffice to say that his highly personal influence, his powers of stimulation, the repercussions of his will and his intellectual vitality were great. He had a genius for recognizing his own.

This is not the moment to speak of the great artist he was, or of his books. Neither emotion nor haste is fitting for a clear consideration, with the rigor that he himself would have wished, of a work so subtle, so masterly, so lovingly pushed to the last extremes of grace, without a thought for time, trouble, or the number of experiments and revisions. When a man has devoted so much energy and ardor, so much patience and thought, to his work, he is entitled to expect that he will be long and carefully studied by those who follow him. The time will come for such respect.

Today, beside the grave of my friend, I feel that I have a duty to perform. Since we are concerned at present with his memory, and since the fate of his name and his reputation will henceforth rest in the hands of those of us who have known him, I think it incumbent on me to bring out a thought which had tormented him for many years, and to which he often returned in his solitude. Although famous, Pierre Louÿs felt that he had not had the proper kind of recognition. Because

one part of his work attracted so many readers who were all too susceptible to descriptions of love, he was convinced that people misunderstood his spiritual aspirations and the guiding principles of his thought. Whatever is erotic and voluptuous in the pages he wrote, all those charming bodies so deliciously portrayed in their tenderest attitudes, with their gentlest beauties, their graceful or passionate gestures, these have easily won for *Bilitis* and *Aphrodite* a host of worshipers.

But such people could only see what they saw. The majority saw nothing in those splendid books but apologies for the flesh and its pleasures. Neither the care and labor required to write such an admirable style, nor the knowledge implied in his descriptions, nor the bitterness and despair that went into them, revealed to their eyes the true features of the author. They thought of him simply as a devotee of pleasure, though the writer of a rather fine and pure style. Their error was shared by people of a very different stamp. I mean those whose frigid or gloomy temperament and whose disgust for things of the flesh roused them to such fury against the work of Pierre Louÿs.

Pierre suffered at being reduced to the sort of character which both parties so naïvely saw in him. He complained that they misunderstood him and did not recognize the real passions of his mind, which were those of an artist. I can bear witness to his complaints and was sufficiently well placed to know that there was substance in them. Thirty years ago, the word "artist" meant for us someone who lived apart, a dedicated person, at once victim and priest, a person who was singled out by his gifts and whose virtues and weaknesses were not those of other men. He was the servant and apostle of a divinity whose nature was just beginning to be understood. At the dawn of our thinking life, we had found our-

selves among the ruins of accepted beliefs. As for positive knowledge, the way in which it had recently been abused metaphysically, and the disillusionment caused by such paradoxical and fanciful use of verifiable discoveries, had put us on our guard against them. But our unknown and unchallenged god was the one who reveals himself through the works of man in so far as these are beautiful and gratuitous. He is a god who only performs miracles; the rest matters very little to him. All the devices of art meet with his approval. Like all gods, he calls for a spirit of renunciation and sacrifice; and the faith in him gives a universal and clearly defined meaning to the pure and naïve pride which is indispensable for the creation of masterpieces. The martyr, the elect of this god, the *artist*, necessarily believes that all virtue lies in the contemplation and cult of beautiful things, and all sanctity in creating them. That is something which could never have been suspected by the majority of Pierre Louÿs's readers, and still less by his enemies.

But though he had sunk into solitude and gloom, he would sometimes turn back to his youth, which had been dedicated to the god of whom I have spoken. And he would invoke against his fame, which seemed to him unjust and unworthy, the magnificent letters he had written to me many years ago. They were filled with an altogether religious exaltation; all the great men of poetry and music were celebrated in them, invoked like the names of the blessed, the most enviable of beings. One particularly beautiful letter contained an account of a stay at the Grande Chartreuse, a week's retreat, but a retreat in his own manner, a retreat with the thoughts and the desires of an artist, with the vows and the introspection of a poet. . . .

I believe that he had no deeper or stronger wish, during

his years of silence and isolation, than to make known one day the person he really was. He wanted to confess the faith of his adolescence, show himself a man of that faith, and he planned a book on himself and on the ardent years of his life, whose title would have been this: *When I Was Nineteen*.

I do not know whether a line of it was ever written.

To Rainer Maria Rilke

Rilke, my dear Rilke, thanks to whom my poems speak in a language I do not understand—everything conspires to deprive me of the time, and almost the strength, to say in fitting terms what I think of you. I should like to bring to the task a grace that is the fruit of calm and leisure. These great boons have been taken from me. Demons all too diverse fight among themselves for the bulk of my time.

Do you remember how astonished I was at the extraordinary solitude in which I found you when we first met? I was passing; you stopped me on my way to Italy and kept me for a few hours. A minute castle terribly isolated in the midst of a vast expanse of rather somber mountains; ancient, dreamy rooms with dark furniture and narrow windows—all this made my heart ache. In your house, my imagination could not but listen to the unending monologue of a mind entirely alone, undistracted from itself and from the feeling of its own uniqueness. I could not conceive a life of such isolation, eternal winters spent in such excessive communion with silence, where so much freedom was given to your dreams, to the essential and too concentrated spirits that come from books, to the inconstant genius of inspiration, to the powers of memory. Dear Rilke, you seemed to me to be enclosed in pure time; I feared for the effect on you of that transparency

of a life too uniform in its pace which, through the sameness of the days, showed distinctly the face of death.

How simple-minded of me to feel sorry for you while your thought was producing marvels out of that void and making time pregnant!

Enviable above all others is your dwelling place with its low tower, the enchanted tower of Muzot. That terrifying peace, the greatness of that quietude seem to me now, as they were for you then, the perfect state. If by some stroke of magic they became mine, I should no doubt be able to accomplish the gracious task of describing in words the admirable lineaments of your soul. I do not know it through its most famous and beautiful works. I am cut off from it by my ignorance. But I know it from direct knowledge; I divine what it awaits; I discern its profundity; I am conscious of its infinite resonance; and nothing is dearer to me than its gentle friendship, pervaded by that mysterious delicacy which is yours.

A Memory of Rilke

AMONG THE rare spirits I have known, one of the most attractive, and to me by far the most mysterious, was Rilke.

If the word magic has any meaning, I should say that the whole of his person, his voice, his look, his manners, everything about him gave the impression of a magic presence. You would have said that he had a way of giving to each word, as he spoke, the power of a charm.

That may be why he often seemed to me so different from myself and sometimes so difficult to understand. He had no doubt developed his thought in a direction completely opposite to the one I had taken and held to for so long. Was it, perhaps, a question of race? The memories he had preserved of his childhood and adolescence were far deeper and richer than my own, and they were always so much alive in him that the spiritual life of the mature man was completely permeated by them. His eyes, which were very fine, saw things I did not see: presentiments, signs or half-signs, significant coincidences, warnings to act or refrain from action on many occasions to which I was surprised to find that anyone could attach importance. I shall not recount the story that he told me of his final meeting with a princess of royal blood at a frontier railroad station. As the train slid noiselessly from its

halting place, gently removing her pale and lofty person standing upright at the door of the last coach, she made a strange sign in the air in which he saw a last farewell, for which he was utterly unprepared. His death shortly afterward showed that he had seen the truth.

Thirteen weeks before his death we spent almost a whole day together on the shores of Lake Geneva. In a park belonging to a friend, where he came to see me, we talked as we walked for hours on end. He had just finished the German translation of my poem on Narcissus. He had read it to a few friends at Lausanne and told me that he was very pleased with it. I replied that I was distressed at not being able to understand his language and that my great good fortune in being translated by such a man as himself must unhappily remain for me a source of abstract joy, since it was only by hearsay that I could appreciate the fine work that he had devoted to my own. Then I talked to him about the theme of Narcissus, which is one of the simplest of dramas. Etc. . . . A little more than two months later came the fatal telegram from Valmont. I could still see him going away on the little white paddle steamer that thrashes the blue waters, trailing and dipping in its furrows the edge and the reflection of its red flag with a white cross. We were feeling pleased with our day and waving our handkerchiefs. I had never seen him looking so well.

I have often thought since then of that perfect afternoon, and I associate it with the regret I feel at having taken so little advantage of Rilke's stays in Paris in order to talk with him at greater length. My time was limited and we lived a long way from each other. We were attracted to each other, and there was also that remarkable and, as it were, transcendent difference between us of which I have spoken. That is to say, we were both "good Europeans."

And that is why to think of him, to think of us, means for me at present to think of many other things. For example, of how much of the future there was in the past, and how much of the past there will be in the future.

Homage to Marcel Proust

ALTHOUGH I have scarcely read a single volume of Marcel Proust's great work, and though the very art of the novelist is an art that I find almost inconceivable, I am nevertheless well aware, from the little of the *Recherche du temps perdu* that I have found time to read, what an exceptionally heavy loss literature has just suffered; and not only literature but still more that secret society composed of those who in every age give the age its real value.

In any case, even if I had never read a line of Proust's vast work, the mere fact that two people with minds as different as Gide and Léon Daudet were agreed about its importance would have been sufficient to allay any doubts; such unexpected agreement could only occur in the case of a virtual certainty. We can be easy in our minds; the sun must be shining if they both proclaim the fact at the same time.

Others will speak with authority and penetration of the power and subtlety of Proust's work. Still others will tell us what manner of man it was who conceived the work and brought it to a glorious conclusion; I myself merely caught a glimpse of him many years ago. I can therefore only put forward a view without weight and barely worth recording. Let it be no more than a tribute, a fading flower on a tomb that will endure.

Since every literary form is the product of a particular way of using speech, the novel takes advantage of the immediate signifying power of language in order to bring before us one or more imaginary "lives," in which it creates the characters, determines time and place, describes incidents linked by a more or less adequate suggestion of causality.

While a poem brings our physical organism directly into play and has as its final term song, which is an exercise in precise and continuous liaison between the sense of hearing, the form of the voice, and articulate expression, the novel aims at awakening the general and intermittent sense of expectation which is the same as that aroused in us by real events; the art of the storyteller is to imitate their erratic occurrence or their normal sequence. And while the world of the poem is essentially closed and complete in itself, being a pure system composed of the ornaments and happy accidents of language, the world of the novel, even the fantastic novel, is bound to the real world in the same way that the *trompe-l'œil* blends into the tangible objects among which the spectator moves.

The impression of "life" and "truth," which the novelist calculates and seeks to create, is based on the continual introduction of the *observed fact*, that is to say, recognizable objects which he incorporates into his design. A pattern composed of actual yet arbitrary details creates a bond between the real existence of the reader and the imaginary existence of the characters; which explains why they are often endowed with a strange power of life that makes them comparable in our minds to real people. Without realizing it, we identify them with all the human beings who exist inside ourselves, because our capacity for living implies the capacity to make live. The value of the work is equal to the amount of life that we ourselves provide.

There must be no essential difference between the novel and the natural description of things that we have seen and heard. Neither rhythms, forms and figures of speech, nor even any definite structure are obligatory. There is only one rule, but it must be kept on pain of death: it is essential—and sufficient—that the sequence of events should carry and even *pull* us toward an end, which may be the illusion that we have been violently or deeply involved in an adventure, or else that we have gained a precise knowledge of fictitious people. It is a remarkable fact—it could be illustrated quite easily by the example of the popular novel—that a collection of signs in themselves completely insignificant and meaningless (since they can be transformed, one by one, into others equally trivial) can arouse the same passionate interest and the same effect as life. This must not be taken as implying a criticism of the novel; at the very most it is a mild accusation against life which turns out to be a perfectly genuine sum total of things, some of which are vain and others imaginary. . . .

It follows that the novel can find a place for anything evoked by and compatible with the orderly functioning of our memory when it recalls and explores a time through which we have lived: not only portraits, landscapes, and what is known as "psychology," but also every kind of thought, allusions to every form of knowledge. It can excite; it can compel the whole mind.

In this respect there is a similarity of form between the novel and the dream; they could be defined by a curious quality which is common to both: *their deviations are an integral part of them.*

It is more the custom to compare poems with dreams, but this seems to me to be a sign of loose thinking.

Unlike poetry, it is possible to give a *résumé* of a novel,

that is to say, it can itself be *related*; it is possible to extract from it an image which resembles it; one whole aspect of it, then, if we choose, can become implicit. It can also be *translated* into another language without losing its essence. It can be *elaborated* internally or *continued* indefinitely, just as it can be read at several sittings. . . . The only limits on its length and diversity are the leisure and endurance of the reader; every restriction that may be imposed on it is the result not of its essential nature but of the intentions and specific decisions of the writer.

Proust turned such a loose and simple structure to the most extraordinary account. He did not seize "life" through action itself; he identified himself with it and, so to speak, imitated it by the superabundance of echoes that the least image awakened in the very substance of the author. He provided endless roots for every germ of analysis that the circumstances of his life had implanted in him. The interest of his work lies in each fragment. We can open the book wherever we choose; its vitality does not depend on what went before, on a sort of *acquired illusion*; it depends on what might be called the *active properties* of the very tissues of the text.

Proust analyzes—and gives us the feeling of being able to go on analyzing indefinitely—what other writers usually pass over.

At each new stage in our lives we have just overlooked *an infinity of possibilities*, which is simply the capacity of all our memories to combine with one another. In order to get on with our external life and adjust ourselves to events, we are bound to neglect this function of imminence which belongs to our deepest nature. We are inwardly made of something that is making itself, and does so at the expense of the possible. We are, by virtue of consciousness alone, completely

inexhaustible—we who cannot pause inside ourselves with-
out at once being assailed by so many thoughts, seeing one
take the place of another, or one developing inside the other,
opening up a vista of parentheses. . . . The mind cannot pre-
vent itself from continually creating and devouring its crea-
tures. At every moment it forms other embryo lives, con-
ceives its monsters and its heroes, sketches out theories, begins
poems. . . . Everything we lose by forgetting, or think we
lose, along with everything we can expect or hope for from
ourselves, the treasure house of all values and of the valueless,
from which each of us extracts the thing he is—that, no
doubt, is what Marcel Proust calls *le temps perdu*, "lost time."
No one, or practically no one, before him had deliberately
made use of its resources. To do so was to make the fullest use
of his being; it was in this way that he consumed it.

Proust was able to apply the powers of his inner life, singu-
larly rich and curiously wrought, to portraying a tiny society
which wanted to be, which had to be, *superficial*. By his crea-
tive act, the picture of a superficial society became a profound
work.

Ought so much intelligence to be lavished on such a task?
Was the subject worth so much trouble and such prolonged
attention? The question deserves examination.

What chooses to call itself "Society" consists entirely of
symbolical figures. No one appears in it except by virtue of
some abstraction. It is clearly necessary that all forms of power
should meet; that somehow *money* should chat with *beauty*;
that *politics* should grow accustomed to *elegance*; that *literature*
and *birth* should get on together and invite one another to tea.
As soon as a new form of power wins recognition, it is not
long before its representatives make their appearance at the
parties given by "Society"; and the movement of history can

be summed up quite well in the gradual accession of the various social species to the salons, the hunts, the marriages and the funerals of the tribe that occupies the top place in a nation.

Since all these abstractions are represented by individuals who are what they are, the result is a series of contrasts and complications which can only be observed on a tiny stage. In the same way that in a sense a banknote is only a piece of paper, so the person belonging to "Society" combines a sort of fiduciary value with a living substance. The combination is marvelously suited to the ends of a subtle writer of novels.

We must not forget that our greatest writers have hardly ever considered anything but the Court. They extracted nothing but comedies from the Town, and fables from the country. But truly great art, the art of simplified figures and the purest types—those abstract beings who make possible a parallel and almost a musical development of the consequences of a quite isolated situation—is bound up with the existence of a conventional milieu where people speak a language adorned with veils and supplied with limits, where *appearance* commands *reality*, and nobly keeps it under a restraint that changes the whole of life into an exercise in presence of mind. . . .

The "Society" of today is not so clearly ordered as the Court of long ago. Yet it has shown itself capable—thanks no doubt to a certain disorder and the interesting contradictions to be found in it—of furnishing the creator of Charlus and the Guermantes with his characters and his themes—some of which are extremely penetrating. But it was in his own depths that Marcel Proust sought the metaphysic which no society can be without.

As for the means he used, they are undoubtedly derived

from our finest tradition. It is sometimes said that his books are not altogether easy to read. But I never fail to reply that we must bless the difficult authors of our day. If they develop a few readers, it is not merely for their personal use. At the same time that they win them for themselves, they give them back to Montaigne, to Descartes, to Bossuet, and a few others who are perhaps still worth reading. All these great men talk in abstractions; they reason; they probe deeply; in a single sentence they may express the entire substance of a complete development of thought. They are not afraid of the reader; they do not count their own labor or his. Given a little more time, we shall no longer be able to understand them.

Funeral Address on Bergson

[1941]

I FELT THAT, at the beginning of a year which finds France at her lowest ebb, exposed to the harshest of trials and with a future almost impossible to imagine, I ought to express in this place the hope of all of us, members of the Academy, present or absent, that the times which lie ahead will be less bitter, less calamitous, less fearful than those through which we lived in 1940 and in which we are still living.

And now, in the very first days of the new year, the Academy has been, as it were, struck on the head. M. Bergson died last Saturday, January 4, at the age of eighty-one—died, it appears, without pain, from a congestion of the lungs. On Monday the great man's body was transferred from his home to the cemetery of Garches, in circumstances that were necessarily of the simplest and most moving. No funeral ceremony; no speeches; but those who were present were no doubt all the more quietly aware, in their meditations, of the exceptional loss we have suffered. About thirty people had assembled, in a drawing room, round the coffin. I expressed the sympathy of the Academy to Mme. Bergson, and she asked me to thank you on her behalf. Immediately afterward the coffin was taken away, and at the door of the house we paid a last tribute to the greatest philosopher of our time.

He was the pride of our Society. Whether or not we were attracted by his metaphysics, whether or not we had followed him in the profound researches to which he devoted the whole of his life, and in the truly creative evolution of his thought, which became steadily bolder and more independent, we possessed in him the most authentic example of the highest intellectual virtues. In intellectual matters his name, universally known, stood for a sort of moral authority. France was able to appeal to that name and that authority in circumstances which I am sure you will recall. He had a large number of disciples who followed him with a fervor, almost a devotion, which no one coming after him in the world of ideas can at present flatter himself that he inspires.

I do not propose to discuss his philosophy. This is not the moment to undertake an examination which would need to be searching and which could only be so if it were done in the light of brighter days and by means of the full and unfettered exercise of thought. The very ancient and for that reason very difficult problems with which M. Bergson dealt, those of time, memory, and above all the evolution of life, were through him given a new beginning, and the position of philosophy as it appeared in France fifty years ago has undergone a remarkable change. At that time, the powerful Kantian criticism, armed with a formidable apparatus for the checking of knowledge and an abstract terminology which had been very skillfully worked out, dominated education and even made its impact felt in politics, in so far as there can be any contact between politics and philosophy. M. Bergson was neither won over nor daunted by the rigor of a doctrine which seemed to decree so imperatively the limits of thought, and he set to work to rescue metaphysics from the state of discredit and neglect into which it had fallen. You know what a

stir was caused by his lectures at the Collège de France, and the world-wide fame that he won for his theories and his analysis. While the majority of philosophers since the eighteenth century had been influenced by physicomechanical theories, our eminent colleague had fortunately been attracted to the natural sciences. He found inspiration in biology. He meditated on the nature of life, and understood and conceived it as the vehicle of mind. He was not afraid to scrutinize his own consciousness, in his search for light on certain problems that will never be solved. But he had performed an indispensable service by restoring and rehabilitating the taste for a form of meditation closer to our own essence than the purely logical elaboration of concepts that, in any case, cannot be satisfactorily defined. The true value of philosophy lies simply in leading thought back to itself. The effort to do this requires of anyone wishing to describe the process, and to communicate what he discovers about his inner life, a special kind of application and even the invention of a form of expression suited to the purpose, for language fails at its own source. This was where the full resources of M. Bergson's genius became apparent. He was bold enough to borrow the magic weapons of Poetry, and combined its powers with the kind of precision that a mind trained in the exact sciences will never allow itself to forgo. The most felicitous, the most original of images and metaphors came at his call, reproducing in the consciousness of other people the discoveries he had made in his own, along with the results also of his inner experiments. This created a style which, though philosophical, avoided pedantry—a fact that disconcerted and even scandalized some, while many others were delighted to find in the flexibility, richness, and grace of his language a freedom and subtlety which are essentially French, but which the previous generation had felt that

serious speculation should studiously avoid. Let me remind you that this revival was roughly contemporary with the one that took place in the world of music when Claude Achille Debussy began to produce his subtle and highly independent works. Both were characteristically French manifestations.

That is not all. Henri Bergson, a great philosopher and a great writer, was also, as he had to be, a great friend of mankind. His mistake, perhaps, was to think that mankind was worth befriending. He worked wholeheartedly for the union of minds and ideals, which he felt should precede the union of political institutions and powers. But may it not be precisely the contrary that must happen? Perhaps, too, we must regard as specifically human the widely varied forms of antagonism which exist among men, including that which divides the partisans of union from those who do not believe in it but regard it as a dangerous myth.

M. Bergson no doubt thought that the very fate of the mind is inseparable from the sense of its presence and universal value; in that respect, and in others besides, he was in sympathy with those forms of thought which are essentially religious. The sense of life, even in its simplest and humblest manifestations, appeared to him to be basically spiritual. All this enables us to imagine what must have been the state of this vast and profound intellect in the face of events which have ruined such noble hopes and changed the face of things so rapidly and so violently. Did he despair? Did he manage to preserve his faith in the evolution of the human species toward a more and more exalted condition? I do not know: being unaware that he had been in Paris since September and only learning of his presence at the very moment I heard of his death, I was unable to go and see him. But I cannot doubt

that he felt wounded to the depths of his being by the total disaster which has overtaken us.

A very lofty, very pure and superior exemplar of the thinking man, and perhaps one of the last men who will have devoted himself exclusively, profoundly, and nobly to thinking, in a period when the world thinks and meditates less and less, when, with each day that passes, civilization is further reduced to the memories and vestiges we keep of its multifarious riches and its free and abundant intellectual production, while poverty, suffering, and restrictions of every kind discourage and depress all intellectual enterprise, Bergson seems already to belong to a past age and his name to be the last great name in the history of the European mind.

APPENDIX

Comment from the Notebooks

Descartes

1900

No one could have taken the *Cogito* less seriously than Descartes—he put it at the head of his work simply because he had to put *something* there. 2:187

1903

The genius of Descartes lay in showing us how to make an endless number of definitions—that is, structures that always amount to a mathematical entity. Wherever there is a uniform structure there is a mathematical entity—co-ordinated variations. . . . Otherwise, natural forms are meaningless to the mathematician. He calls them nonanalytical functions. . . .
 3:89

1910

"I think, therefore I am." This is not a piece of reasoning. It's a fist coming down on a table, to corroborate words in the mind. . . . 4:487

1911

His naïveté: pinching himself to make sure he is not dreaming. This is Descartes and his *Cogito*. 4:508

1913

The Cartesian *Cogito* should not be construed in itself. As an argument it is not self-sufficient—taken alone it means nothing.

It's a magnificent shout, the climax of a drama, a literary slogan—a decisive act, a mind's *coup d'état*.

It marks the point where the man and the philosopher meet—the passage from imitative youth to thinking manhood. 5:144

1924

Descartes created the ideal language of physics—one requiring geometry and algebra. . . . 9:702

I wonder if Descartes read Montaigne? 9:794

> Life said: "I am sad, therefore I weep."
> Music said: "I weep, therefore I am sad." 10:103

Descartes and Clarity. No *occult* qualities whatever. His greatest effort was toward *clarity*. He was hardly dead when gravitation, electricity, and later on, life, etc.—energy.
10:103

Portrait of Descartes: the lifted eyebrow—the imbalance suggests a dual vision. 10:251

Descartes sees the *power* of thought, Pascal its impotence.
10:350

A crucial question.

Imagine 2 humanities, one governed by the spirit of Descartes, the other by the spirit of Pascal. Choose. Both men

were extraordinary—one by rule, the other by accident (even in matters of religion).

I like Descartes because of the great, simple purity of the man, the solidity of his thought, the general air of honesty and order apparent in his whole manner. 10:359

Cogito—and the world divides.

Two directions:
 One toward the infra—toward God (supra).
 The other toward concise, measurable knowledge.
 I first thought of the *Cogito* as a magic formula—*Fiat lux*: the knowable world divides, the land is separated from the waters, the rigid from the flexible, the measurable from the irrational, etc.
 Later, as a postulate—thought and self as parallels. 10:374

1926

Pascal is more exciting to the mind than Descartes; Descartes excites the will.

Pascal is a turbulent sort of agitator. He changes his mind, reverses his direction, upsets everything, shatters himself, destroys his own arguments by citing the prophets, etc. Descartes brings control. Pascal is a sort of drug, violent and depressive. Descartes regulates, he is a tonic—he puts God himself to use. 11:381

Descartes tries to find something objective in the subjective.
 11:770
1927

Descartes, genius of order;
Pascal, of general disorder. 12:483

1928

Find what Descartes wanted, what it was possible for him to want (in the 1640's), what he coveted if only half consciously —there's the base, the strategic point to be clarified.

Once that is settled, the *man* follows his own trajectory, but the directions are known. 12:615

1929

Cogito. . . . This is to give great importance to the verb *to be!* Believing that it has a specific meaning, and the meaning an object or *value.* The object of a meaning is the value of that meaning in observable "reality."

Thus, a "centaur" is a meaning without an object.

Ergo sum. Sum! the magic word:

Descartes staging a *coup d'état.* 13:449

1935

"Descartes": *Cogito*

I'd like to catch him—if there were any way—*in the act*: the *self* intervening *in person,* becoming a philosopher. "I" becoming a factor—a point of reference—in short . . . an *oracle!*

In the *Cogito,* 2 curious points: a mythical value is given to the word *be,* and the knowledge of a certain "reality" is based on the self. 18:174

1936

Cogito

You must confess, Monsieur des Cartes, that to say "*I am*" is to say absolutely nothing; and to say "*I think*" is to say: "I

312

talk to myself, I see, or operate, in a certain way—I compare."

19:375

1937

Descartes:

Soldier plus man of leisure and curiosity.

Discourse on Method:

The novelty was *man* coming back into philosophy—the old-fashioned measure of things.

Since Aristotle, man had been left out; in his stead, analysis of discourse.

(In short, look for what was not there before Descartes.)

But, man in person (the method is the man): there's the bottom of the "I am." At a single stroke:

1) The hierarchy of subjects was transformed. It was the body that interested him—anatomy, etc.

2) Whence, perhaps, the co-ordinates—geometry.

3) Physics and mechanics—the world system—mathematics clarified. 19:803

Descartes:

"Clear and distinct ideas."

This depends on our ability. It leads to constructing knowledge out of the components of our ability.

In any case, we inevitably assume that all *real* things are *real* only in so far as they contain nothing that could not be turned into *clear* ideas. Anything that cannot be conceived as a clear idea *does not exist*. There is no such thing as the *not clear* in itself. That's the position of Cartesius. The real is that which has been, or can be, determined.

It leads to *matter and movement*, i.e., to solid bodies. But . . .

19:859

313

May 1940

The *Cogito* has (or has had) immense value, but it has never had any meaning. 23:292

Descartes—antiphilosopher. His first concern was with application. The *Cogito* meant "no more philosophy." His God was a fundamental postulate, to clear the ground. Then came his truly great ideas: a *universe* represented entirely in mathematical terms, and this brought him to the idea (new at the time) of *conservation*—since the whole unified system of reference had to be expressed in an equation—and then the idea of the *product* as a form. . . . 23:481

1945

Descartes' famous distinction between the physical world and the other can be verified, as it has been by subsequent events, that is to say by the spectacular success of the quantitative analysis of phenomena. 29:895

Pascal

1900

Pascal. . . . Actually, he had a taste for rigorous thought, a taste that was both a thing of the past and ahead of his time. . . . It was the moment when the infinitesimal calculus was being developed, and it was better not to look at things too closely.

<div align="right">2:180</div>

1904

There is something childish about Pascal. 3:486

1912

Pascal missed a very fine chance to drive a team of two if not three.

 He beat his horses—when the supreme tact would have been to harness them elegantly, since they were his, and to spare their mettle.

<div align="right">4:803</div>

1920

"Pascal, or the sin of pride . . . against pride." 7:415

1924

Pascal used rigorous reasoning on fanciful texts, to which he added, as given, the subjective notions of Montaigne and the

like—about life, the vanity of all things, relativity, etc.—
 that the Scriptures are true—as fact;
 that the Scriptures are enigmas—as reasoning;
 that everything is either evil or nothing. 9:703

Pascal (in matters of religion) was educated by men who knew nothing about mysticism, and had either forgotten their theology or had contempt for it. 10:79

Pascal, enemy of the human race. Apologists are a disagreeable lot. The indecency of any man who wants to convince, or charm—the *ambivalent* nature of the work he produces.

 10:194

Pascal's Wager: an offense against religion—or rather against God, if God could be offended—and a scandal in science. But worse—it is not even an anxious inquiry, it's a device in apologetics. 10:272

Pascal:
 I hate confusion—
 I hate to see a man putting into mathematical form things to which number and measure do not apply, and doing it merely to be impressive—and that this should be obvious. Above all when the man doing it is a great mathematician. . . .
 I hate to see the "infinite" abused, since it is nothing but a word, and even if it means something, that something is none of our affair. I hate to see affectation mixed with sincerity— it's a matter of the art of writing.
 I hate to see a man using artifice to turn others against their lot, when they are in it in spite of themselves and are doing what they can to make the best of it; to see a man trying

to persuade others that they must expect the worst, must always keep in mind the most intolerable notion of their predicament, and be alert to whatever is most unbearable in it—which is precisely the notion of nothingness, the void, the notion of suffering and risk, and anxiety about the risk—using the notion of eternity as an almighty weapon, and developing it by the artifice of repetition.

A great intelligence—a small mind—not much originality —no artist at all—no imagination—*petit bourgeois*.

A miser, a skinflint.

If all the borrowed ideas and stupid notions were struck out of the *Pensées!* 10:342

"Pascal against civilization." 10:400

1925

Pascal: a profound mind with petty views (his speculations on the infinite are naïve). 10:537

Pascal made fun of a Jesuit who said that light was the light-producing movement of luminous particles. Those particles are now coming back, under the name of photons. 10:627

Style:

Pascal's famous revision—changing "too much light dazzles" to "too much light obscures"—is a nice argument:

1) against Pascal as a so-called inspired writer—since it's a piece of rhetoric, a fake window, not even nicely placed. It's an effect—P. is a rhetorician.

2) against the silly devotees of clarity—

"Obscures" is no doubt right, but from wanting "too much light." 10:682

Pascal, enemy of the human race.
Everything in Pascal is against man.
Man has the right to defend himself. 10:706

January 1929

The malice in Pascal is obvious.
Charity . . . !
The Jansenists put a rigor into the *heart* that belongs in the mind. 13:417

1932

What I detest in Pascal is the *mixture* (in a man whose greatest quality should have been *purity*). That is why the Romantics took him up. The mixture makes him *probable—average—*too human. But what becomes of his greatness? 16:109

1933

Pascal is reductive: the sublime at half price; death, a means. Among his *Thoughts* there are not many that can help to transform a man into more than man; but plenty that can flatten him.

In short, an enemy of the human race. 16:201

My complaint against Pascal is that he wanted to *persuade*; and for his purposes—as it always happens in such cases—he distorted, overstated, withheld, etc.

For me this is shocking—I've caught him in the act of *literature*. As I see it, if a man has something to say and thinks it should be said, he should put it just as it is in his mind—that is, with his objections, etc., always included. Exactly as it is.

16:592

Pascal. The Wager is absurd, since it names only one alterna-
tive and concludes with a hope in mathematics, whereas the
gain and the loss are on the one hand inconceivable, and on
the other as indefinite as the terms of the Wager. The interest-
ing thing is the idea of putting this great question in the form
of a wager. He could have made something of that. 17:13

1934

Pascal & Co.

I have said but one thing—the book or collection of
Pensées is not *serious*.

To base one's argument on the prophets of Israel, when
on the other hand one is Pascal and the great mathematician
that he was, is to my mind a *comedy*.

To invoke the "eternal silence," when, after all, it was
invented to fit the needs of a beautiful phrase—same conclu-
sion. 17:389

1935

To translate Pascal: "The heart has its reasons," etc., means
"the heart has its powers of excitement which the faculties of
judgment and exact knowledge do not recognize." 17:835

Among all the most gifted of men, Pascal is the most envious.
He loathes Descartes, the Jesuits, the nobility, the army, the
courts, the arts—(Scholasticism).

No belief in the progress of the sciences, no foresight. A
merciless critic, a great mathematician. A physicist with a
narrow outlook. *Esprit de finesse*. 18:311

(January–February) 1936

Pascal: "eternal silence" and "infinite space." Two images falsified by the way they are expressed. He neither heard, nor looked. Therefore ... "poetry"—but in a work offered as something quite other than poetry. 18:724

December

Pascal: a bad end, a good beginning. At first, serious and sound—with a will to see clearly and to do the duty of a man of profound mind. Being ambitious, he was jealous—even to the point of borrowing an idea here and there.

Ending in such a state of misery that he took up apologetics, and his fame is the invention of such comedians as B. and others. 19:716

1943

Pascaliana: Pascal believed only in witnesses who end on the gallows!

Nonsense. If they are stupid enough to get themselves hanged, they are as credulous as they are stupid.

To end on the gallows makes no sense except in defense of something one is not sure of, but is determined *at any cost* that it shall be true, or thought to be so.

But when one is sure! There is nothing to do but shrug one's shoulders. 28:83

There are certain mystical writers, women especially, who give the impression that they are playing with Christ as children do with a doll, making him talk, teasing him, etc. Pascal was one of those. 28:219

1945

"The heart has its reasons" . . .

No—they're not *reasons*, but something quite different: they are *powers*.

. . . "that reason does not know."

It knows them only too well. 29:747

Pascal proves and demonstrates, again and again, the nothingness of man; but he doesn't seem to see that his well-founded condemnation falls at the same time on all that man is able to think and believe, and therefore on his God.

Isn't he saying: Theology, what Vanity! 29:895

Bossuet

Modern theories of the unconscious—a form of degeneration. They tend to destroy the highroad so painfully built up by the Occident, and so magnificent—Bossuet as the example.

4:332

1922

The problem of Bossuet's great passages; his "clinchers"—a problem in statistics and aesthetics. 9:42

Swedenborg

April 1936

About Swedenborg—I am working on him, *per accidens*, these days. He is a case (with every possible doubt about "the sincerity of anything in writing") of rather sudden transmutation—etc.

Related questions:

The transposition of psychic events into language;

Why I doubt the validity of describing *daydreams*;

The role of language—the spoken and the written phase;

Recourse to articulate language necessarily brings in elements of a very different *order* from the instantaneous elements of immediate, subjective, raw perception;

There is a sort of *finish*, or shaping, that *destroys what would be of the greatest interest* to know, the *chrono-molecular* structure. As if one were studying a living person (a real moment is a sort of *living person*)—

Expressing something in words is an operation that radically alters the immediate nature of subjective phenomena (two different moments are involved), introducing the *fact of re-cognizing them*, and it is impossible to *recognize* them without unconsciously *producing* the recognition—cancelling their uniqueness and spontaneity. So we give them a sequence, a . . . *narratability* that presupposes an observer independent of them, as well as connections and separations, discontinuity

and continuity, *which are certainly no part of the moment itself.*

In particular, the action and reaction *between the self and its perceptions* is [sic] completely stopped—and yet, that is the important thing. A system of inner forces is very different from a system of external ones.

So invention comes in. 19:81

Voltaire

As a literary critic, Voltaire had the most positive, the most technical, the boldest intelligence. 4:477

1917

Voltaire is the classic par excellence, much more classical than the 17th-century authors, for the simple reason that he was prodigiously intelligent and came later. He knew their art, and he judged them as a whole.

This is the man who "discovered" Shakespeare. And it was he who said, so admirably: poetry is made of nothing but beautiful details—the truest and profoundest of remarks . . . one that opened the way to all modern poetry. . . .

. . . What Voltaire calls *beautiful details* is simply the continuous condition of the poetic—whether the detail is an image, a turn of syntax, a sound, etc. . . . 6:450

1926

A quick wit is as good as profundity. 11:529

April 1945

Ego—more and more 18th century. . . .

I've been drunk on Voltaire (the letters) for the past month.

A capital figure. He had the gall to believe in nothing, or to think he did. And he forced his view onto the public. Freedom of thought has belonged *ever since* to the general public —no longer the preserve of the few.

He makes all the great men of the *Age of Louis XIV* look like boys—Racine, etc.: choir boys caught at their idle chatter. Cf. what Voltaire says about Pascal.

In short, Voltaire is a divide in the history of Europe. After him, all religious thought became a special case, a paradox, or a prejudice. 29:722

May [*1945*]

Dear old Voltaire! . . . in these letters, I keep coming on things very much my own. But what zest he had—at my age! And he says he laughs! . . . 29:846

Goethe

The "wisdom of Goethe" was simply a matter of living for a very long time with his powers unimpaired, and in a very unsettled period. 2:729

Goethe was an actor. He played the comedy of the intellect— his role, intelligence. The trouble with the role was that he couldn't *be*, if he had to *seem*, intelligent. It is impossible to impersonate, and at the same time really to be, the dominant intellect. So Goethe's "wisdom," as they say, was compounded of borrowing from both sides—but more from the theatrical. 2:906

1907

Goethe, prince of impresarios. He gave its most "elegant" form to the charlatanism discovered by Voltaire who, at a favorable moment, made of the man of letters a universal, political, prostitute-idol, a sort of Augustus Caesar elevated by popular opinion—as if the truly superior man could be recognized by the crowd. Then came Lamartine, Hugo, the dissolution of the Empire, and the thousands of little Caesars of the press and telegraph. 4:183

August 1930

Mass production:

"Shakespeare, Dante, Cervantes, Goethe." Prefabricated idols. Literary bogeymen. A street-vendor's wares. Models for four engravings. "Great writers," for the people and the nation.

Such deification precludes reading and "admiring."

14:538

1931

Goethe—the Profound Comedy. 15:142

January 1943

An actor in the Comedy of Culture.

Goethe: above all, a great actor—an actor of genius in the role of a man of genius, much more than he was a *man of genius*.

Goethe's handsome physique served his fame—and perhaps (No!—certainly) had its influence on *him*. It suggested, even required, a pose.

Nietzsche, an entirely different sort of mind—greatly superior to Goethe. But corrupted by "history." A first-rate intellectual ex-sensibility. Philology and neurology.

Zarathustra (in translation) bores me. Allegory. 26:695

April 1945

Ego—I am struck, reading Robert d'Harcourt's *Gœthe et l'art de vivre*, to find that Goethe and I have a great many "phobias" and obsessions in common—with certain essential

differences, of course. But it's remarkable how many, and how striking, are the traits we have in common.

My hand closely resembles his (the cast at Abbé Mugnier's), and both very different from Hugo's. Yet, a number of contrasts: the sense of order, the art of escape, etc. I have nothing of these.

Addendum: I am also finding in this book certain aspects of Goethe that turn up in *My Faust*—I was unaware of them before I wrote it.

For instance, the disciple scene in *Luste*, and the big scene in II.

I have no idea how I manifest these similarities in *egoesthesia* to Goethe.

Whereas, in the matter of differences, he seems to me a great deal like Gide. Plants, insects, escape, studied poses, disciples, etc. . . .

Perhaps there are *chrononomic* waves. 29:721

Stendhal

1900

Stendhal—"nerve" as a normal social practice.　　　　2:158

1907

Stendhal—his talent is presence of mind.　　　　4:211

1908

Stendhal—the exact opposite of Mallarmé.

"In a certain sense" the difference is one of *distribution*. In the former, everything signifies—that is, he will have nothing to do with signs, he substitutes reality for them. He "realizes" (in the sense of *realizing a fortune*), turns literature into a definite, immediate pleasure of the same order as real things, the pleasure of seeing clearly—excitement defined its object.

Anything "poetic" he puts into song. There is a strange phrase in *Rome, Naples, and Florence*—a phrase not too far from Mallarmé.

For the latter, form is everything—it defines without naming, indicates by omission. . . .　　　　4:481

1918

My complaint against Stendhal is that he didn't understand

or have any real feeling for any but the social being, and for *him* only as he was to be seen in the comic view. Stendhal's people are all "learning" society, seeing it in contrast to their own "sensibility"—and with a great deal of intelligence.

In any case, for me characters in novels are all unbearable.

7:155

1928

Take any sentence in Stendhal, for example: was it written for an effect, or is it an observation?

Did he *think* it, without reference to a likely audience? or did he deduce it from his notion of that audience? Does it aim to be clear in itself? Or is it aimed at someone?

It is a function of what?

That's the whole question!

Now in writers P, Q, and R (Hugo), it is clear that everything is an *effect*. They are consistent (con-sis-tent). But in such writers as Pascal, Rousseau, and even Stendhal, it is not clear —there's something equivocal.

I am aware of this in myself, constantly having to write things that are not simply drawn from my own nature and circumstances, but complicated by irrelevant considerations.

13:17

Stendhal lived at a time when there was such a thing as *passion* —I mean suffering, a kind of acute illness (which it is), a quality, a kind of nobility, etc.—"genius" in the order of feeling. . . .

Wherefore, hypocrisy in passion—simulation. . . . But how is one to be sure? . . . 13:17

February 1940

Stendhal—3 postures: a man of wit, a man of knowledge (positive), a man of passion. 23:117

331

1942

Stendhal—Voltaire

Stendhal's characters—just as "alive," and just as fake or conventional, as the characters in Voltaire's tales. They are stimulants. The life in them is the whole of their author's wit —a species of diabolism that sets the intelligent *ingenu* against the established order of things.

Actually such faking is quite justified. . . . 26:133

1943

Beyle, like Goethe, belongs to the class of *actors*. His way of talking about love, etc., always front stage, with very amusing "suggestions."

I say *actors* (no doubt because of some remnant of 18th-century influence), and I account for this notion by another: that is, we sense that there's not very much behind the writing —behind the wish *to write*. *To write* is the great thing. *To produce an effect* on someone is always *a principle of comedy*. . . .

26:776

Stendhal belongs to the literary type of actors—that is, those whose works are simply a role they are playing—and they *watch* their audience, never take their eyes off it. The genre is terribly irritating—their motives are always obvious.

Yet the actor in question is an excellent actor.

But you can hear the *prompter*—that is, the determination to succeed by using passion and the pretense of never being the dupe—except perhaps of oneself as a lover. The scheme is obvious in every line, and this is what I call "the prompter."

After a hundred pages you can predict—every time—Stendhal's reaction to anything at all.

But again, an excellent actor. Wonderfully good in his 3 or 4 roles. His "young lead," his "bores," his "villains"—always a bit the same, and more and more "period," but perfectly realized.

Comment: in literature, any marked *sincerity* is the sign of the actor.

In this I find that Stendhal, whether he will or not, is like certain illustrious (or not) writers of the religious or pious type.

To be completely oneself before an audience is quite simply . . . to wear a disguise. 26:882

1944

Moments of ridiculous naïveté in Stendhal. So, his intelligence, quick as it was, didn't react when he was overtaken with wanting to appear to his reader as the man of passion? Or to show him how to fight with a pistol? Someone should make a list of his pretensions. In these, he is 19th century, and less 18th. He can sometimes say, vividly, something stupid— and it's nearly always when he is writing about himself. He draws his caricature, not his portrait. We can see him listening to himself. He is alone—with onlookers. 29:18

Flaubert

1903

. . ."as boring as Flaubert." 3:51

1909

Flaubert had the bad luck to convince himself that there is one and only one way to describe a matchbox. Once the way is found—fame and immortality. 4:369

1915

Bouvard and Pécuchet—a fairly stupid book, like its author:

A series of pigeonholes, a device the "Naturalists" found useful.

It's taken by some as a sort of intellectual *Ecclesiastes*—the vanity of all knowledge.

If that's the intent, the means are absurd. What he should have done was not to take a pair of idiots, but to show the stupidity of the great—Pascal, Kant, on their own stage.

5:659

1916

Reading Flaubert is unbearable to anyone who can think—he's incompatible with thought. 6:141

1921

To put it briefly, the art of Flaubert and his ilk is a taste for the *trompe-l'œil*, for making marble out of cardboard—things and people out of words. 8:349

Re Flaubert—
Gabbing gets you nowhere. 8:365

1924

Flaubert's style (*Ibrahim, sans se détourner, de temps en temps, criait la manœuvre à ses matelots*) describes by juxtaposition— it's impossible to find the order. Another vice of this style— there's always room for one more detail. 10:46

Verlaine

1925

Verlaine—wretched—a career of poverty.
Crude manners, habits, ideas—but what a voice! 10:609

January 1932

Verlaine—that *mélange*—that garbage—or rather slop bucket.
 Verlaine and Rimbaud, angels chanting *Merde!* in chorus.
 15:475

Nietzsche

Nietzsche is not a nourishment but a living force. 2:702

1905

Not the *will* to power, not at all—merely the wish. 3:499

1915

Nietzsche—precisely the naïve professor, like the Normal School student who doesn't dare admit he is one. The "grind." The notion of "the class," the prize competition, "originality." Cf. Taine and the like.

Nietzsche, an episode in the overthrow of the school-masters.

Determined to be taken seriously. . . . 5:689

1921

Nietzsche (and many another): creative syphilis. 8:465

October 1929

(Merely a stimulant, not a nourishment.)

Nietzsche doesn't represent a "philosophy" (fortunately for him)—he's both composer and composed . . . a "poet" of

the nervous system. And all his effects are reactions transposed (into language)—objections, answers, contradictions—endless *escapes*, etc. in which the excitement, the substitutes, the grouping, etc., take "ideas"—that is to say, sign-words—as their mode of expression. . . . The only figure I can think of to illustrate this generality is a hand with each finger capped by a little head. *The life in this puppet is the life of the hand*, and it appears to be five characters. The spectator sees a comedy. The puppeteer in this case may *believe* in his characters.

One of these may represent the "universe," another "sexuality," or metaphysics, or nature, etc. This can be done (and everyone does it) because of the nature of *language*—which makes it possible to express and combine "notions," with *extraordinary freedom* as regards their *origin* and actual *meaning*—and in spite of these—and by means of the mechanism, or the real automaton, which is the nervous system.

14:36

May–June 1931

Nietzsche. How could this man (really a *lonely* man, I believe) bear to write such rant, to transpose so naïvely such bits of ideas into a warrior's bluster and bragging, or rather the declamations of some Biblical hero or Assyrian monarch? . . . His sense of being above mankind, a notion common to all thinkers, and commonplace enough—or at least usual in this sort of "talker."

(A *thinker* is a *talker* before the fact.) 15:114

1932

The nonsense in Nietzsche and his followers:
Let's get tough, etc. Cf. patriotic songs. A braggart and a bully. *Cheap stuff.* A weak man's need.

Nietzsche is one of the weak—Cf. his fear of the Decadents.
16:21

January 1939

Nietzsche's *eternal return*, Heraclitus' *river*: these are ab-
surdities—notice the observer counting the returns, or watch-
ing the flow. But they *are* true products of sensibility—
complementaries.

How can such ideas be *thought about?* . . . Anyone who tries
it, destroys them. 21:911

1943

Reading Nietzsche. The thing that's false (and he is among
those I admire most in the realm of ideas) is the emphasis he
puts on *others*, on polemic, and everything having to do with
theories. He sees things too much as if they were already
Literary History—and himself the victor over Socrates and
Kant.

Also his magic word: *Life*. But that's too easy. 26:711

I know of nothing crazier than Nietzsche's famous question:
Would you care to live this life of yours over and over again?
But ignoring this absurd and unthinkable ghost of an idea,
the Eternal Return, one might reply that it offers a choice be-
tween a return that's no return (if the one before is forgotten)
and a boring repetition—in fact, unbearable to think of.

Compare this with Faust's apostrophe: "Stop, Moment"
. . . etc. Maybe there's some connection between these two
poses. They are nothing but poses. . . . 26:799

April 1945

"Nietzsche—exciting humbugology." 29:715

Rilke

29 December 1926

A telegram tells me Rilke is dead. 11:883

November 1928

Yesterday at Marthe de Fels', saw Dr. Emmerli, of Valmont, who had telegraphed me at the time of Rilke's death. He said Rilke used to talk to him constantly about me, so he knows a great deal about me without knowing me. Rilke's end: he pricked his finger on a rose thorn—leukemia—he was covered with black pustules—suffered horribly. Would allow narcotics to be given him only up to the point of losing consciousness—agreed to crook his little finger as a sign that it was enough. 13:314

Proust

Montesquiou–Proust–Lucien–3 tarts, and what falsettos!
Spoiled on fine literature, acute nonsense. Deadly bores, not
a whit of intellectual force. But every dessert and confection
in the world—all of them poison. Frills and curls. 13:679

1931

Proust is baroque. 15:353

Proust—descriptive "psychology"—vulgar ideas, double
meanings—the fake truth of the novel. 15:353

August 1934

26/8/34. Have 2 vols. of Proust Letters. Lord! how far I am
from all this.

I can't conceive how anyone could write such letters—
always clamoring to be reviewed. 17:454

341

Bergson

Bergson told me yesterday that he wiped the slate clean in 1890 and began his system by studying memory, bringing together the data relating to amnesia, which he considers fundamental in the matter.

I noted—to myself—that I set about my own philosophy two years later (in 92)—and no need to wipe the slate clean, since there was nothing on mine. And as for method, I trusted in nothing but *my own way of seeing* the mind—being somehow repelled by documents.

He talked about his system, about the limited function of the brain, which merely connects the mind with our actions. This seems the opposite of my view. I believe thought and consciousness are not to be distinguished from a *kind of act*.

Memory, to my mind, is not free, being rigorously bound to repeat the *order* of events—without exception (save the apparent one: images of simultaneous things which can then be enumerated in some order or other).

I gave Bergson the example of the dynamo, which cannot be understood in the absence of an electric current. Examination in that case tells us nothing about it. 10:67

1925

10 Nov. Went to call on Bergson. To my surprise, I met him in the street, going home—walking with a limp.

He recognized me, invited me in, seemed delighted to see me. Kept me for a long time—an uninterruptible flow of talk —his notions of melody—tonics—phases.

Then poetry—*subjective* . . . mystical—and I talked about the kinds of composition—

We talked about a psychic event, the production of a word (for example): something that wants to be expressed *in order* to evoke the exact word that will express it. . . . 11:202

Saw Bergson—a long talk. Poetry—it intrigues him. Then painting. Said he knows little about Wagner. . . . I talked about Cause–Thing–Process. He said he had never thought about this. 11:217

1926

16 June. Ran into Bergson at the Institute library. We talked. He spoke of *Rhumbs*, and again used his image of "tangents to thought," which he finds in this collection.

On this point, he told me that what he writes is a *résumé* of the work he is continually doing on a large number of subjects. 11:516

1929

8 Nov. Heitz-Boyer told me that Bergson was in room 88, for treatment of his bladder, and that he would be glad to see me—took me in to him. B. was in bed, his round head very large, with heavy eyebrows, his eyes a bit sunken. We talked for a long time—I entertained him with gossip. 14:95

12 Nov. Long conversation with Bergson, toward 6 o'clock. His idea of life is curious. He always sees it in contrast with

"matter," and thinks its aim or law is to produce *unexpected actions*. I didn't dare pursue this thought, which he tells me is the result, for him, of considering everything that distinguishes life . . . etc.

We talked aesthetics, in connection with a book he had in his hand—R. Rolland's *Beethoven*. He said that what R. R. says about the "architecture" in Beethoven surprised him (making Beethoven a less sentimental creator than anyone had thought), and that it seemed to make Beethoven and me more alike. I developed my own idea, since he spoke of my "intellectualism." I told him not to be mistaken, that I am a *formist*—and that the fact of beginning with forms, going from the form to the "matter" of works or ideas, gives the *impression* of intellectualism, by analogy with logic—but that forms are *intuitive* in origin—and I explained to him my theory of ornament: that the sensibility produces something to fill a vacancy, following local-general laws (contrasts and symmetries).

He asked me, several times, whether I agree with what Gillouin says about my sonnet *Grenades*. 14:103

January 1930

Called on Bergson. Found him looking brighter. He talked about his condition—a prostate operation by electric cautery —local anesthetic. . . . Told me that, *interdum*, he was making psychological observations.

We talked about evolution—I told him we'll end by thinking the future is the cause of the past, that the problems in this field are greater than ever and our only consolation is that now physics is getting to be as troublesome as biology.

He complimented me on my essay *Conquête de l'ubiquité* —he had seen extracts of it in the *Figaro*.

Later we talked about this Swedish "business" of mine.

14:250

1932

Bergson's ideas are combinations of elements or terms that seem to me arbitrary, historical, didactic—and I cannot accept them without first going back and putting them under headings I can recognize as usable.

The most questionable kind of thinking is speculation on *divergent* terms—that is to say, terms at once abstract (or theoretical) and undefined. A scandal in philosophy. 15:504

Pentecost. Finished the *Manet* as best I could—

At Bergson's, at 3 o'clock. He was expecting me. The *Idée Fixe* in front of him, with bits of paper inserted here and there.

He seemed to have put on a bit of weight. Thin hands, puffy. Eyes bright as ever. He greeted me—compliments on the book, lying open. I explained that it's an *Alimentary Farce*, which amused him—he said I should have used that as a subtitle. He remarked that I draw no conclusions, offer no solutions—and said that he can't keep from concluding.

He seemed to insist on this point and on the kind of *decision* he makes after thinking for a long time, finally making a choice by eliminating one conclusion after another.

"So," I told him, "you fall on what is *yours* like a great bird of the desert, hovering for a long time, finally dropping like a stone on a barely perceptible sheep."

He said that he has often thought that if he had been differently oriented in his youth, his decisive mind would have made him a man of action—strenuous action!

I said, "So! You are a Mussolini *manqué*—a brute! I see!"

I compared him to a kind of Hercules entangled in his own problems—*The After-Life, Evil,* etc.—grasping and subduing them, etc.

We spoke of what I say in the *Idée Fixe* about the *orgasm*—that acute pleasure so much like pain, and so near it—and I counted up for him the critical muscular states comparable to it which accompany the *rarer* forms of elimination: vomiting, childbirth . . . We talked about the strange economy of the body, which uses the same organs for very different functions. And he said: "Nature has found no way to avoid using the same organ for love and urination." I replied that she economizes on drainpipes! . . . Then we talked about schooldays. He said he was a good student—didn't know Greek very well, translated it with a dictionary. But in philosophy, when he read Plato's dialogues he was so interested that he wanted to see the original, and at first he used a translation to help him but after only a few pages he could read quite easily.

I told him that, as for me, Greek . . . etc.

We criticized the University.

Talked about Intellectual Co-operation. He told me how he had suggested it to Léon Bourgeois. We talked also about novels and novelists: I told him about my inability to accept the arbitrary—he talked about their pretense of thinking of their characters as alive and independent of them. Flaubert's arsenic. . . .

I left at 4:15. . . . 15:627

1934

2 Oct. MCMXXXIV. At 3 o'clock, Bergson—who kept me for 2 hours. He too thinks of sensibility as a kind of *resistance.* I was surprised.

We also talked about diction—then Nice. 17:559

Thérèse Murat tells me that Bergson, as they were talking about me, said:

"*Ce qu'a fait Valéry, devait être tenté.*"

("What Valéry has done, had to be attempted.")

A respectable line of verse—I'll remember it. It's a motto, my "necessity," and also defines me. Does Bergson mean it to refer particularly to my poems and "poetics"?—or to everything (published?). 17:792

1940

Sunday, 5 January '40. A telephone call from Le Roy, telling me Bergson is dead. Funeral tomorrow at 2. . . .

Jan. 6th.

At Bergson's, 2 o'clock.

In a room at the back, the casket on trestles, and about 30 people. Mme Bergson tells me he had talked to her about me in the last few days. Others there: Brinon and Lavalle [sic] representing Vichy. Le Roy, Carcopino, Faral. I represent the Academy. Bellessort not there! Some men come in and take away the casket . . . we all go out. Only Mme Bergson and her daughter ride. We walk away through the snow. In normal times, it would have been the Pantheon. 24:149

1941

It's surprising that several people have tried to derive me from Bergson, whose philosophy I still (August '41) only know from hearsay, and had never heard of it when I was *taking my own shape*—between '92 and 1900. Thibaudet decided, on the evidence of one word in *La J. P.*, that I had been "influenced" by B. And yet he knew me! Raymond (at Geneva) said the

same thing recently. The fact is, I am hardly able to read philosophers (and understand them even less)—they bore me, they go on too long and their language is disagreeable.

If anyone knew how little Plato I've read—and that little in translation! Yet I've written "Socratic dialogues"! It's the *form* that interests me. The *substance* of thought is nothing. Theories that don't lead to *methods* (since these prove the thesis) have no meaning whatever for me. Spinoza. In Descartes, it's the *man* that I see. Etc.

Aristotle, a few formulas . . .

As for Bergson, I met him at Thérèse Murat's (in 192–?). . . . I had some excellent talks with him, at rather long intervals, and he was always very gracious indeed. I think I rather interested him. I am very fond of his remark (passed on to me), "What Valéry has done had to be attempted"—both justification and praise, and a very keen insight into the said V.

24:762

1943

A portrait of Kant—reminds me of Bergson, the shape of the skull showing through, the head held at a slant, and the unfocused look in the eyes, so characteristic. These traits struck me as quite definite. Then I thought of various other "intellectual" eyes. H. Poincaré: weary. Mallarmé: distant.

28:86

1943

It seems to me that in Bergson (whose ideas I know only from hearsay—I can't read philosophers) his actual observations are a kind of *accessory*—either arguments or stimulants useful to his system, but the system is the thing—the aim and end.

28:169

9 November '44. Rivet tells me that at Bogotá (in 1942) Jouvet read my "funeral speech" on Bergson from the stage, the audience standing to listen. . . .

It was confidential in Paris! 29:255

NOTES

NOTES

ABOUT THE TITLE *Masters and Friends*.

Maître et ami is a traditional mode of address in letters and dedications. It conveys affectionate respect and admiration for the teacher, the older writer or artist. Baudelaire used it in the dedication of *Les Fleurs du mal* to Théophile Gautier.

Valéry gave it a slightly different turn, using it as the title of a collection of essays—*Maîtres et amis* (1927). That volume, in which a number of the present essays were included, has served as a model for this one. And it was my distinguished master and friend John Crowe Ransom who persuaded me that the French title could be brought straight over into English. "Why couldn't it be translated (even imperfectly)," he said in a letter, "and appear over this particular book of philosophers, poets, fictionists, etc., as *Masters and Friends?* It sounds warm and nice, and suits the author. It indicates no more topical order than there actually is in it."

If it were my privilege to dedicate this volume, it would be to John Crowe Ransom.

The Appendix is made up of passages selected from the whole range of Valéry's personal notebooks, the twenty-nine big volumes of the *Cahiers*. These sketchy entries written at intervals over the better part of a lifetime bring us into

Valéry's confidence, giving us his intimate and often more objective view of the writers he has dealt with in the foregoing essays and speeches. (The selections and translations are mine.)

In the preparation of this volume I am indebted at every point, and particularly in the Notes, to Paula Deitz, Assistant Editor of the Valéry series. I am also grateful to Catherine David, once again, for her fine-tooth criticism of the translations. And to Diane Amussen for her thoughtful treatment of the text at every stage of manuscript and proofs. The index is also hers.

The notes which follow are bibliographical and explanatory by turns. The latter are not meant to supply general information. They are limited, with a few exceptions, to clarifying the allusions and other references that a French reader might be expected to catch but an American or English reader might not. The bibliographical notes indicate for each work the occasion of its composition (when that is known), its first publication, and, if republished, one later collection where it may be readily found. Except where otherwise noted, the place of publication is Paris and the publisher is Gallimard.

<div style="text-align: right">J. M.</div>

Acknowledgment is gratefully made to Crown Publishers, Inc., for permission to quote from Albert Einstein, *Relativity: The Special and the General Theory* (copyright 1961), and to Holt, Rinehart and Winston, Inc., for permission to quote from P. Hume Brown, *Life of Goethe* (copyright 1920).

Introduction, by Joseph Frank

xii. *"Defines the mysterious echo . . ."*: from Valéry's letter of April 18, 1891, in his *Lettres à quelques-uns*, p. 47.

xvi. *"This crisis set me against my 'sensibility' . . ."*: is from "Propos me concernant," Valéry's preface to *Présence de Valéry*, by Berne-Joffroy (Chez Plon, 1944); see "Remarks Concerning Me," Collected Works, Vol. 15.

xvii. *"I told him [Mallarmé] one day . . ."*: see Valéry, *Œuvres I*, Pléiade (1957), p. 635; and "Letter about Mallarmé," Collected Works, Vol. 8.

xviii. *"Donner un sens plus pur aux mots de la tribu"*: "give a purer sense to words on every tongue," a line from Mallarmé's sonnet, *Le Tombeau d'Edgar Poe* (*The Tomb of Edgar Poe*); see Mallarmé, *Œuvres Complètes*, Pléiade (1945), p. 70 and note (p. 1492).

xx. *"In reality, I named as a man . . ."*: from "Introduction to the Method of Leonardo da Vinci," see Valéry, *Œuvres I*, Pléiade (1957), p. 1155; also Collected Works, Vol. 8.

xxi–xxii. *Non, non! . . . Debout! . . .*:

> No, no! . . . Arise! Into the successive age!
> Break, my body, this pensive form!
> Drink, my breast, the birth of the wind!
>
> • • •
>
> Let us run into the waves to re-emerge alive!
>
> (Tr. by William McCausland Stewart)

(See Valéry, *Œuvres I*, Pléiade [1957] p. 151; also Collected Works, Vol. 1.)

xxix. *"The charlatanism discovered by Voltaire . . ."*: *Cahiers* 4:183.

xxx. *"That is the fact . . ."*: *Cahiers* 29:909.

3. PONTUS DE TYARD: "Pontus de Tyard," first published in a special issue of *La Muse Française* (Feb. 10, 1924) devoted to the Pléiade poets; in *Œuvres*, Vol. G (1937); see *Œuvres I*, Pléiade (1957).

4. *Those sublime big-bellied bottles:* "ces bouteilles dives et pansues." *Dive* is archaic. The phrase in French evokes Rabelais and his *Oracle de la Dive Bouteille* (*Oracle of the Sublime Bottle*), at the end of his Fifth Book.

O calme nuit qui doucement composes:

> O calm night that so softly composes
> In my favor a shade more alive
> Than ever Morpheus in his smoky hall
> Painted from the nothingness of his metamorphoses . . .
>
> (Tr. by Martin Turnell)

6. SKETCH FOR A PORTRAIT OF DESCARTES: "Fragment d'un Descartes," appeared first in *La Nouvelle Revue française*, May 1, 1925; in *Maîtres et amis* (Beltrand, 1927); see *Œuvres I*, Pléiade (1957).

In August of 1894 at Montpellier, Valéry was writing "An Evening with Monsieur Teste" and reading Descartes. In a letter to Gide at the time, he said: "I have lately reread *The Discourse on Method*. It is really the modern novel as it might be done. Don't forget that later philosophy rejected the autobiographical. This is the part that must now be revived, and someone must write *the life of a theory*—too much has been written about the life of passion (in bed). But, this is not so easy: puritan that I am, I want the theory to be better than the fake stuff in *Louis Lambert*. . . ." (Gide-Valéry, *Correspondance*, p. 213.)

7. *Abbé Picot*: the translator of Descartes' *Principes de la*

philosophie (1647) from the Latin. "The preface to the *Prin-ciples*" took the form of "A letter from the author to the one who translated the book."

8. *Surmounted by cannon balls with plumes of flame*: "sommée de bombes panachées de flammes"; the phrase describes the emblem of the French *gendarmerie*—the national military force responsible for maintaining law, order, and public safety.

Baillet: Adrien Baillet (1649–1706), a priest and scholar, the earliest (almost contemporary) biographer of Descartes. His two-volume *Vie de Descartes* (1691) and his abridged version in one volume (1693) remain useful and interesting sources. (See Valéry's note, p. 36.)

Polytechnique: The École Polytechnique is an institute for advanced scientific and technical training similar to the Massachusetts Institute of Technology. It is connected with the War Ministry. Admission, by competitive examination, to the École Polytechnique carries great prestige in France.

13. DESCARTES: "Descartes," first published as "Discours prononcé à la Sorbonne pour l'inauguration du 9ᵉ Congrès International de Philosophie le 31 juillet 1937," in *Revue de Métaphysique et de Morale*, Oct. 1937; in *Variété IV* (1938); see *Œuvres I*, Pléiade (1957).

Mr. President, Mr. Minister: The Government was repre-sented on this occasion by Albert Lebrun, President of the Republic 1932–40, and Jean Zay, Minister of National Educa-tion 1936–40.

22. *What is thought to be his skull*: In his notebooks Valéry gives a plainer account: "*23 Nov. 1931*. At the Museum, in Rivet's office, spent a long time handling Descartes' skull. Teeth gone, no lower jaw. The skull beautifully balanced.

Well preserved. I noticed that to a large extent the sutures no longer hold." (*Cahiers* 15:400.)

"The Museum" is the Museum of Natural History in the Jardin des Plantes, Paris, where Paul Rivet was professor of anthropology.

25. *Fresnel*: Augustin Fresnel (1788–1827), a French physicist, who did much to establish the wave theory of light.

26. "*Least action*": Valéry liked this term and used it often. The principle, first formulated by the French mathematician and astronomer Pierre de Maupertuis (1698–1759), is displayed where "the amount of energy expended in performing a given action is the least required for its execution" (J. R. Newman, *The World of Mathematics*, II, p. 882). (See Collected Works, Vol. 10, p. 8 & *n.*, and Vol. 13, p. 206 & *n.*)

31. "*Alors comme alors!*": A fairly untranslatable expression no longer in common use, meaning approximately "we shall see when the times comes."

The remark of Stendhal's which Valéry has in mind is probably this: "[Napoleon's] education, being far from complete, never helped him to predict the historical consequences of events. Instead of calculating them coldly, he would sense the dangers he might encounter, and then his great spirit would respond with the words: *Alors comme alors*!" (Stendhal, *Napoléon* [Honoré Champion, 1929], II, p. 229.)

32. *World-line*: "ligne d'univers."

Valéry was well acquainted with Minkowski's contribution to relativity theory. The whole of the paragraph that follows ("And lastly, if the sense of Self achieves . . .") is based on a figurative use of Minkowski's conception of a "world-line."

In Minkowski's "world," space and time form a four-dimensional continuum, called in French *univers*, in English,

"world." The unbroken succession of events that make up the life of any particle of matter in space-time is a "world-line" (*ligne d'univers*).

Here is Einstein's own presentation of Minkowski's idea:

... the world of physical phenomena which was briefly called "world" by Minkowski is naturally four-dimensional in the space-time sense. For it is composed of individual events, each of which is described by four numbers, namely, three space co-ordinates, x, y, z, and a time co-ordinate, the time-value t. The "world" is in this sense also a continuum; for to every event there are as many "neighboring" events (realised or at least thinkable) as we care to choose, the co-ordinates x_1, y_1, z_1, t_1, of which differ by an indefinitely small amount from those of the event x, y, z, t originally considered. That we have not been accustomed to regard the world in this sense as a four-dimensional continuum is due to the fact that in physics, before the advent of the theory of relativity, time played a different and more independent rôle, as compared with the space co-ordinates. It is for this reason that we have been in the habit of treating time as an independent continuum. ...

The four-dimensional mode of consideration of the "world" is natural on the theory of relativity, since according to this theory time is robbed of its independence. ... But the discovery of Minkowski, which was of importance for the formal development of the theory of relativity, does not lie here. It is to be found rather in the fact of his recognition that the four-dimensional space-time continuum of the theory of relativity, in its most essential formal properties, shows a pronounced relationship to the three-dimensional continuum of Euclidean geometrical space. ...

These inadequate remarks can give the reader only a vague notion of the important idea contributed by Minkowski. Without it the general theory of relativity ... would perhaps have got no farther than its long clothes. [Albert Einstein, *Relativity: The Special and the General Theory* (New York: Crown Publishers, 1961), pp. 55–57.]

34. *Bourdaloue*: Louis Bourdaloue (1632–1704), a Jesuit and one of the great French preachers of the seventeenth century. His reputation at the time was greater even than Bossuet's.

36. A VIEW OF DESCARTES: "Une Vue de Descartes," preface to *Les Pages immortelles de Descartes choisies et expliquées par Paul Valéry* (Éditions Corrêa, 1941); in *Variété V* (1944); see *Œuvres I*, Pléiade (1957).

38. *A society where you can have some fun*: "le monde où l'on s'amuse." The French phrase is the title of a well-known comedy (1868) by Édouard Pailleron, who also wrote *Le Monde où l'on s'ennuie* (1881).

40. *A little twenty-one-year-old lieutenant . . . in his room at Valence*: Napoleon as a young artillery officer garrisoned at Valence experienced one of his most intensive moments of self-realization and intellectual development.

The point of interest here is that Valéry brings together two of his principal heroes—the hero of pure intelligence and the hero of intelligence in action—at similar moments of their lives, moments of formative crisis. He surely has in mind also his own crisis of self-determination in the autumn of 1892, at the age of twenty-one. (See pp. 41ff & *n.*, and p. 170 & *n.*)

41–43. These pages on Descartes' "extraordinary intellectual drama" should be read with Valéry's own early crisis in mind. We have Henri Mondor's word for it that Valéry "sometimes consented with a smile to compare [his own] to Descartes' crisis."

During 1891–92, from the age of twenty to twenty-one, Valéry passed through a period of intense spiritual conflict. Caught up in a kind of visionary love-obsession with a

woman ten years older than himself, whom he did not know and had only glimpsed occasionally in the street, he was at the same time undergoing a profound intellectual reformation, under the enlightening shock of his encounter with Poe, particularly in *Eureka*, and with the poems of Mallarmé and Rimbaud.

The great crisis of his life seems to have occurred on the night of November 9, 1892, in Genoa, where young Valéry was spending a vacation with relatives—a stormy night, brilliant with lightning, which he spent sitting upright in bed, in sleepless agitation and distress: "My whole fate being played out in my head."

In his letters and notebooks Valéry has left various accounts of this formative experience, dealing less with the circumstances than with the substance of the conflict and its resolution. Out of the struggle "between me and me," as he says, the first "me" withdrew to become the detached onlooker, the superior "I"—that pure awareness which is the unmoved observer of all else that exists, not only of its own body and the world outside but also of that secondary "me" which is emotion, sensation, and thought itself.

Looking back on this critical experience many years later, Valéry wrote: "At the age of twenty, I had to take very serious measures against *Idols* in general. At first it was a matter of only one that obsessed me, making life almost unbearable. The power of absurdity is unbelievable. . . . What could be more humiliating to the mind than the disturbance caused by such a trifle as this: an image, a mental component destined to be forgotten? . . ."

See Valéry, *Cahiers*, *passim*; Henri Mondor, *Précocité de Valéry* (Gallimard, 1957), pp. 301–27; Octave Nadal, *A mesure haute* (Mercure de France, 1964), pp. 151–64.

48. *The n-tuple flexibility of Gauss's curvilinear co-ordinates*: Karl Friedrich Gauss (1777–1855), German mathematician and physicist, has been ranked with Archimedes and Newton.

Gauss transformed Descartes' straight-line co-ordinates into curved co-ordinates that measure curvature in two, three, or four dimensions. Einstein describes the function of Gauss's co-ordinates in this way:

> If we are given a surface (e.g. an ellipsoid) in Euclidean three dimensional space, then there exists for this surface a two dimensional geometry, just as much as for a plane surface. Gauss undertook the task of treating this two dimensional geometry from first principles, without making use of the fact that the surface belongs to a Euclidean continuum of three dimensions. . . . Gauss indicated the principles according to which we can treat the geometrical relationships in the surface, and thus pointed out the way to the method of Riemann of treating multi-dimensional, non-Euclidean *continua*. Thus it is that mathematicians long ago solved the formal problems to which we are led by the general postulate of relativity. [Albert Einstein, *Relativity*, p. 86.]

51. *Regulae: Regulae ad directionem ingenii* (*Rules for the Direction of the Mind*), published in 1701, fifty years after Descartes' death. Valéry cites here from Rule IV.

Lully: Raymond Lully (c. 1235–1315), a Catalan mystic, writer and missionary.

53. *Pangloss*: In *Candide* Dr. Pangloss is Voltaire's version of a disciple of Leibnitz. Valéry here agrees only halfway with the good doctor, who thought that "indeed everything is for the best in this best of all possible worlds."

55. "*Simplici mentis intuitu*" : from Descartes' *Meditationes de prima philosophia:* "*neque etiam cum quis dicit, ego cogito, ergo sum sive existo, existentiam ex cogitatione per syllogismum deducit,*

sed tanquam rem per se notam simplici mentis intuitu agnoscit"
(Paris, 1641; Amsterdam, 1642, p. 75).

In Clerselier's French translation (*Méditations*, 1647), the phrase is "connue de soi" (Descartes, *Œuvres et Lettres* [Bibliothèque de la Pléiade, 1952], pp. 375 f.). Valéry makes it "connue par elle-même," which Martin Turnell translates as "self-evident."

Entretien avec Burman: It is obvious from the foregoing note that Valéry was mistaken in his reference.

56. *We have only to read this passage*: from *Méditation Seconde: De la nature de l'esprit humain; et qu'il est plus aisé à connaître que le corps.* "Of the nature of the human mind, and that it is more easily known than the body." The original text of this fine passage will be of interest to readers who know French:

> *Prenons pour exemple ce morceau de cire qui vient d'être tiré de la ruche; il n'a pas encore perdu la douceur du miel qu'il contenait, il retient encore quelque chose de l'odeur des fleurs dont il a été recueilli; sa couleur, sa figure, sa grandeur sont apparentes; il est dur, il est froid; on le touche, et si vous le frappez, il rendra quelque son. Enfin, toutes les choses qui peuvent distinctement faire connaître un corps se rencontrent en celui-ci.*
>
> *Mais voici que, cependant que je parle, on l'approche du feu....*
> [Valéry, *Œuvres I*, Pléiade (1957), p. 826.]

69. A SECOND VIEW OF DESCARTES: "Seconde vue de Descartes," first published as "Croquis d'un 'Descartes'" in *Domaine Français*, *Messages* (Geneva: Éditions des Trois Collines, 1943); with its present title, in *Variété V* (1944); see *Œuvres I*, Pléiade (1957); tr. by Anthony Bower as "Sketch for 'Descartes,'" in *Selected Writings* (New York: New Directions, 1950); hereafter cited as Bower, *Selected Writings*.

72. THE RETURN FROM HOLLAND: "Le Retour de Hollande," first appeared in *La Revue de France*, March 1, 1926; in *Maîtres et amis* (Beltrand, 1927); in *Variété II* (1929); see *Œuvres I*, Pléiade (1957).

John Crowe Ransom has said: ". . . it came more and more to seem to me that the best single revelation which V. offers in an essay is in the informal sketch 'The Return from Holland.' . . . [There] he cites all the stances of the mind, all its self-dispositions including both the rational ones and the most grotesque fancies; he runs the whole gamut, from mechanism to art. He grasps the multiplicity of mind more freshly and easily than Bergson, and knows all the time that his art is a fiction, that is to say, a kind of metaphysic, while at the same time he quite understands the tight hold that mathematics can enfold the mind in, like a straitjacket."

76. *Omitting nothing*: "rien omettre." The phrase is meant to remind us of the fourth and last of Descartes' rules for the right conduct of his reason: "Et le dernier, de faire partout des dénombrements si entiers et des revues si générales que je fusse assuré de ne rien omettre" (*Discours de la Méthode, II*). ("The last was in all cases to make enumerations so complete and reviews so general that I should be certain of omitting nothing": *Discourse on Method*, tr. by Elizabeth S. Haldane and G. R. T. Ross.) See also Collected Works, Vol. 10, p. 52 & *n*.

85. *Nicolas Rameau*: Valéry surely must have in mind the French composer Jean-Philippe Rameau (1683-1764).

86. VARIATIONS ON A "PENSÉE" (Text with the Author's Notes): "Variation sur une 'Pensée.' " This essay first appeared, without the Author's Notes, as part of the "Troisième centenaire de Pascal," in *La Revue hebdomadaire*, July 14, 1923;

in *Variété* (1924); as a brochure, with the Author's Notes, *Variation sur une "Pensée," annotée par l'auteur* (Liége: Éditions du Balancier, 1930); see *Œuvres I*, Pléiade (1957); tr. by Malcolm Cowley (without Valéry's Notes) as "Variations on a Theme from Pascal," in *Variety* (New York: Harcourt, Brace, 1927), hereafter cited as Cowley, *Variety*; tr. in part by Bower as "Man and the Night, Extract from 'Variations on an Idea of Pascal,' " in *Selected Writings*.

Several years before the publication of this famous essay, Valéry had written in a letter to Pierre Louÿs (May 21, 1917): "I have notified my future brain of the principal points for a savage attack on Pascal's *Pensées* . . ." (*Lettres à quelques-uns*, p. 121).

He began the attack with a warning salvo two years later (1919), in the following passage from the "Note and Digression" on Leonardo, clearly identifying Pascal but contemptuously refusing to name him:

Leonardo was totally unaware of the coarsely defined opposition between the spirit of finesse, or art, and the spirit of geometry that would be proclaimed, three half-centuries later, by a man who was completely insensitive to the arts and could not conceive of any such delicate but natural union of distinct talents; who thought that painting was vanity and that true eloquence laughed eloquence to scorn; who involved us in a wager in which he drowns all finesse and all geometry; and who at last, having changed his new lamp for an old one, wasted hours sewing papers into his pockets, at a time when he might have honored France by discovering the infinitesimal calculus. . . . [See Valéry, *Œuvres I*, Pléiade (1957), p. 1210; also, Collected Works, Vol. 8.]

A few days after his essay on Pascal first appeared, Valéry wrote disparagingly of it to his boyhood friend Pierre Féline: "The article on Pascal is everyday stuff; nothing worth com-

municating to any but the 40,000 readers of the *R.H.*" (i.e., *Revue hebdomadaire*). (See Pierre Féline, "Souvenirs sur Paul Valéry," *Mercure de France*, July 1, 1954, p. 417.)

89. "*The heavens declare . . .*": In this and the next passage Valéry is using his own translation from the Vulgate, Psalm 18:2–5 (Authorized Version, Ps. 19:1–4):

> *Les cieux énoncent la gloire de Dieu,*
> *et l'ouvrage de ses mains est proclamé par le firmament.*
> *Le jour vomit au jour la parole divine,*
> *et la nuit enseigne la nuit.*
> *Ce ne sont point des babillages, ni de ces propos*
> *qui peuvent échapper à l'oreille,*
> *mais leur résonance se prolonge aux extrémités de la terre . . .*
>
> *Caeli enarrant gloriam Dei,*
> *et opera manuum ejus annuntiat firmamentum.*
> *Dies diei eructat verbum,*
> *et nox nocti indicat scientiam.*
> *Non sunt loquelae, neque sermones,*
> *quorum non audiantur voces eorum.*
> *In omnem terram exivit sonus eorum . . .*

"*Non sunt loquelae . . .*": In the Authorized Version, Psalm 19:3–4:

There is no speech nor language, where their voice is not heard.
Their line is gone out through all the earth, and their words to the end of the world . . .

"*The stars of the morning shouted for joy*": Job 38:7:

Alors que les étoiles du matin éclataient en chants d'allégresse,
Et que tous les fils de Dieu poussaient des cris de joie?

[Authorized Version]
When the morning stars sang together, and all the sons of God shouted for joy?

91. *"Coelum et terram ego impleo"*: from Jeremiah 23:24, *Numquid non caelum et terram ego impleo? dicit Dominus* (Do not I fill heaven and earth? saith the Lord).

100. *Based on the Wager*: "au raisonnement du Pari." See Pascal's *Pensées*, Everyman's edn., Sec. III, "Of the Necessity of the Wager"; also, Collected Works, Vol. 5, p. 32 & n.

106. *The Mystery of Jesus*: "Le Mystère de Jésus," title of the section (*Pensées*, Pléiade edn., Article 736) from which Valéry cites: "Console-toi, tu ne me chercherais pas si tu ne m'avais trouvé" ("Console thyself, thou wouldst not seek Me, if thou hadst not found Me": *Pensées*, Everyman's edn., Sec. VII, par. 552).

Bourdaloue: See p. 34 & *n*.

Father Noël: Estienne Noël, Jesuit Rector of the Collège de Clermont (Paris) in Descartes' time. In an exchange of letters with Pascal, Father Noël took the defense of Descartes' physics. Pascal broke off the exchange, writing instead to a friend, M. Le Pailleur, and indulging at length in the "mockery" to which Valéry refers. (Pascal, *Œuvre*, Pléiade edn., pp. 151 ff.)

107. *Cavalieri*: Francesco Bonaventura Cavalieri (1598–1647), Italian mathematician, student of Galileo. His "method of indivisibles" was developed in his *Geometria indivisibilibus continuorum nova quadam ratione promota* (Bologna, 1635).

Saccheri: Girolamo Saccheri (1667–1733), a Jesuit priest of San Remo, whose book *Euclides ab omni naevo vindicatus* (Milan, 1733) helped to found the first non-Euclidean geometry.

108. BOSSUET: "Sur Bossuet," first appeared as "Lettre au Directeur du *Bien Public*, à Dijon," in a special issue of the *Bien Public* (1926); under its present title in *Commerce XIII*,

Autumn 1927, and in *Variété II* (1929); see *Œuvres I*, Pléiade (1957); tr. by Bower, in *Selected Writings*.

110. SWEDENBORG: "Svedenborg," first published in *La N.R.F.*, June 1, 1936; as preface to *Swedenborg*, by Martin Lamm (Stockholm, 1936); in *Variété V* (1944); see *Œuvres I*, Pléiade (1957).

114. *Mr. Martin Lamm's book*: Martin Lamm (1880–1950), a Swedish writer, author of the study of Swedenborg (Stockholm, 1915), which Valéry used.

119. *Actio praesentiae*: "An act of presence."

123. *How is a Swedenborg possible?* "Comment un Svedenborg est-il possible?" This question, in one form or another, was habitual with Valéry. Beneath the wit it had a deeper resonance in his mind, where the idea of possibility was fundamental.

Ten years earlier he had posed the counterpart of this question in his preface to *Monsieur Teste* (1925); "Why is M. Teste impossible?—That question is the *soul* of him. *It turns you into M. Teste*. For he is none other than the very demon of possibility." M. Teste is "a monster," and therefore "cannot survive in reality for more than a few quarters of an hour." The implication in the present essay is that Swedenborg too is a kind of "monster," both possible and impossible, real and unreal.

It may well be that the question first took shape in Valéry's mind from his early reading of Montesquieu's *Persian Letters*, where he encountered the famous and not so ridiculous question, "Comment peut-on être Persan?" "How can anyone be a Persian?" (Or: "How is it possible to be a Persian?") In his essay on the *Persian Letters* (1926), Valéry gave his own reply: "The answer is a further question: How is it pos-

sible to be what one is? No sooner does the question occur to us than it takes us out of ourselves, and at once we see how impossible we are." A year later (1927) in his essay on Stendhal, Valéry, still preoccupied with the idea, turns again to what must have been his source. "In the eyes of people who are indifferent in matters of religion there is a mystery about the priest. The problem exists and precisely because those people who look at religion from the outside also exist. The intelligent unbeliever necessarily regards the priest as something of a puzzle, a monster—part man, part angel—who surprises him, makes him smile, and quite often disturbs him. He says to himself: *Comment peut-on être prêtre?*—"How is it possible to be a priest?" (See p. 204.)

124. *Haec vera sunt quia signum habeo*: These things are true because I have the sign.

126. *A new Key to Dreams*: "une nouvelle Clef des Songes." *Clef des Songes* is the generic term for those popular "dream books" that circulate among the superstitious and the ignorant—the "concierges." Valéry had his own ideas about dreams, and usually took a bantering tone toward the prevalent modern theories. For instance: "She . . . asks me if I practice analyzing my dreams as is done in Central Europe, where no right-thinking person fails to fish up out of his own depths every morning some abysmal enormity, some obscenely shaped octopus he is proud to have fostered." ("A Fond Note on Myth," in Collected Works, Vol. 10, p. 37.)

130. VOLTAIRE: "Voltaire," an address delivered at the Sorbonne on Dec. 10, 1944, the 250th anniversary of his birth; first published as *Voltaire: Discours prononcé le 10 décembre 1944 en Sorbonne* (Coll. Au Voilier, Domat-Montchrestien, 1945); in *Morceaux choisis* (1950); see *Œuvres I*, Pléiade (1957).

Valéry's daughter, Agathe Rouart-Valéry, has given this account of the circumstances of the address:

Soon after . . . [the liberation of Paris, August 1944], he began work on an important speech on Voltaire, rereading his work with great admiration. He delivered it in the "great amphitheatre" of the Sorbonne on Dec. 10, 1944, with an extraordinarily moving authority and majesty. It was the first time he had spoken at an official ceremony since 1940. And it was the last time he was ever to be heard on such an occasion. [Agathe Rouart-Valéry, "Vie de Paul Valéry," in *Paul Valéry Vivant* (Marseilles: Cahiers du Sud, 1946), p. 20.]

In his notebooks Valéry set down his own impression of the occasion: "Sorbonne—Voltaire—'Ovation'! I was nervous but read well." (*Cahiers* 29:333.)

133. *Its pomps, but not its works*: "De ses pompes, mais non de ses œuvres," an indirect reference from the Catholic ritual of baptism, in which the candidate is asked whether he renounces "Satan, and all his works, and all his pomps?"

135. *Got himself cudgeled and crowned with laurel*: Valéry here has in mind two famous incidents in Voltaire's life: the first, when the Chevalier de Rohan had the young Voltaire summoned from the Duc de Sully's dinner table and whipped by lackeys at the entrance gate, while Rohan looked on from his coach and directed the beating; the second, Voltaire's apotheosis at the very end of his life, on the occasion of the presentation of his last tragedy, *Irène*, at the Comédie Française. From his box in the theater, Voltaire looked on while his bust was set up on the stage and crowned with laurel, amid prolonged acclamation.

136. *Intellectual value lasts only for a flash*: "une valeur d'esprit ne dure qu'un éclair." Valéry is paraphrasing a line from a popular eighteenth-century love song, *Plaisir d'amour*, which begins:

Plaisir d'amour ne dure qu'un moment,
Chagrin d'amour dure toute la vie.

The pleasure of love lasts but a moment,
The sorrow of love endures a lifetime.

The lines are from *Célestine* by Jean-Pierre Claris de Florian (1755–1794); the music, by the German conductor and composer J. P. E. Martini (1741–1816), professor at the Paris Conservatory and superintendent of music at the French court. (See Collected Works, Vol. 5, p. 22 & *n.*)

Sang the praises of Newton in verse: Voltaire's poem *Sur la philosophie de Newton* (1736).

137. *Products of the new age:* "les enfants du siècle nouveau"; Alfred de Musset's autobiographical novel, *La Confession d'un enfant du siècle* (1836), brought the phrase into common use.

But contrary to what the proverb says, it is not everybody who has more wit than Voltaire.

This whole passage, pp. 137–38, is Valéry's counterattack against the Romantics and their view of Voltaire, implying that their reaction had long since become the commonplace view held by "everybody." The "proverb" referred to had its origin presumably in a remark made by Talleyrand in a speech before the Chamber of Peers, July 24, 1821: "*Il y a quelqu'un qui a plus d'esprit que Voltaire, c'est tout le monde*" (There is somebody who has more wit than Voltaire, and that is everybody).

138. *His "hideous smile":* "son 'sourire hideux.' " Valéry jibes not only at "the proverb" (see note above), but more specifically at Alfred de Musset, and probably at Chateaubriand as well. His use of quotation marks would indicate that he expected his readers to recall the following words of Musset, from *Rolla*, part IV:

Dors-tu content, Voltaire, et ton hideux sourire
Voltige-t-il encor sur tes os décharnés?

Do you sleep content, Voltaire, and your hideous smile,
Is it hovering still over your fleshless bones?

From his early youth, Valéry had detested Alfred de Musset and particularly the character of Rolla. (See Collected Works, Vol. 10, p. 220 & *n*.)

Chateaubriand also had applied the word "hideous" to Voltaire: "Il n'aperçoit partout que le côté ridicule des choses et des temps, et montre trop souvent, sous un jour *hideusement gai*, l'homme à l'homme . . ." (Everywhere he sees only the ridiculous side of things, and of the times as well, and too often he reveals man to men in a *hideously merry* light . . .). (*Le Génie du Christianisme*, Pt. 2, Bk. 1, Chap. 5.) Cf. Alfred de Musset, *Poésies complètes* (Pléiade, 1957), p. 283 and note (p. 717).

145. *The royal decree that abolished torture*: the ordonnance issued by Louis XVI at the beginning of the Revolution (October 9, 1789).

147. ADDRESS IN HONOR OF GOETHE: "Discours en l'honneur de Gœthe," delivered at the Sorbonne on April 30, 1932, in commemoration of the 100th anniversary of Goethe's death; first published in *La N.R.F.*, June 1, 1932; in *Variété IV* (1938); see *Œuvres I*, Pléiade (1957).

This address grew, in part, out of Valéry's participation in the work of the League of Nations' Permanent Committee on Arts and Letters, of which he was a leading member. As early as July 1931, at its first meeting in Geneva, the committee had accepted an invitation from the city of Frankfort to hold the first of its annual *Entretiens* there the following year, in celebration of the Goethe centennial.

Meanwhile, in Paris, a French national committee for the Goethe centennial was formed, with Valéry as one of its vice presidents. Such committees were organized throughout Europe.

By January 1932 Valéry was at work on his speech, an "official chore," as he said to Gide at the time (*Cahiers* 15:449). At the end of January he spent an afternoon with Charles Du Bos at Versailles, where they had "a long conversation on Gœthe" (*Cahiers* 15:496).

Valéry's "official chore" was one that he was to perform several times over. First at the Sorbonne:

Saturday 30th of April, the Goethe speech. I was completely exhausted from working on it. . . . Auditorium jammed . . . officials seated on plain benches . . . badly organized. I am obviously a sort of State poet. . . . I was annoyed reading my piece, knowing it was much too long. Three-fourths of the audience of 3000 couldn't hear. [Cahiers 15:604]

Two weeks later (May 12) when the League of Nations' *Entretiens* opened in Frankfort, Valéry was absent, detained in Paris to attend the funeral of President Doumer. A short version of his speech, with the title "Comment je vois Gœthe" was read in his absence. He arrived the next day, in time to take part in two days of discussions.

Valéry read his "Gœthe" again at Zurich on May 26. (Cf. Agathe Rouart-Valéry, "Introduction biographique," in Paul Valéry, *Œuvres I*, Pléiade, 1957, p. 67.)

His true feeling about the Goethe speech is plain in a letter to Gide written soon afterward (June 7, 1932):

I owe everything that's all good, *true*, in that document . . . to Du Bos and Gide—i.e. you,. Napoleon: filler, fetched in. Remember what audience I was talking to. Had to cut out what I had

really *thought through* (which was entirely different), and put in the easy, the "more or less all right." The final week—from five in the morning till eight at night—without stopping!! I gave the "Goethe" again at Zurich, at the University!! Altogether I had read only *Faust* and the Martens translation of the things on biology (1837, excellent!). Skull and plant. I *really liked* that old tome. Couldn't find the theories on light. You are probably right about my French. I have never written so loosely, at such a gallop on Remington. Disgusting even to read it over.

That's what it's like to have to play Bossuet to the Third Republic!! [Gide–Valéry, *Correspondance*, 1955, pp. 512 and 513.]

In a letter to René Berthelot, Valéry wrote: "There is something about Goethe that bothers me. I have the feeling that he has a *trick for seeming profound.*" (René Berthelot, "Lettres échangées avec Paul Valéry," in *Revue de métaphysique et de morale*, January 1946, p. 2.)

151. *The mysterious game of intelligence and chance*: "le jeu mystérieux de l'Intelligence et du Hasard," a variation on the title of Marivaux's comedy *Le Jeu de l'amour et du hasard* ("The Game of Love and Chance"; 1730). (See p. 221 & *n.*)

153. *No longer the war of Louis XV and Monsieur de Thorane, which taught French to young Goethe and introduced him to our tragic dramatists*: Count Thorane, King's Lieutenant to Louis XV, was billeted in the Goethe home during the Seven Years' War. Some account of his influence on the Goethe family may be of interest here:

As a result of the Seven Years' War, 7,000 French troops took possession of Frankfort in the beginning of 1759, and occupied it for more than three years. In the ways of a foreign soldiery at free quarters, the Frankforters saw a strange contrast to their own decorous habits of life, but the French occupation was brought more directly home to the Goethe household. To the disgust and indigna-

tion of the father, to whom as a worshiper of Frederick the French were objects of detestation, their chief officer, Count Thorane, was quartered in his house. Goethe has told in detail the history of this invasion of the quiet household—the never-failing courtesy and consideration of Thorane, the abiding ill-humor of the father, the reconciling offices of the mother, exercised in vain to effect a mutual understanding between her husband and his unwelcome guest. As for Goethe himself, devoted to Frederick though he was, the presence of the French introduced him to a new world into which he entered with boyish delight. With the insatiable curiosity which was his characteristic throughout life, he threw himself into the pleasures and avocations of the novel society. Thorane was a connoisseur in art, and gave frequent commissions to the artists of the town; and Goethe, already interested in art through his father's collections, found his opportunity in these tastes of Thorane, who was struck by the boy's precocity and even took hints from his suggestions.

A theatre set up by the French was another source of pleasure and stimulus. The sight of the pieces that were acted prompted him to compose pieces of his own and led him to the study of the French classical drama. In the *coulisses*, to which he was admitted by special favor, he observed the ways of actors—an experience which supplied the materials for the portraiture of the actor's life in *Wilhelm Meister*. A remark which he makes in connection with the French theatre is a significant commentary on his respective relations to his father and mother, and indicates the atmosphere of evasion which permanently pervaded the household. It was against the will of his father, but with the connivance of his mother, that he paid his visits to the theatre and cultivated the society of the actors, and it was only by the consideration that his son's knowledge of French was thus improved that the practical father was reconciled to the delinquency. The direct results of his intercourse with the French soldiery on Goethe's development were at once abiding and of high importance. It extended his knowledge of men and the world, and, more specifically, it gave him that interest in French culture and that insight into the French mind which he possessed in a degree beyond any of his contem-

poraries. [P. H. Brown, *Life of Goethe* (New York: Henry Holt, 1920), pp. 14–16.]

154. *August fathers . . . sublime fathers*: These phrases are meant to evoke the closing scene of *Faust*, Part Two. (See p. 169 & *n*.)

169. *The "Mothers," those "goddesses who are unknown to mortals" . . .*: from the "Dark Corridor" scene in Act I of the Second Part of *Faust*. It is obvious, from this point to the end, that Valéry is turning the meeting between Goethe and Napoleon into a sort of parody of the closing scenes of *Faust*, or perhaps a scene in a possible, but as yet unwritten, Faust drama, "a Third Part of *Faust*," as he says (p. 172).

170. *The empire founded on intelligence in action and the empire of intelligence in its free state*: Valéry compares Napoleon and Descartes in the same terms. (See p. 40 & *n*, and p. 171.)

What a moment! It was 1808 . . . the priceless moment when the Star reached its zenith: Napoleon had the most daring kind of superstitious confidence not only in his genius but in his luck, which he called his "star." (See Louis Madelin, *Histoire du Consulat et de l'Empire* [Hachette, 1937], II, p. 210.)

172. *A Third Part of Faust*: Valéry imagines Goethe dreaming of a continuation of his two Faust plays, taking Napoleon as his hero.

But it was Valéry himself who later on wrote the continuation he had in mind, two Faust plays of his own, which he brought together under the title *Mon Faust* (My Faust), and often referred to them as *un troisième Faust* (a Third Part of *Faust*). The subject of both these plays was . . . not Napoleon . . . but, predictably, "a great mind contemplating the remnants of its thought."

175. *Pater Aestheticus*: Surely this is a pun on Goethe's "Pater Ecstaticus." (See p. 169 & *n*.)

176. STENDHAL: "Stendhal," appeared first as "Essai sur Stendhal (A propos de *Lucien Leuwen*)," in *Commerce*, XI, Spring 1927; under the title "Préface—Au Sujet de Stendhal —A propos de Leuwen," in *Œuvres complètes de Stendhal, Lucien Leuwen* (Honoré Champion, 1927); in *Variété II* (1929); see *Œuvres I*, Pléiade (1957); tr. by W. T. Bandy, in *This Quarter* (Paris), March 1930; same privately printed (Paris, At the Sign of the Black Manikin, 1930); tr. by William A. Bradley, in *Variety, Second Series* (New York: Harcourt, Brace, 1938); hereafter cited as Bradley, *Variety II*.

Most French editions of this essay carry, below the title, this dedication: *A Monsieur Jules Cambon, Ambassadeur de France.*

As Ambassador to Washington, 1897–1902, Jules Cambon took a leading role for Spain in negotiating the end of the Spanish-American War. This made his reputation and took him to Madrid as Ambassador, 1902–07. In Berlin during the troubled years 1907–14 he clearly foresaw the coming of the First World War. He was elected to the French Academy in 1918, and died in 1935.

179. *Ranuce-Ernest*: Ranuce-Ernest IV, prince of Parma, a character in *La Chartreuse de Parme.*

Dr. Du Poirier: "le docteur Du Poirier, le premier médecin du pays" (. . . the best doctor in the country), a character in *Lucien Leuwen.*

185. *Alors comme alors!* See p. 31 & n.

Nets strung too high: Stendhal liked this figure, *Vous tendez vos filets trop haut* ("you string your nets too high"), which he attributed to Thucydides—in whose writings it is evidently not to be found.

193. *Hypotheses non fingo*: "I make no hypotheses." The phrase is Newton's, from the "General Scholium" which he

added to the second edition of his *Principia* (1713): ". . . hypotheses, whether metaphysical or physical, whether of occult qualities or mechanical, have no place in experimental philosophy." (Tr. from the Latin by Andrew Motte.)

Permutations: *trespres = prestres* (*prêtres*)

ligionre = religion

197. *A great saint who undressed in the market place*: the reference is doubtless to St. Francis of Assisi.

202. *The first night of Hernani*: At the famous first performance of Hugo's *Hernani* (at the Théâtre-Français, February 21, 1830), a fight broke out between the Romantics and the Classicists. The incident became the subject of a painting by Albert Besnard, "La Bataille d'Hernani," now in the Victor Hugo Museum in Paris.

Allies: "les Alliés" were the powers which, in 1814–15, invaded France and brought about the restoration of the Bourbons.

The Grand Army: "La Grande Armée" of Napoleon was the first "European army."

Institute: The Institut de France comprises the five academies: the Académie française, the Académie des inscriptions et belles-lettres, the Académie des sciences, the Académie des beaux-arts, and the Académie des sciences morales et politiques.

203. *Polytechnique*: See p. 8 & *n*.

205. *Faraday . . . head of a sect called the Sandemanians*: Michael Faraday (1791–1867), the English chemist and physicist, was an elder in the small dissident Presbyterian sect named for Robert Sandeman.

206. *Visse, scrisse, e amó*: "lived, wrote, and loved," a line from the epitaph which Stendhal wrote for himself in 1821, at the age of thirty-eight:

Qui giace
Arrigo Beyle Milanese,
Visse, scrisse, amó
Se n'andiede di anni . . .
Nell 18—

(Here lies
Henri Beyle of Milan
Who lived, wrote, loved
And passed away at the age of . . .
In the year 18—)

Valéry cites the line almost as Stendhal wrote it, and not as it appears on his tomb in the Montmartre Cemetery in Paris:

Arrigo Beyle, Milanese
Scrisse, amó, visse.

207. *Follow the practice with which they began . . .*: "Suivez la manière par où ils ont commencé . . ." is from Pascal's *Pensées*; see the Everyman's edn., Sec. III, "Of the Necessity of the Wager," par. 233.

211. *But this Gaudissart who puts up at the Grand Hôtel de l'Europe et de l'Amour*: Gaudissart is the typical nineteenth-century traveling salesman, a noisy, trivial, bragging bore created by Balzac in *L'Illustre Gaudissart* (1832).

213. GÉRARD DE NERVAL: "Souvenir de Nerval," preface to *Les Chimères* by Gérard de Nerval (Pour les amis de poésie, 1944); as a brochure with the title, *Au Sujet de Nerval* (Textes Prétextes, 1944); see *Œuvres I*, Pléiade (1957).

A "Michel-Lévy": one of those inexpensive volumes in a series of contemporary authors published by Michel Lévy, who founded the Calmann-Lévy publishing company in 1836. Other writers represented in the Michel-Lévy collec-

tion: Dumas, Balzac, Hugo, Stendhal, Baudelaire, Flaubert, Gérard de Nerval, and Anatole France.

Bug-Jargal: Victor Hugo's novel (1820) dealing with a Negro uprising in Santo Domingo led by Bug-Jargal, a character modeled on Toussaint L'Ouverture, who headed the actual revolt in the late eighteenth century.

Han d'Islande: another of Hugo's novels (1823), about a monster who terrorized Norway in the seventeenth century.

Pont Neuf: the oldest of the Paris bridges, begun in 1578, completed in 1606.

214. *Moréas*: Jean Moréas (1856–1910), a French poet of Greek origin, one of the early Symbolists, who later turned to classical forms.

215. *Senlis, and the noble Forest of Compiègne*: town and forest are both in the Île-de-France, north of Paris.

216–17. *Saint-Martin*: Louis Claude de Saint-Martin (1743–1803), called the "Unknown Philosopher," devoted himself to Illuminism and the theosophical speculations of Jakob Böhme. He wrote a number of books, among them *Le Tableau naturel des rapports qui existent entre Dieu, l'homme et l'univers (1782)*.

217. *Peau de Chagrin*: (The Wild Ass's Skin), a novel (1831) by Balzac. A poor young man is given the skin as a talisman that will grant him every wish, but each time a desire is fulfilled the skin shrinks. When it is gone, he will die.

219. *Alors on vit sortir du fond du Purgatoire* . . .: the third stanza of *La Tête armée* (The Armed Head):

> Then, emerging from the depths of Purgatory, was seen
> A youth wet with tears of Victory,
> Holding out his unsullied hand to the rulers of the skies.
> (Tr. by Geoffrey Wagner)

221. *The play of wit and chance*: "des jeux de l'esprit et du hasard." Valéry is again playing a variation on the title of Marivaux's comedy, *Le Jeu de l'amour et du hasard* (1730). (See p. 151 & *n*.)

Méryon: Charles Méryon (1821–1868), a French artist known mainly for his etchings of Paris.

222. *Luc Albert Moreau*: (1882–1948), a French painter; he had made the lithographs for the edition of Nerval's *Les Chimères* for which Valéry wrote this preface.

223. THE TEMPTATION OF (ST.) FLAUBERT: "La Tentation de (Saint) Flaubert," introduction to *La Tentation de Saint Antoine* by Gustave Flaubert, illustrated by J. G. Daragnès (J. G. Daragnès, 1942); in *Variété V* (1944); see *Œuvres I*, Pléiade (1957).

227. *Already burned everything that can be worshiped*: "déjà brûlé tout ce qui peut s'adorer." Valéry is echoing a proverbial injunction attributed to Saint Rémy, who, as Archbishop of Rheims, is said to have baptized King Clovis (A.D. 496) with the words: *adore ce que tu as brûlé, brûle ce que tu as adoré* (worship what once you burned, and burn what once you worshiped). (See Collected Works, Vol. 3, p. 21.)

232. VILLON AND VERLAINE: "Villon et Verlaine," a lecture given at the Université des Annales, Jan. 12, 1937; first published in *Conférencia*, April 15, 1937; in *Œuvres*, Vol. K (1939); see *Œuvres I*, Pléiade (1957); tr. by Bradley, in *Variety II*.

235. *Clément Marot had already observed*: the passage cited by Valéry is from Marot's preface "Aux Lecteurs," to his edition of Villon (Galiot Du Pré, 1533).

236. *Pierre Champion*: (1880–1942), French scholar, son of the publisher Honoré Champion. Valéry's reference is to his book *François Villon, sa vie et son temps* (1913).

238. *Femme je suys povrette et ancienne* . . .: "I am a poor little old woman; know nothing, have never read a word; at the church where I am a parishioner, I see a painted paradise where there are harps and lutes. . . ." (Tr. by Martin Turnell.)

239. *Longnon*: Auguste Honoré Longnon (1844–1911), a medievalist and founder of the study of historical geography in France, professor at the Collège de France from 1892. Among his many works are a scholarly edition of Villon's poems and an *Étude biographique sur François Villon* (1877).

Marcel Schwob (1867–1905): French novelist, poet, and literary historian, a friend of young Valéry during his early years in Paris. Valéry greatly admired Schwob's researches on Villon, which were the subject of many of their conversations. See Schwob's *François Villon et son temps* (1912). (See also Collected Works, Vol. 10, p. xii & *n.*, Vol. 12, p. 186 & *n.*, and Vol. 13, p. 257 & *n.*)

243. *The Hôtel-Dieu*: The oldest hospital in Paris, founded A.D. 600, near the Cathedral of Notre Dame.

245. *Foie, poumon, et rate qui respire*: "Liver, lungs, and spleen that breathe." (Tr. by Martin Turnell.)

246. *Dictes-moy où, n'en quel pays?*: "Tell me where, in what country . . . ?" (Tr. by Martin Turnell.)

248. *Calmes dans le demi-jour* . . .: The opening lines of Verlaine's *En Sourdine*:

> Calm in the half-light
> That the high branches make . . .
> (Tr. by Martin Turnell)

250. *Mais où sont les neiges d'antan?* ...:

> But where are the snows of last year?
>
> Will you leave him here, the poor Villon?
>
> Tell me where, in what country ... ?
>
> What has become of that bright forehead,
> That yellow hair, those arched eyebrows ... ?
> (Tr. by Galway Kinnell)

253. VERLAINE PASSES BY: "Passage de Verlaine," first appeared as "Autour de Verlaine," in *Le Gaulois*, Jan. 27, 1921; with the present title, in *Maîtres et amis* (Beltrand, 1927); in *Variété II* (1930); see *Œuvres I*, Pléiade (1957).

254. *Polytechnique*: See p. 8 & n.

259. FOUR LETTERS ON NIETZSCHE: "Quatre Lettres de Paul Valéry au Sujet de Nietzsche," published with a "Notice" by Valéry in *Cahiers de la Quinzaine*, April 1927.

The four letters are dated: November 11, 1901; December 10, 1902; August 4, 1903; October 1907. They were addressed to Henri Albert, whose translations of Nietzsche were then appearing in the *Mercure de France*.

260. *Cahiers de la Quinzaine*: founded by Charles Péguy in January 1900, after his break with the socialist group of the Société nouvelle de librairie et d'édition. The review appeared regularly until July 1914.

263. *In spite of Clausius' theorem, which would seem to rule it out*: R. J. E. Clausius (1822–1888), a German mathematical physicist; his restatement of Carnot's principle did much to make thermodynamics a science. In a paper presented to the Berlin Academy in 1850 he enunciated the second law of

thermodynamics in its well-known form, "Heat cannot of itself pass from a colder to a hotter body" (*Encyclopedia Britannica*).

This was doubtless the theorem of Clausius which seemed to Valéry to rule out the notion of "Eternal Return."

265. RECOLLECTIONS OF J. K. HUYSMANS: "Souvenir de J.-K. Huysmans," first published as a preface to Huysmans' *Durtal* (Edouard Champion, 1925); under the title *Huysmans*, with etchings by Ch. Jonas (À la Jeune Parque, 1927); in *Maîtres et amis* (Beltrand, 1927); under the present title, in *Variété II* (1930); *Œuvres I*, Pléiade (1957).

Sûreté Générale: called, since 1934, the *Sûreté Nationale*— the French National Police and Intelligence Agency under the Ministry of the Interior. Huysmans worked there for twenty-two years. "On the stroke of eleven, he arrived at the offices of the Sûreté Générale in the Rue des Saussaies. Here he spent the next six hours, copying out official letters, adding up columns of figures, and—like so many other young authors employed in various French ministries—working on his own books and articles." (Robert Baldick, *The Life of J.-K. Huysmans* [Clarendon Press, 1955], p. 66.)

269. DURTAL: "Durtal," first published in the *Mercure de France*, March 1898; as a brochure, no. 3 in the Collection "Les 49 Ronins du Quai Malaquais" (Edouard Champion, 1925); in *Maîtres et amis* (Beltrand, 1927); in *Œuvres*, Vol. G (1937); see *Œuvres I*, Pléiade (1957).

284. AT THE GRAVE OF PIERRE LOUŸS: "Sur la Tombe de Pierre Louÿs," first published under the title "Que voulez-vous . . ." ("How can I possibly . . .") in *Les Nouvelles Lit-*

téraires, June 13, 1925; in the collection *Le Tombeau de Pierre Louÿs* (Les Éditions du Monde moderne, 1925); as "Sur la Tombe de Pierre Louÿs," in *Petit recueil de paroles de circonstance* (Plaisir de Bibliophile, 1926); in *Vues* (1948); tr. by J. H. Lewis as "Pierre Louÿs, 1870–1925," in *The Dial*, *LXXX*, January–June, 1926.

290. TO RAINER MARIA RILKE: "A Rainer Maria Rilke," first published with other pieces honoring Rilke in *Les Cahiers du Mois*, August 1926; in *Petit recueil de paroles de circonstance* (Plaisir de Bibliophile, 1926); tr. in *Literary World* (New York), December 1934.

292. A MEMORY OF RILKE: "Souvenir de Rilke," in *Le Figaro littéraire*, Dec. 16, 1941; in *Vues* (1948).

295. HOMAGE TO MARCEL PROUST: "Hommage à Marcel Proust," first appeared as "Hommage" in *Hommage* à *Marcel Proust*, a special number of *La N. R. F.*, Jan. 1, 1923; in *Variété* (1924); see *Œuvres I*, Pléiade (1957); tr. as "A Tribute," by Malcolm Cowley, in *Variety*.

302. FUNERAL ADDRESS ON BERGSON: "Discours sur Bergson," delivered before the French Academy, Jan. 9, 1941; first published in *Suisse Contemporaine* (Geneva), June 1941; not published in France until 1948, in a posthumous collection, *Vues*; see *Œuvres I*, Pléiade (1957).

"This speech, which was little known in France at the time, made its way abroad by clandestine means and was greeted, especially in England, as a profession of faith and an act of courage." (Agathe Rouart-Valéry, "Introduction bio-

graphique," in Paul Valéry, *Œuvres I*, Pléiade [1957], p. 67).
See also Appendix, above, p. 349.

303. *France was able to appeal to that name and that authority in circumstances which I am sure you will recall*: Even such an indirect remark as this was an act of courage in Paris under the German occupation. The reference is to Bergson's missions to Spain and the United States during the First World War to plead the cause of France and the ideals of French culture. He was twice in the United States, at the two worst periods of the war, January–May 1917 and May–September 1918. (See Bergson's pamphlet, *La Signification de la guerre* [Bloud, 1915].)

During a previous visit to the United States (1912–13), Bergson had been Visiting Professor at Columbia University, where he received an honorary doctorate of letters, February 3, 1913.

Appendix

320. *Such comedians as B.*: a reference to the eighteenth-century Abbé Boileau, who probably originated the legend of Pascal and the abyss. He wrote in one of his letters: "Ce grand esprit *croyait toujours voir un abîme* à son côté gauche, et y faisait mettre une chaise pour se rassurer" (this great mind *believed that he always saw an abyss* beside him on the left, and would have a chair put there to reassure him). (*Lettres de l'abbé Boileau*, 1737, p. 207.)

329. *Abbé Mugnier* (1853–1944): a priest with literary interests, a brilliant talker well known in the Paris *salons*, a friend of Marthe de Fels. He is said to have been responsible for Huysmans' final conversion.

340. *A telegram tells me Rilke is dead*: See "A Memory of Rilke," p. 292.

Marthe de Fels: The *salon* of the Comtesse de Fels, sister-in-law of the Duchesse Edmée de La Rochefoucauld, was one of the most brilliant in Paris during the 1930s; political and literary in tone, it was frequented by Valéry, Gide, Claudel, Fargue, Pétain, and Laval as well as such foreign figures as Hemingway, Eisenhower, Churchill, and others. The star of her *salon* was no doubt her great friend the poet St.-John Perse, who at the time was an important government official at the Quai d'Orsay.

Valmont: Val-Mont is the sanatorium at Montreux (Switzerland) where Rilke died.

341. *Montesquiou*: Robert, Comte de Montesquiou-Fezensac (1855–1921), descendant of a famous family, a writer of "precious" oddities, novels and verse. His most interesting work is his memoirs, *Les Pas effacés* (1927), published after his death.

Lucien: Lucien Daudet (1883–1946), son of the novelist Alphonse Daudet, and himself a writer. See his *Autour de soixante lettres de Marcel Proust* (1929).

343. *Heitz-Boyer*: Dr. Maurice Heitz-Boyer, professor in the School of Medicine, was treating Bergson.

344. *What Gillouin says about my sonnet Grenades*: René Gillouin, critic and biographer, author of two books on Bergson, *Henri Bergson* (ca. 1900) and *La Philosophie de Bergson* (1911), and several volumes of essays. The remarks in question were made in an essay, "Paul Valéry, poète métaphysique," in *Le Destin de l'occident* (Éditions Prométhée, 1929).

345. *This Swedish "business" of mine*: a reference to efforts being made to nominate Valéry for the Nobel Prize.

346. *Talked about Intellectual Co-operation. He told me how he had suggested it to Léon Bourgeois*: In 1921, Léon Bourgeois (1851–1925), the principal French representative in the League of Nations, proposed the creation of an international committee to study questions of intellectual co-operation.

On January 4, 1922, the Council of the League created an International Committee on Intellectual Co-operation as a consultative organ. This Committee of twelve members met for the first time in August 1922 and elected Henri Bergson its first president. Other members of the group were Albert Einstein, Gilbert Murray, Madame Curie, *et al.*

In 1925, the parent committee created a Sub-Committee on Arts and Letters, which Bergson persuaded Valéry to join. It was under Valéry's influence that the subcommittee was transformed, in 1931, into the "Permanent Committee on Arts and Letters" with a program reflecting his own turn of mind. As President of the Permanent Committee from 1935–1940, Valéry was largely responsible for the program of meetings and debates held in many countries of Western Europe and once in South America.

We also talked about . . . Nice: Their talk was about the fifth session of *Conversations* (*Entretiens*) to be held in Nice, April 1–3, 1935, by the League of Nations' Committee on Arts and Letters. The occasion also included the inauguration of the Mediterranean University at Nice, of which Valéry was the newly appointed Administrator.

347. *Thérèse Murat*: Another *salon* where Valéry was often seen was that of the Comtesse Joachim Murat, great-granddaughter of the painter David. She was a close friend of Abel Bonnard and André Suarès and welcomed those associated with *Action Française*. She was also a disciple of Bergson long before it was fashionable to be so.

Le Roy: Edouard Leroy (1870–1945), philosopher and mathematician, a disciple of Bergson; held the chair of philosophy at the Collège de France from 1921; French Academy, 1945.

Brinon: Fernand de Brinon (1885–1947): as editor of the *Journal des Débats* (1920–1932) he favored a Franco-German political entente, and was the first French journalist to interview Hitler (1933); fled to Germany in 1945, but was later condemned to death by the *Haute Cour* and executed.

Lavalle: Pierre Laval (1883–1945), Minister of Foreign Affairs after the assassination of Barthou (1934); signed the Treaty of Rome with Mussolini (1935); Minister of State under Pétain (1940); arranged Pétain-Hitler meeting. Arrested by Pétain. Condemned to death and shot (Oct. 1945).

Carcopino: Jérome Carcopino (1881–), remarkable Hellenist and historian of the Roman Republic. Minister of Education under Pétain (Vichy, 1940–41); was later tried and found not guilty because of his work for the resistance (1945). Professor at the Sorbonne from 1951; French Academy, 1955.

Faral: Edmond Faral (1882–1958), Professor of French Literature and Medieval History at the Collège de France from 1925; Administrator, 1937–1955.

Bellessort not there!: André Bellessort (1866–1942), French writer and traveler in behalf of French culture (South America, Japan, Romania). He wrote books on Balzac, Voltaire, Hugo; French Academy, 1935.

Bellessort had been appointed, with Valéry, to represent the French Academy.

Thibaudet: Albert Thibaudet (1874–1936). The most respected literary critic of the period between the two wars: author of *La Poésie de Stéphane Mallarmé* (1912 and 1926); *Flaubert* (1922); *Paul Valéry* (1924); *Stendhal* (1931); etc.

Raymond (*at Geneva*): Marcel Raymond (1897–), scholar and literary critic, professor at the University of Geneva.

349. *Rivet*: Paul Rivet (1876–1958), Professor of Anthropology at the Museum of Natural History, Paris. (See p. 22 & *n.*)

Jouvet: Louis Jouvet (1887–1951) was France's most famous actor in the period between the two world wars. During the Second War, he toured with his troupe in South America; then returned to France, where he continued as director of the Athénée Theater.

INDEX

INDEX

*This colophon was chosen from a number of drawings by Paul Valéry of
his favorite device.*